Praise for
PROJECT MANAGEMENT IN THE

"*Project Management in the Hybrid Work]* world of projects–formal and informal. It's essential reading for project management professionals and the rest of us who just work on projects. (So, everyone?) I'm adding it to my recommendation list for new grads and anyone needing a boost in a new or current job."

—TERRI L. GRIFFITH, Keith Beedie Chair in Innovation & Entrepreneurship, Simon Fraser University and author of *The Plugged-In Manager*

"There can be no better guides for getting stuff done in the maze of the new hybrid workplace and its associated technology than Phil Simon and his book *Project Management in the Hybrid Workplace*."

—NICK MORGAN, President, Public Words Inc. and author of *Can You Hear Me?*

"Only an idiot would attempt to manage a project in the post-COVID hybrid world without Phil Simon's book. From social capital, piloting, and collaboration tools to the importance of clear writing, he covers it all, with clear prescriptions and terrifying case studies. Trust me: you should read this book before you start your next project."

—JOSH BERNOFF, bestselling author or co-author of six books including *Writing Without Bullshit*

"COVID-19 forced us to embrace the new world of remote and distributed work and to recognize that people have re-evaluated their personal and professional priorities. In *Project Management in the Hybrid Workplace,* Phil Simon explains why the way we manage projects and launch products must change as well. In a humorous and readable fashion, Phil provides practical advice on technology, training, and managing human capital. Read this book if you want to maximize each employee's personal contributions, minimize cognitive biases, and work smarter."

—MICHELLE GITLITZ, General Counsel, Flexa Network Inc.

"A great book. Simon makes essential points about contemporary operations in a fun and interesting way."

—DR. PETER CAPPELLI, Professor of Management, University of Pennsylvania Wharton School and author of *The Future of the Office*

"With unquestionable tech chops, relentless research, and perfectly placed pop-culture references, Phil Simon provides the ultimate guide to getting projects done in the hybrid workplace. Get ready to learn ... and at times, laugh out loud."

—**KARIN REED**, **CEO, Speaker Dynamics and author of** *Suddenly Hybrid: Managing the Modern Meeting*

"I learned more in these pages than I did in 13 years running an all-remote professional services company. Terrific and timely, this book is required reading for all team leads and managers."

—**JAY BAER**, **co-author of** *Talk Triggers: The Complete Guide to Creating Customers with Word of Mouth*

"Phil Simon shows us how to get things done, whether your team is next door or 10,000 miles away. This is a book we all desperately need."

–**DORIE CLARK,** *Wall Street Journal* **bestselling author of** *The Long Game* **and executive education faculty, Duke University Fuqua School of Business**

"Simon's no-nonsense approach details the why, the what, and the ever-important how of contemporary project management."

—**DARREN MURPH**, **Head of Remote at GitLab and author of** *Living the Remote Dream*

"A multi-disciplinary take on what it means to manage work successfully in a world where people could, and frequently are, anywhere. If you're feeling fried by the cognitive load of hybrid and remote work, this book will help you think and act differently. You'll feel better for it."

—**ELIZABETH HARRIN**, **author of** *Managing Multiple Projects*

"The way we work has changed, but too many leaders haven't changed their methods. This book will teach you how to modernize your approach to project management."

—**DAVID BURKUS**, **author of** *Leading From Anywhere*

PROJECT MANAGEMENT IN THE HYBRID WORKPLACE

PROJECT MANAGEMENT IN THE HYBRID WORKPLACE

PHIL SIMON

Award-winning author of *Message Not Received*
and *Reimagining Collaboration*

Copyrighted Material

Project Management in the Hybrid Workplace

Copyright © 2022 by Phil Simon. All rights reserved.

No part of this publication may be reproduced, stored in a retrieval system, or transmitted, in any form or by any means—electronic, mechanical, photocopying, recording, or otherwise—without prior written permission from the publisher, except for the inclusion of brief quotations in a review.

For information about this title or to order other books and/or electronic media, contact the publisher:

Racket Publishing | www.racketpublishing.com

ISBNs
ISBN: 979-8-9858147-2-9 (hardcover)
ISBN: 979-8-9858147-0-5 (paperback)
ISBN: 979-8-9858147-1-2 (ebook)

Printed in the United States of America

Cover design: Luke Fletcher | www.fletcherdesigns.com
Interior design: Jessica Angerstein

Also by Phil Simon

Reimagining Collaboration: Slack, Microsoft Teams, Zoom, and the Post-COVID World of Work

Zoom For Dummies

Slack For Dummies

Analytics: The Agile Way

Message Not Received: Why Business Communication Is Broken and How to Fix It

The Visual Organization: Data Visualization, Big Data, and the Quest for Better Decisions

Too Big to Ignore: The Business Case for Big Data

The Age of the Platform: How Amazon, Apple, Facebook, and Google Have Redefined Business

The New Small: How a New Breed of Small Businesses Is Harnessing the Power of Emerging Technologies

The Next Wave of Technologies: Opportunities in Chaos

Why New Systems Fail: An Insider's Guide to Successful IT Projects

Agile: The Insights You Need from Harvard Business Review (contributor)

To Volodymyr Zelenskyy and the people of Ukraine

"Runnin' things. It ain't all gravy."

—JON POLITO AS JOHNNY CASPAR, *MILLER'S CROSSING*

CONTENTS

List of Figures & Tables	xv
Preface	i
Introduction	1

✪ Part I ✪
The Brave New World of Work

Chapter 1	The Worm Has Finally Turned	23
Chapter 2	No Small Challenge: Managing the Hybrid Workplace	39
Chapter 3	Revisiting the Great Efficiency Debate: The Return of Resilience	65

✪ Part II ✪
Contemporary Project Management: Old Habits and New Challenges Collide

Chapter 4	PM 101: An Insanely Brief Overview of Contemporary Project Management	93
Chapter 5	The Exasperating Second-Order Effects of Hybrid Work	119

✪ Part III ✪
Prescriptions for Success: How to Manage Projects in Hybrid Workplaces

Chapter 6	Reevaluate Your Vetting Criteria	145
Chapter 7	Come Together	157
Chapter 8	Settle Early on the Tech	179

Chapter 9	Perform a Project Premortem	205
Chapter 10	Conduct a Project Pilot	217
Chapter 11	Provide Formal Employee Application Training	231
Chapter 12	Institutionalize Clear Employee Writing	249
Chapter 13	Embrace Analytics	269
Chapter 14	Reconsider Employee Evaluations and Rewards	283
Coda	A Tale of Two Companies	295
Acknowledgments		297
Bibliography		299
About the Author		303
Index		305
Endnotes		315

LIST OF FIGURES & TABLES

Figure P.1: The Geography of a Hybrid Writing Project

Figure 1.1: US Employee Engagement Trend

Figure 1.2: The Pendulum Has Finally Swung Toward Employees

Figure 1.3: The Longer We Work Remotely, the Less We Want to Return to Pre-COVID Work Conditions

Figure 1.4: Percentage of Americans Who Are Choosing Not to Return to the Office

Figure 1.5: Why Americans Are Working From Home (Percentages)

Figure 1.6: The Work Legacy of COVID-19

Figure 2.1: Number of Days/Week People Want to Work in the Office

Figure 2.2: Employee Responses When Asked How Many Days Per Week Their Employers Will Let Them Work Remotely in 2022 and Beyond

Figure 2.3: Percentage of Companies Surveyed That Reported Offering Remote Work

Figure 2.4: Percentage of Executives Who Cited the Potential for Inequities to Develop Between Remote and In-Office Employees as Their Top Concern

Figure 2.5: Proximity Bias vs. Location

Figure 2.6: The Work/Location Pendulum

Figure 2.7: The New World of Work

Figure 3.1: The Bullwhip Effect

Table 3.1: Simple Stocking Options for AirPods at an Apple Store

Figure 3.2: Efficiency vs. Resilience

Figure 3.3: Predicting the Post-COVID Supply Chain

Table 3.2: Sample Problems and Solutions for Digital Books

Figure 3.4: A Balanced Approach to HCM

Figure 3.5: An Extremely Efficient Approach to HCM

Table 4.1: The Three General Project Categories

Table 4:2: Ten PMBOK v6 Knowledge Areas

Table 4.3: PMI Performance Domains and Hypothetical Issues

Figure 4.1: Goldratt's Theory of Constraints

Figure 4.2: Generic Asana Gantt Chart

Table 4.4: How Mainstream Deployment Approaches Compare

Figure 4.3: Simple One-Week Sprint

Figure 4.4: The Build-Measure-Learn Loop

Figure 4.5: Project Success Percentages

Figure 4.6: Poll Results on Difficulty of Managing Projects in Remote and Hybrid Workplaces

Figure 5.1: Employee Work Preferences: Time and Place

Figure 5.2: Media Richness Theory

Figure 6.1: Pearl Lemon Website: Tools We Use

Table 6.1: A Tale of Two Design Firms

Figure 7.1: Trust and Social Capital on a Hybrid Project

Figure 7.2: Relationships Matter

Figure 7.3: Slamming Colleagues: The Medium Matters

Figure 7.4: Proximity vs. Project/Product Complexity

Figure 8.1: The Need for a Proper PM Application vs. Project Size and Complexity

Figure 8.2: Technology, People, and Homogeneity

Figure 8.3: Simon's Law of Tool Overlap

Figure 8.4: Tool Overlap Scenario #4: Don't Even Bother

Figure 8.5: Tool Overlap Scenario #5: We Can Make This Work

Figure 9.1: Project Premortems: Size Matters

Table 10.1: Factors to Consider When Deciding to Conduct a Project Pilot

Figure 11.1: The Relationship Between Employee Proximity and Workplace Applications

Figure 12.1: Overcoming the Proximity Problem With Clear Writing

Figure 13.1: Generic Project Management Dashboard

PREFACE

"I think we all would have been a lot happier if they hadn't landed a man on the moon. Then we'd go, 'They can't make a prescription bottle top that's easy to open? I'm not surprised they couldn't land man on the moon. Things make perfect sense to me now.'"

—JERRY SEINFELD, *SEINFELD*, SEASON 5, "THE DINNER PARTY"

On July 20, 1969, Neil Armstrong took that historic "one small step." To this day, NASA's stunning scientific and technological achievement leaves me in awe. I still can't get my head around the degree of coordination and collaboration involved in that remarkable feat. As a rabid fan of Jerry Seinfeld's eponymous show, I've often pondered the depth of his astute assessment of the moon landing, including several times when I've worked on projects with people in different locations.

Like the one that I describe next.

Wanted: Professional Scribe

An up-and-coming software vendor claimed to have built a better mousetrap in a critical business area. (Call it Bluth here, but it's a pseudonym.) If a tree falls in a forest and no one is around to hear it, though, does it make a sound?

To help build buzz, Bluth bigwigs wanted to create a short but slick ebook to give away on its website in exchange for email addresses. Nothing earth-shattering here. For years, this marketing stratagem was standard industry practice to gather viable leads.

To this end, in mid-2021 Bluth commissioned a prominent multinational publisher—call it Sitwell here—to write and produce a 30-page ebook.* Bluth needed the final product within three months, but ideally it would arrive sooner. Sitwell charged mid-five figures for its efforts—significant, but hardly ginormous for a well-funded company with grand ambitions such as Bluth.

Sitwell reached out to my agent, Matt, in search of a suitable ghostwriter. He in turn contacted me and explained the project to gauge my initial interest.

On the surface, the project fell squarely in my wheelhouse. After all, I'd called myself a professional scribe for nearly 15 years by that point. The topics also jibed with my writing and professional backgrounds: I had to fuse technology, enterprise software, analytics, productivity, collaboration, and automation.

Distant Early Warnings

Still, it didn't take a rocket surgeon to identify the project's copious red flags. For starters, I'd be trying to please two masters in two countries in two time zones. Figure P.1 shows a highly unscientific map of everyone's physical locations.

---

* Yes, these are all *Arrested Development* references. RIP, Jessica Walter.

The Geography of a Hybrid Writing Project

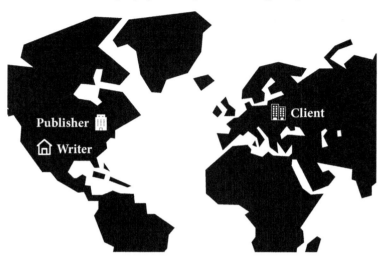

Figure P.1: The Geography of a Hybrid Writing Project

Now, if we'd all been working in the same location, I still would have been concerned. There's always a learning curve when working with new people and organizations. A project consisting of remote or hybrid work only makes the curve steeper.

Second, given the end-product's expansive and subjective nature, I wasn't keen on writing five pages without clear marching orders, let alone thirty. Not to worry, Matt had informed me. A Sitwell VP, Oscar, had told him that Bluth had previously signed off on the ebook's outline. Without having seen it, though, I knew that squeezing all of Bluth's requisite topics into a short yet cohesive ebook would be tight. Every paragraph was going to count.

Then there was the tech. During the preliminary call, I expressed my reservations to my agent and my primary Sitwell contact whom I'll call Lucille here. Here's one critical exchange from that seminal phone conversation:

Me: "Although this is our first time collaborating, I've got some concerns about how we'll work together based upon my previous experiences on remote and hybrid projects."

Lucille: "Such as?"

Me: "Sitwell wants to rely upon email—and that's just not going to work here. We won't be successful if we try to manage this project in our inboxes."

Lucille: "Well, Phil, we have been at this for a while, but I'll bite. What exactly did you have in mind?"

Me: "At a minimum, we need to use a proper communication and collaboration hub like Slack, Zoom, or Microsoft Teams. Each is tailor-made for this type of gig. I don't want to brag, but I wrote books on the first two and know the last one reasonably well. Pick a tool. I'll happily show everyone the ropes as a bonus."

Lucille: "Hmm. I don't know."

Me: "Not to be rude, but this is a dealbreaker for me. I'll pass on this opportunity if we all have to use email. I feel that strongly about it."

Lucille: "Fine. We've got a company license for Teams, but we have never given it a shot. I've heard good things. You can be our guinea pig."

Despite the apparent victory, I wasn't doing cartwheels after the call. Several things still gnawed at me. First, although Microsoft Teams is a powerful communication and collaboration tool, it does not replicate the functionality of a proper project management (PM) application à la Trello, Basecamp, and Asana. I'd broached the subject with Lucille after she agreed to use Teams, but she resisted embracing yet another new application.

Second, I didn't know how many Bluth employees would be working with me—and in which capacities. Was I collaborating with a single client contact or four? In hindsight, I also should have insisted that all of us formalize our roles and responsibilities in a simple matrix. Again, however, I didn't make this demand because I'm at least a little self-aware. I knew that I'd already pushed the envelope with this fusty publisher by drawing a line in the sand over email.

My reservations notwithstanding, I remained cautiously optimistic that our initial dialogue had laid the groundwork for a successful project. After the call, I signed on for a modest flat-rate fee. I was ready to proceed to Phase II: virtually meeting the Bluth folks and starting the writing process.

If we'd all lived happily ever after, I wouldn't be starting the book with this little yarn, but you probably deduced as much already.

The Project Kickoff

A few days later, I participated in the introductory conference call with several Sitwell and Bluth stakeholders. I again voiced my concerns about how we'd communicate on and manage this project. (As Reagan said, "Trust, but verify.") Lucille's assurances aside, I was still a skosh skeptical. It's not like I had anything in writing at this point. What's more, I've known for decades that, when it comes to how we work, old habits die hard. I was also aware of the power dynamics of these types of engagements—a topic that undergirds this book.

For decades, Sitwell's standard operating procedure on these types of projects involved—you guessed it—email and Microsoft Word attachments. Those tools may have sufficed in 2001, but it was 2021. There were far better ways to get things done on remote and hybrid projects.

To that end, I floated the idea that we all use Google Docs in lieu of Word. Doing so would:

- Let everyone collaborate on the same document in real time.
- Prevent multiple versions of the ebook from spiraling out of control. (Without traditional email attachments, no one could claim that they were looking at an old draft of it.)
- Let me rewind the document and reverse anyone's mistakes.

Stan, my primary Bluth contact, wholeheartedly concurred with me. I could tell he was tech-savvy. Like me, he realized that the processes Sitwell required everyone to follow were antiquated.

It didn't take long for Lucille to put the kibosh on that idea. She told everyone on the call that Sitwell had tried Google Docs years ago. Converting the file from Google Docs to Microsoft Word and then to Adobe InDesign for final layout had resulted in significant formatting issues that delayed the project. (You can't win 'em all.)

At least we all agreed that Teams would serve as the project's north star. *In theory,* this meant no email; everyone would be on the same page without having to search their inboxes for the latest updates. (I advised the group that I'd be creating a simple Google Sheet to track each chapter's progress. No, it wasn't a proper PM tool, but it did allow all project stakeholders to view a real-time snapshot of where everything stood.)

Although we'd ostensibly settled on the tech, another issue was gnawing at me. During the call, I picked up on a vibe that multiple Sitwell stakeholders would be chiming in on the ebook's content. All else being equal, the more cooks involved in this type of creative project, the greater the opportunity for conflict, pissing contests, misunderstandings, and delays.

Familiar Patterns Derail the Project

Fast-forward one month. Despite my best efforts and the verbal commitments of key stakeholders to stay the course, the simple ebook project had quickly devolved into a morass of confusing email threads, logistical challenges, and miscommunications.

Case in point: the final ebook outline. Oscar had indicated that it was a *fait accompli* before I'd signed on. In fact, no one had even started it; there was no document for anyone at Bluth to approve. I'd have to create one with Stan from scratch. Multiple Bluth *stakeholders* (plural) would have to bless it.

I'd worked with Stan over the course of two days to create a logical roadmap for the ebook that checked all his boxes. I was waiting for his input on the latest version of the outline when, without warning, he suddenly went off the grid on an IPO-related trip. This delay stopped my progress in its tracks.

Stan resurfaced two weeks later and shared the final outline with his colleagues. As I'd feared from the onset, Bluth execs refused to stay in their lanes and started chiming in. Several had offered structural, unsolicited, and contradictory feedback on the ebook's direction.

I was receiving a fixed fee for this project, and I'd already put in thrice as much work as I'd anticipated. It should surprise exactly no one that, at this point, we were already well behind schedule. The project's foundation was cracking—and fast. The parties were starting to get testy, myself included. Apart from that, though, things were going great. (Yes, I'm being sardonic.)

One Final Hail Mary

I went old school, picked up the phone, and spoke with Lucille. It was high time that everyone talked. Exchanging more asynchronous messages would only exacerbate the issues, raise our temperatures, and further delay the project. Lucille wholeheartedly agreed with me about the need for a group call and ran the idea by Oscar. All systems go.

To find a mutually convenient time to meet, I created a scheduling poll in Doodle and shared it with everyone in the group. It clearly showed an array of options accounting for our different time zones. (Today the popular booking tool Calendly now does the trick, although plenty of folks foolishly believe that using it represents the acme of arrogance.)

Within two days, we'd all voted on our preferred options for a meetup. I finalized the mutually convenient meeting time and date in Doodle, automatically notifying everyone in the process. I then spoke privately again with Lucille. The two of us were sanguine that we could resolve the issues undermining the project and frustrating everyone involved.

The morning of the meeting, I awoke, brewed a cup of coffee, and checked my inbox. At the top was an urgent message from Stan to everyone on the chain. "This meeting time doesn't work for me," he wrote. "We will have to reschedule." (Stan didn't cite a last-minute emergency. Why he'd selected that Doodle slot in the first place mystifies me to this day.)

Back to square one.

Brass tacks: The very problems that I'd identified and tried to address prior to joining the project were nevertheless hindering it anyway. I'd come to the realization that this endeavor wouldn't end well. Despite my best efforts to set expectations and keep us on

Preface

track, my initial doubts about the project had metastasized. I politely exited stage left, and Sitwell paid me for my services rendered.

Postmortem Reflections and Outcomes

In the days after I exited the engagement, I occasionally reflected on how a promising project had run off the tracks. To be sure, failure wasn't inevitable. Early conversations like the one I had with the Bluth and Sitwell stakeholders—and the ostensible buy-in they produce—should have greased the communication wheels. There's just one caveat, though: When project participants agree to use a set of tools and to follow a certain process, they must abide by those commitments. Mind-blowing, I know.

In hindsight, the ebook project stumbled out of the gate for a bevy of reasons. Participants' refusal to embrace new ideas, tools, and processes sits at the top of the list. Plain old stubbornness and aversion to change are alive and well.

To some extent, the team would have had to overcome these challenges if everyone had worked in a colocated environment. Make no mistake, though: The hybrid nature of the project exacerbated its underlying problems—and created new ones. The fact that the parties were located thousands of miles away from each other made sticking the landing even more challenging.

Coming Full Circle

Let's recap.

More than half a century after the historic Apollo 11 landing, two successful companies and an experienced, tech-savvy writer located in three different time zones embarked on what appeared to be a short, straightforward writing project. The objective: to bang out a short ebook for mid-five figures within two or three months.

Initial project planning and discussions had produced participant commitments and assurances. Unfortunately, those had gone quickly by the wayside. As a result, the project stumbled out of the gate. Colocated employees at the two firms unsuccessfully tried to use technology to bridge the considerable proximity gaps. Communication among team members soon broke down, simple coordination proved challenging, and frustrations began mounting. Efforts to remediate the project failed. Within six weeks, the project had completely unraveled and the writer exited.

The short ebook finally saw the light of day more than six months *after* its initial deadline—costing the client untold leads. In the end, the project took thrice as long as its captains had originally conceived.

What does that woeful tale say about our ability to successfully complete more complex projects when we're not all in the office at the same time? Ditto for launching new products.

As usual, Seinfeld was right.

That's the cynical view. Believe it or not, though, I consider myself an optimist. Yes, projects in hybrid and remote workplaces pose a daunting array of human, technological, and logistical obstacles. Despite these realities, though, we *can* overcome them through a combination of new and proven techniques.

After all, we put a man on the moon.

INTRODUCTION

"I know that progress has no patience
But something has to give."
—RUSH, "SECOND NATURE," LYRICS BY NEIL PEART

During my days as a college professor, I lost count of the number of students who asked me if an upcoming exam would be hard. (No one is judging. I did the same thing when I was all of 19 years old.) After a few semesters of seasoning, I started answering the question with one of my own: Compared to *what?*

For context, college-level exams are harder than, say, becoming an Uber driver. (At least they *should* be. I believe in desirable difficulty. Students are products, not customers, but I digress.)

In his 2019 book *Super Pumped: The Battle for Uber,* Mike Isaac of the *New York Times* wrote about a new program that the controversial ride-sharing company had developed called UberX:

> ... an ambitious, low-cost model that turned nearly anyone on the road who had a well-conditioned car and could pass a rudimentary background check into a driver for the company. Allowing random citizens to drive other people around for money opened up a slew of problems, most notably that no one had any idea whether or not it was legal. At Uber, no one really cared.

In the eyes of Uber's less-than-scrupulous management at the time, its drivers should only need a pulse, a valid license, a smartphone, and a vehicle. After that, the drivers were pretty much good to go. This frictionless onboarding process was deliberate. Back then, Uber routinely asked municipalities for forgiveness *after* entering local markets, not permission *before* setting up shop.

At the other end of the spectrum is the pathway to becoming a chartered financial analyst, or CFA. It only requires passing three notoriously difficult four-hour tests. Topics include economics, derivatives, financial models, complex valuations, and ethics. You know, breezy stuff.

The CFA Institute reported in November 2021 that only 27 percent of test-takers passed Level I of the test.[1] Think of the CFA exam as the antithesis of Uber's driver-approval process.

Becoming a PMP

Now let's turn to another valuable professional credential: the certified Project Management Professional, or PMP.

In terms of difficulty, the PMP exam lies somewhere between becoming an Uber driver and a licensed CFA. Getting your PMP ticket punched is a relatively straightforward and inexpensive process, but I can't provide its pass rate. The Project Management Institute hasn't published an official one since 2005.

Exam success rates aside, however, real-world project management is no walk in the park. The words *simple* and *easy* have never applied to the art of project management, no matter how many letters follow your name.

Exhibit A: Amazon lists more than 30,000 books with the keywords *project management* published *before* March 2020.[2] As a discipline, it has *never* been static and straightforward. The move to remote and hybrid work only adds another layer of complexity.

A tech-savvy twenty-four-year-old who aces her PMP test will soon learn three vital lessons when she starts applying her trade on the job. First, as is usually the case, practice is far messier than theory. Next, as the example in the Preface illustrates, the success of an ostensibly simple endeavor is hardly a given. Foolish is the soul who believes otherwise. Finally, even similar projects can suffer from vastly different issues. Having spent a career working on all sorts of projects, I should know.

Entering the Time Machine

I'm turning back the clock. Don't worry: You'll still have a smart-phone when you arrive.

It's now 2014.

Guardians of the Galaxy and Taylor Swift's *1989* rule the day. Outside of the entertainment world, technology lets you do plenty of things from the comfort of your own home: see a doctor, get in a workout, pick up a new skill by taking an online class, order millions of products for home delivery, and wildly overshare on social media.

To pay your bills, you've worked for the past decade as a dedicated PM for an old-school manufacturer. Last week, your employer took an unexpected step by hiring a trendy, tech-savvy digital-ad agency to run an unconventional digital marketing campaign.

As an experienced PM, you ask yourself the following questions about the forthcoming engagement:

- What are the project's objectives, and how will we measure them?
- What's the deadline to launch the campaign?
- What's the budget?

- What tools will employees use to communicate, collaborate, and manage the project?
- What are the project's risks?
- What's the definition of *done?*

The answers to queries such as these will in part determine whether this project is ultimately successful. Equipped with no additional information, you're pessimistic. The two companies' disparate cultures aren't likely to jibe.

Again, you're no neophyte. You're well aware of the challenges related to managing projects and launching products. What's more, you know that these obstacles aren't confined to client-vendor relationships like the previous one. They plague all sorts of arrangements in which people from different organizations attempt to build something from scratch.

Another Scenario

Let's stay in 2014 for a moment but slightly change the circumstances. Two different departments *within the same organization* launch a new product. Surely, things will go relatively smoothly, right?

Not necessarily.

Even when the same logo adorns everyone's business card, it's folly to assume that everyone in these two groups will play nice with each other. Cohorts under the same roof sometimes despise each other. (As many of those 30,000 PM books detail, projects involving "internal customers" frequently suffer from the same problems that vex client-vendor relationships.)

Back to Reality

Now let's return to the present day. You no doubt own a better smartphone than you did in 2014 but, thanks to COVID, the world

Introduction

is dramatically different on a number of levels. The pandemic accelerated many existing trends, as the following statistics demonstrate:

- **Healthcare:** The number of physicians offering telehealth jumped from 25 percent in 2018 to almost 80 percent in 2020.[3]
- **Ecommerce:** Worldwide, it increased 19 percent from its prepandemic level in 2020.[4]
- **Home fitness:** With gyms closed, millions of people started working out at home. Many industry types wonder if traditional gym memberships will ever revert to their prepandemic levels.[5]
- **Higher education:** The number of enrollments in online courses grew 93 percent between fall 2019 and fall 2020.[6]

Perhaps no change has been more significant—and more welcome—than how we work.

No Going Back (to Work)

It's tough to envision any of these trends suddenly reversing—especially the explosion in remote and hybrid work. Most of us freakin' love the flexibility that our new professional digs afford us. (The one regular exception: cranky old-school managers, but we'll get to them later.)

Americans aren't alone in clamoring for fundamental and permanent change in where and when they clock in. In February 2022, Belgium became the latest country to mandate four-day workweeks. Citizens can now legally ignore their bosses' entreaties after the workday ends without fear of reprisal.[7] Take *that*, Belgian Lumbergh.

Count me among the millions of people who are saying *good riddance* to the unspoken, arbitrary, and archaic rules around office hours. We won't miss workplace cultures that value face time over results. My disdain for each impeded my career progress. More than once, my temerity to leave work at a reasonable hour on a normal workday led to a heated conversation with colleagues or my manager.

Still, a world predicated on hybrid and remote work isn't all sunshine and lollipops. With respect to completing projects and launching new products, our new work environs introduce all sorts of thorny problems and exacerbate existing ones.

Size Matters: Lessons From *Small Giants*

In his 2007 book *Small Giants: Companies That Choose to Be Great Instead of Big,* Bo Burlingham describes how some small-business owners paradoxically *declined* growth opportunities because of their greater ambitions. (Yes, you read that sentence correctly.) A few of these contrarians even decided to voluntarily shrink their businesses—and not because investors had pressured them to do so.

Perhaps this counterintuitive move isn't so odd after all. To paraphrase a line from the *Cheers* theme song, some people would rather work at places where everybody knows their name. Employers often benefit too from cozier environs, as workplace friendships can improve a company's bottom line. Apart from reduced turnover, three decades of research have demonstrated that workplace collegiality generally enhances employee productivity and morale. You're less likely to slam Milton in accounting over email if you enjoy playing tennis with him every Saturday morning.

Now, I don't want to overstate Burlingham's case. No company is perfect, Small Giants included. (In his book, he doesn't contend otherwise.)

Size matters, but so do time and location. Two simple but magical things *can* happen when we work with our colleagues in the same physical location at the same time: We get to know who they are, and we get to know what they do.

Also, just because we work at the same time and location as our colleagues doesn't mean that we know what makes them tick, much less what they're up to. (Dunbar's number is alive and well.) Conversely, just because we work remotely doesn't mean that we don't know our colleagues, much less what they're doing on any given day. As I detail in my previous book *Reimagining Collaboration,* internal collaboration hubs such as Slack and Microsoft Teams promote organizational transparency when used properly.

Indeed, projects and new products can still break bad under ideal circumstances. Neither amicable workplace relations nor complete transparency ensures success. The act of creating, building, or launching something new is anything but simple.

The Big Question at the Heart of This Book

Now, consider less-than-ideal circumstances—the antithesis of a Small Giant. Picture a decidedly impersonal generic remote or hybrid work environment. Say that you've never met your colleagues in real life, or IRL, as the kids say.

This type of virtual room is much harder to read. As a result, we're much less likely to intuit each of the following essential three pieces of information:

1. Where our colleagues, direct reports, and managers are working.
2. When they're working.
3. What they're working on.

And good luck learning about other key constituencies, such as our clients, partners, and vendors.

Let the following meaty question serve as the fulcrum of *Project Management in the Hybrid Workplace:* How are we supposed to successfully complete projects when we often don't know where and when essential contributors are working and what they're doing?

This book argues that the world of work has fundamentally changed—for good. As such, ways in which we manage projects and launch products must change also. We don't need to start with a blank slate, but we need to reevaluate old doctrines and see if they still apply. In some cases, they certainly do. In others, however, we need to adopt some new norms and prescriptions—ones that specifically address the realities of remote and hybrid work environments.

The Choice to Emphasize Project-Based Work

Thanks to COVID, we do lots of things differently, some less frequently, and others not at all. (Been to the movies lately?) At least one thing has remained constant during the pandemic, however: the distinction between the types of work that employees perform. Regardless of who's doing it and where or when it takes place, work generally falls into one of two buckets:

1. Project-based work, including project management and product launches.
2. Routinized or standardized endeavors, such as answering calls or processing insurance claims.

This book examines the former and intentionally ignores the latter. I feel compelled to explain my rationale.

The late coach of the Oakland Raiders and iconic broadcaster John Madden once said, "If you've got two starting quarterbacks, then you've got none." As a parallel, to write an effective business book, authors need to make conscious choices. The well-intentioned

Introduction

scribe who pens a book for *everyone* in fact writes it for no one in particular.

Let me be absolutely clear: My decision to concentrate on project-based work is neither a snub nor some type of moral judgment about the value of certain types of jobs. This type of work isn't inherently "better" or more valuable than its routine or standardized counterpart.* It just poses different challenges—ones complicated when people work in different locations and time zones.

On a different level, certain jobs have remained *relatively* unaffected by the shift to remote and hybrid work. Examples include dental hygienists, short-order cooks, and DoorDash delivery drivers. Not all that much has changed.

Alternatively, what if you worked as a customer service representative prior to March 2020? Lockdown changed *where* you worked, but not the following:

- ☺ How you worked.
- ☺ When you worked.
- ☺ What you needed to accomplish while on the clock.

In fact, many of the nearly three million customer service representatives in the United States[8] have been fielding calls from their homes for years. I'm sure that I've even met a few of them. (I live about 30 minutes from LiveOps headquarters in Arizona, a company that some have termed *the Uber of call centers*.[9])

---

* Celine Dion and Britney Spears reportedly earned about $500,000 per show during their Las Vegas residencies.

A Trip Down Memory Lane

I know a thing or two about answering calls all day long.

Between college and grad school, I worked for a year at Sony Electronics in its northern New Jersey office as a customer relations representative. From 8 a.m. to 5 p.m. every day (with an hour for lunch), I answered calls from customers displaying varying degrees of vitriol. Parents with busted camcorders hosting a birthday party for their young child next weekend were often apoplectic from the moment I uttered the words, "Thank you for calling Sony. This is Phil. How can I help you?"

Sony made quality CD players and car stereos, but happy customers don't wait on hold for ten minutes because everything's fine. (Hello, availability bias.) To be fair, I understood their anger. (Over the past three years, I've politely but firmly laid into the Dacor reps over my refrigerator—and subsequent replacements—malfunctioning, but I digress.)

Had I still been working in the same capacity when COVID-19 hit, I can say two things with absolute certainty. For starters, I could have performed my job at home. Truth be told, my current home office beats my old gray cubicle hands down.

Location aside, however, I'd be miserable. A person can only take so much abuse. The Quality Assurance and Training Connection reported in 2015 that call center turnover typically runs at between 30 and 45 percent per year.[10] I can't imagine that number dropping during the Great Resignation, but we'll get to that shortly.

A Multidisciplinary Approach

This book is far wider than deep. In the pages that follow, I reference and stitch together a panoply of different fields, books, studies, and theories. This decision is very much deliberate; there's a method to my madness.

Whether they've garnered their PMP certification or not, experienced PMs know that theirs is a multifaceted field encompassing a slew of indispensable domains. Managing a project or launching a product isn't easy, regardless of your specific role, business function, organization, or industry.

Consider Val, a hypothetical PM who exhibits excellent interpersonal, technical, organizational, and delegation skills. He's a nice enough bloke. Despite repeated coaching, however, he's just not able to see how his projects fit into his company's long-term strategy. As a result, Val often makes questionable project and product decisions that frustrate his colleagues and hurt his employer's bottom line. It's only a matter of time before he'll have to move on.

Who Should Read This Book

Project Management in the Hybrid Workplace casts a wide net and targets a diverse set of readers. A number of groups come to mind.

Product Peeps

The first cohort consists of what I'll affectionately call *product peeps*. As its name suggests, *a head of product* oversees product development within an organization. The individual in this critical role is ultimately responsible for:

- Setting the long-term vision and strategy for the company's product(s).

- ☺ Delivering new features for existing products and products altogether.
- ☺ Ensuring that the product meets a company's target audience and keeps up with competing offerings.

Note that the nomenclature around this position is anything but uniform. For instance, since its 2006 founding, Twitter has employed many people in the role of *VP of Product.*[*] (Twitter and executive stability have never been synonymous.) A company down the street might use the moniker *chief product officer* for essentially the same role. *Product manager* is a more junior position.

Seasoned PMs

You realize that the struggles on projects in remote and hybrid workplaces are real. Specifically, the same PM techniques that worked so well pre-COVID no longer hold water. You're wondering if you need to tweak your tried-and-true approach to your craft. This book will help you overcome the new challenges that you're going to face when everyone works in different places and at different times.

Service Providers

We've seen an explosion of people who run marketing, design, and other types of shops. The same holds true for freelancers who routinely build things for—and provide services to—their clients. Make no mistake: These are projects.

---

[*] It's accurate to call the company's early culture dysfunctional, as Nick Bilton describes in his fantastic 2014 book *Hatching Twitter.*

Introduction

People Who Hire Service Providers

The next cohort represents the flip side of that coin.[*] Examples here include:

- ☺ Executives who make decisions on which partners to contract.
- ☺ Small business owners.
- ☺ People who work in their organizations' project management offices.

At a high level, many old-school business owners didn't exactly embrace remote and hybrid work—and perhaps they still don't. I get it. They didn't get to work from home, so why should their employees? However understandable that mindset, employers who attempt to revert to the prepandemic M–F/9–5 model will have a hard time filling their open positions. Rather than fight the inevitable, why not get on board? This book will help mature and successful business owners think about project and product management in the context of the brave new world of work.

Individual Contributors

Let's say that your profession and current job regularly involves working on internal projects. I'm talking about coders, web designers, testers, and other folks with no PM responsibilities. Maybe you've never viewed your work through the lens of a proper project before.

PM Newbies

Maybe you're new to the field of project management or you're thinking about getting into it down the road. In either case, you won't have trouble paying your bills. PMI estimates that employers

---

[*] Yes, I'm thinking of DeNiro's iconic scene with Pacino in *Heat* as I write these words.

worldwide still need to fulfill tens of millions of positions involving project management.[11] You won't learn *everything* you need to know about the subject here. Think of this book as a primer—one that provides a broad overview that may whet your appetite to learn more.

Students of Project Management

Untold numbers of colleges and universities offer classes, certificates, and undergraduate and even graduate degrees in the field of project management. Students taking related PM classes will benefit, as will professionals who have enrolled in executive-education programs.

No, this book doesn't supplant the need for formal project management textbooks. These massive tomes typically emphasize theory over practice. In this vein, *Project Management in the Hybrid Workplace* serves as a valuable, real-world complement.

To state the obvious, these groups can and do overlap. For instance, a graphic designer is working toward her MBA at night. A management consultant is pondering going in-house and taking a client-side job.

What Else You Need to Know

We live in an era of listicles, short attention spans, modularized content, and TikTok videos. Reading a decent-sized book on a subject might seem like a big commitment. Here are some beneficial things to know from the start.

Story Matters Here

On March 31, 2009, AMC, the pioneering TV network behind *Mad Men* and *Breaking Bad*, launched a splashy new marketing campaign under the slogan: "Story Matters Here." The three-word motto has deeply resonated with me ever since.

Introduction

This book adheres to a similar philosophy. In the following pages, you'll find plenty of statistics, charts, citations of academic studies, and references to books. To underscore certain points, I've deliberately included detailed case studies and examples, many of which reflect others' experiences. My goal is to strike the right balance between theory and practice. Ideally, each element complements the others.

In a similar vein, the examples and case studies in this book run the gamut. I've balanced wise decisions from Amazon, Automattic, GitLab, and others with cautionary tales from other companies, a few of which I referenced in the Preface.

Assumptions

I'm also making several assumptions about you, dear reader:

- **You're intelligent and curious.** You don't just want to know what; you want to know *why* as well. To sate your quest for knowledge, you'd like easy access to references and links. I've provided them in footnotes and endnotes. Skip them if you like, but you won't have to go hunting for sources if one piques your curiosity. (Thank you, Google and the Internet Archive.)
- **You prefer a conversational writing style to an academic one.** You respond better to simple and direct sentences. You'd rather the author of a book avoid using polysyllabic words such as, well, polysyllabic. (I'm with you. *Use*, never *utilize*.)
- **You've got a sense of humor and appreciate a little snark.** If you believe that plenty of business and PM texts are difficult for readers to digest, then you've found the right book. This one's not like that. I'm a fan of pop-culture references and humor, although my allusions and jokes won't always land.

There are plenty of boring speakers and writers, but there's no such thing as a boring topic. Project management is no exception to this rule.

Truth in Advertising

The following pages provide essential guidance for managing projects and launching new products in remote and hybrid workplaces. The prescriptions are both tactical and strategic. Together, they will help employees, product and project teams, departments, and entire organizations avoid the pitfalls that frequently plague these endeavors.

Let me be clear: This book doesn't advance a new methodology for managing projects or launching products. Its context and advice apply equally to the existing methodologies. In this sense, *Project Management in the Hybrid Workplace* is less of what some might call a big-idea book than its predecessor.

By comparison, my previous book *Reimagining Collaboration* revolved around a big idea: the hub-spoke model of collaboration. Teams, informal groups, and even entire companies can—and should—integrate all their workplace applications into a single, cohesive whole. By doing so, they can realize manifold benefits: improve their communication and collaboration, reduce multitasking and employee burnout, and build the foundation for the forthcoming advancements in artificial intelligence and machine learning.

Yes, there's a certain degree of overlap between the two books. In both, the author brings his inimitable style, penetrating insights, sharp wit, and brooding intensity. (Too soon?)

Kidding aside, the two books are complements, not substitutes. Communication, collaboration, and project management are adjacent business disciplines. Apples and coconuts they are not. A team

Introduction

of web designers building a new site for its client can't manage the project in isolation. Finally, and as mentioned earlier, both books tackle their respective subjects in multidisciplinary manners.

Plan of Attack

This book consists of three parts. Part I provides a quick overview of the massive changes that have reshaped countless workplaces since March 2020. The ramifications for traditional project and product management are, in a word, profound. More than ever, successfully building new things and launching new products requires adopting a different mindset. Some prior PM tools and methods undoubtedly still apply; others, however, need to move from optional to imperative.

Part II offers a high-level overview of project management. It then analyzes the second-order effects stemming from the explosion of remote and hybrid work. To be sure, employees have welcomed its arrival. Still, as the story in the Preface demonstrated, we now must overcome greater friction and different challenges when working on projects and launching new products.

We then move on to Part III, the crux of this book. Each chapter provides a prescription to increase the odds that projects succeed in hybrid and remote workplaces. Collectively, these recommendations will help informal groups, formal teams, professional-service firms, and organizations of all types navigate this new world of work.

An Essential Disclaimer

In his excellent 2011 book *How: Why How We Do Anything Means Everything*, Dov Seidman advocates adopting a few guiding principles rather than creating a labyrinth of individual rules.

For example, consider Google's famous internal "Don't be evil" credo. Those three simple words obviated having to create dozens of disparate, confusing, and possibly contradictory dicta governing employee behavior. The number of people who love reading and writing detailed policy manuals is exactly zero.

Maybe a Googler did something questionable or behaved in an unethical manner. (Hello, Andy Rubin.[12]) Against a backdrop of "Don't be evil," the resulting conversation with the offending employee is relatively simple; the question never hinged upon whether he technically violated an obscure HR policy. (Interestingly, Google updated its internal code of conduct in May 2018. Employees should now strive to "Do the right thing."[13] I suspect that company lawyers sanctioned the change.)

This book abides by the same principle-based approach as Seidman advocates and Google's management follows. General prescriptions matter more than a slew of individual rules or a detailed checklist. On any given project, adhering to the advice in Part III guarantees exactly zilch. Rather, the guidance only increases the chances of a successful outcome. The following blackjack analogy will illustrate my point.

Hit Me

Say that you've got 15 and the dealer is showing a six and no, you're not counting cards à la *Rainman*. Should you hit or stick?

In this simple case, standing maximizes your chances of winning the hand. The dealer has to hit and will bust 42 percent of the time. Although standing is no guarantee of success, it's the correct statistical play and maximizes your chances of winning. Take a card if you like, but don't be surprised if your more experienced tablemates promptly walk away upon completion of the current hand. They know that

Introduction

19

> you don't understand the correct strategy, and they don't want you screwing things up for them.

By the same token, following all the advice in this book won't ensure that you'll meet your project's objectives in any type of work environment, never mind all of them. Ignore all this book's recommendations, and your project may still miraculously wind up a rousing success. Neither extreme, however, is likely.

Strap in. Get ready.

PART I

The Brave New World of Work

Chapter 1

THE WORM HAS FINALLY TURNED

"That's what the money is for."

—JOHN HAMM AS DON DRAPER, *MAD MEN*

Let's light this candle with a tricky *Jeopardy!* question. (RIP, Alex Trebek.)

Answer: Papua New Guinea, a few island countries in the Pacific Ocean, and the United States.

Question: Of the 193 members of the United Nations, which are the only countries that don't require employers to provide paid time off for new parents?

Paid Leave: A Microcosm of the Typical American Workplace

Passed in 1993, the Family and Medical Leave Act, or FMLA, only guarantees American employees *unpaid* job protection. Even then, it's complicated. (I used to assist organizations in setting up enterprise systems that tracked employee leave, among other things. Simple they were not.) In a way, though, FMLA makes sense against the backdrop of US federal labor laws.*

As I learned in grad school a million years ago, American labor legislation has been decidedly pro-employer for decades. When it comes to paying parents while they care for their newborns, the United States is a far cry from Estonia, Canada, and France.

Sure, certain states have passed more progressive legislation, perhaps none more than California. For their part, scores of companies go well beyond the bare minimum. Prominent, deep-pocketed firms such as Microsoft, Netflix, Volvo, and ~~Facebook~~ Meta are downright generous in granting new parents *paid* time off. It's good PR. Recruiters at these organizations smartly tout the policy when wooing applicants. They should. The policy serves as a signal that their future employer values its employees, not to mention a potential point of differentiation from other firms.

In September 2020, Oxford Economics surveyed members of the Society for Human Resource Management about their paid-leave practices. SHRM members reported offering some type of paid leave between 35 percent and 55 percent of the time, depending on the type of leave in question.[1] Many respondents provide it because state law currently mandates it.

The numbers may be ticking up on paid parental leave, but it's still a mixed bag at best. This leaves one to wonder if it's a priority for the American workers.

It most certainly is. According to an April 2021 YouGov poll, more than four in five Americans favor it.[2] In sum, the demand for paid leave is strong, but the supply is wanting. The gap is considerable.

---

* For a stunning visual on differences among countries, check out https://tinyurl.com/rpm-paid-leave.

If paid leave is so important to many American workers, it's reasonable to ask why more companies don't offer it.

The short answer is because they don't have to. Many companies won't offer an employer benefit unless they're compelled—either by regulation or the economic necessity of attracting workers.

Apart from exhibiting a general reluctance to offer new employee benefits, employers aren't above rolling back existing perks. Exhibit A: employer-funded retirement plans. Throughout the twentieth century, American employers routinely offered their employees defined-benefit plans—aka *pensions*. Starting in the 1980s, however, they began steadily shifting the responsibility of retirement to individual employees via defined-contribution plans.[3]

It worked.

In the early 1980s, defined-benefit pension plans covered three in five private-sector workers. CNN Money reports that the corresponding figure today is a paltry 4 percent.[4]

The Erosion of Labor Unions

At this point you may be wondering, Where are unions in all this? Aren't they supposed to protect their members' interests?

We're a long way from 1954, arguably the halcyon days for organized labor. Back then, more than one in three US workers belonged to a labor union. As of January 2022, that number had plummeted to one in ten.[5] (In case you're curious, that number in Canada is 30 percent.[6] Again, context matters here.) Unions are often powerless to force management to adopt employee-friendly policies these days.

For many employers, 10 percent is still far too high. Amazon may not have hired Pinkerton guards à la Carnegie Steel during the 1892 Homestead Strike, but it has fervently fought employee-unionization efforts since its inception. It's also been successful as of this writing, although I'm betting that Amazon will be reluctantly certifying its first union by the end of 2022.[7] The Everything Store isn't above employing questionable, possibly illegal, tactics in the process.[8]

Scaling back employee benefits or fighting unions is one thing, but what about laying off significant portions of the workforce, even when a company is clearly in the black?

Compared to other nations, American laws and overall attitudes toward layoffs differ dramatically from their European counterparts.[9] As but one case in point, the late CEO and turnaround specialist "Chainsaw" Al Dunlap prided himself on cost cutting (read: mass layoffs), company profitability be damned. He earned his other nickname, "Rambo in Pinstripes," after he posed for a photo wearing an ammo belt across his chest.

Churchill once said, "Democracy is the worst form of government, except for all those other forms that have been tried from time to time." The very same maxim applies to capitalism.

Now, if this book were a critique of American capitalism, then I'd continue by exploring the following adjacent labor-related subjects:

- Automation.
- Stagnating middle-class wages.
- Outsourcing.
- The extensive reliance upon independent contractors. (Hello, Uber.)
- The meteoric rise in CEO pay. In 2020, the top CEOs earned 351 times more than the typical worker. (The same ratio was a mere 20:1 in 1965 and 61:1 in 1989.) Again, this rise is most pronounced in the United States.[*]

---

[*] See https://cnb.cx/3vcpNuY.

But *Project Management in the Hybrid Workplace* isn't that kind of book. The opening part of this chapter serves to establish that, for decades, American companies have generally held more power than their employees have. Compared to their brethren in other countries, the employer-employee power asymmetry is inarguable.

How have American workers felt about this reality and, by extension, their jobs? Are they engaged?

Employee Engagement on the Job

We've all met people who love what they do. Somehow, they mesh with their managers, colleagues, and employers. They never complain—nary a bad day. Ever. Maybe you're one of these fortunate few. And then there are others who loathe everything about their current professional stations in life.

Anecdotes aside, what does the data say about employee satisfaction?[*]

Consider a revealing statistic from Gallup. In August 2018, the hallowed analytics and advisory firm reported that a mere 34 percent of American workers reported being "engaged" while on the job. More specifically, only one in three was "enthusiastic about and committed to their work and workplace."[10]

Without context, that number in isolation may seem pitifully low. (As you know by now, I like context.)

Here's the rub: 34 percent represented its apex since Gallup began reporting that national figure back in 2000. Despite a recent postpandemic bump (possibly stemming from being able to work remotely), the statistic has never even crossed 40 percent, as Figure 1.1 demonstrates.

---

[*] I'll use the terms *engagement* and *satisfaction* interchangeably. I'm aware that technically you can be one without the other, but fine semantic distinctions just don't interest me.

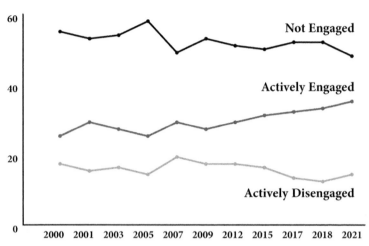

Figure 1.1: US Employee Engagement Trend (Source: Gallup)

As a corollary, the percentage of American workers who claim to be "not engaged" has never fallen below half. At least worker malaise isn't confined to the red, white, and blue. Far from it. Across the pond, in 2017 Gallup reported that 10 percent of Brits were engaged at work.[11]

For at least two decades, rare is the American who has been a happy camper while on the clock. Yet at least in the short term, most of us have grudgingly tolerated the grind of M–F/9–5 work for two main reasons:

1. Employers set the rules over where and when employees work.
2. We need to pay our bills.

Don Draper's iconic quote at the start of this chapter accurately sums up how many Americans think about work. In the eyes of many, Maslow's Hierarchy of Needs and other highfalutin theories about self-actualized employees are best left for academics and wonky management theorists. Sure, there are exceptions, but we collectively suck it up because people have drilled the idea that "work isn't supposed to be fun" into our heads for decades. Welcome to the real world, sparky.

Those looking to escape private-sector employment often find that things aren't so different in other walks of life. That is, many ostensibly uncommercial American institutions liberally borrow from the playbooks of their corporate brethren.

The prominent social critic and political activist Noam Chomsky has written and spoken extensively about the corporatization of American universities.[*] (As a recovering college professor myself, I can confirm that he's absolutely right. Even public universities are fundamentally businesses—and that reality impacts how they view their employees. Rare is the institution of higher learning that offers anything more than a nine-month employment agreement to its nontenured faculty. The fact that so many K–12 teachers need to purchase their own supplies for their students should sicken anyone with a conscience.[†]

All of this is to say that American workers have been waiting for the pendulum to swing their way for a long time. To quote from the 1976 film *Network*, workers have been "mad as hell and they're not gonna take it anymore."

Beginning in March 2020, that swing finally began taking place, gradually and then suddenly. We've now clearly entered a new era of work—a decidedly more employee-friendly one. Figure 1.2 shows the change.

---

[*] Watch one of his talks at https://tinyurl.com/noam2-rpm.

[†] The statistics from the National Center for Education Statistics are not for the faint of heart: https://tinyurl.com/nces-rpm.

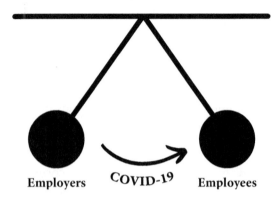

Figure 1.2: The Pendulum Has Finally Swung Toward Employees

The Newly Emboldened Workforce

As you've no doubt heard by now, we're smack dab in the middle of the Great ... something. Call it the *Great Resignation,* the *Great Reset,* or something else if you prefer.

Irrespective of moniker, "something infectious is spreading through the workforce," as Emma Goldberg of the *New York Times* writes in an excellent January 2022 piece.[12] COVID-19 caused people to reevaluate their personal and professional priorities. Troves of individuals realized that their companies needed them more than the other way around. A record 4.4 million Americans quit their jobs in September 2021.[13] (The Job Openings and Labor Turnover Survey provides a fascinating look into who's quitting and why.[14])

Millions of people decided to hang their own shingle when the mask wearing began. (If not now, when?) The US Census Bureau reported that seasonally adjusted new business applications spiked 20 percent from 2020 to 2021 to a record five million.[15] Oodles more started gigging. More than 60 million Americans freelanced in

2021.[16] The stock of freelancing site Upwork started taking off in May 2020. While currently down from its high, it's still worth $3 billion as of this writing.

The US labor market is historically tight. Wendy's employees aren't making $15/hour because franchisees are feeling particularly generous.[17] Fast food restaurants need people, and they have no other choice but to pay their employees more.

Easier, Not Easy

The regulatory environment in the United States has tilted toward industry for decades, especially compared to other industrialized countries. That's not to say, however, that entrepreneurs don't work hard or that starting a business is easy. Far from it.

The data from two types of businesses is eerily consistent.

The US Small Business Administration Office of Advocacy in 2018 reported that roughly half of small businesses survived past the five-year mark. Only about one in three restaurants, Pilates studies, and law firms reached the ten-year mark.* As someone who hung his own shingle twenty years ago, I can attest that the obstacles are still formidable.

Startups differ from restaurants and law firms in one fundamental way: Their business models are unproven. Back in 1997 Netflix was a startup, as was Uber in 2009. In 2019, the failure rate of startups hovered around 90 percent.[18]

---

* Read more at https://tinyurl.com/rpm-smadvoc.

Two Different Pandemic-Related Work Scenarios

Socrates famously said, "The unexamined life is not worth living." In that vein, it's instructive to review two alternate realities from the one that ultimately came to pass.

Number 1: The Blip

COVID-19 turned out to be a minor annoyance that lasted a few weeks to a month.

I wish.

If this scenario had played out, workers would have viewed the work-from-home (WFH) period as the equivalent of a few snow days or a *workation*. For a short, joyous time, they would have taken a brief respite from the normal drudgery of putting their faces on, commuting to the office, enduring obnoxious colleagues, and working in environments that rarely compared to the comforts of their homes. When the dust finally settled, I suspect that most employees would have returned to the office, if somewhat grudgingly.

Number 2: COVID-19 Kept Us Home but Unproductive

Employees tried, but ultimately realized, that they couldn't effectively do their jobs outside of their organizations' physical walls. Physical proximity to our colleagues is essential to get *anything* done.

No dice on this scenario either.

Throughout the pandemic, employees have reported being as productive if not more productive while working from home—and then, from anywhere.

Shocker, right? What would you expect them to say? Remarkably, however, the majority of *employers* agree with that assessment. In August 2020, the management consulting outfit Mercer published a survey finding that an astonishing 94 percent of the 793 employers surveyed agreed that "productivity has remained the same or improved since employees began working remotely."[*]

Upon reading that last paragraph, you may well be thinking, "I told you so."

What's more, you may be miffed that it took a pandemic to validate your thesis: You can be productive away from the office. At least you can take solace in the fact that this belief is neither surprising nor new. Employees have long yearned for remote work. It's not hard to locate a slew of turn-of-the-century articles on the subject.[†] And a WFH gig is not just a mild preference either. A 2017 survey found that nearly three-quarters of workers would leave their current jobs for remote ones.[19]

The idea that we could be just as productive away from the office didn't just occur to us when COVID arrived. We've long believed that we didn't need to be in the office.

We've become accustomed to this new way of working. We like it. As Figure 1.3 shows, every day that we work effectively out of the office makes us less likely to voluntarily revert to our prepandemic work conditions.

That's my story, and I'm sticking to it. Still, it's based on hard data.

In February 2020, the nonpartisan Pew Research Center conducted an extensive survey of 10,000 adults about all aspects of their work.[20] Of particular relevance here is the rise in the percentage of workers opting to do their jobs outside of the confines of their reopened offices. See Figure 1.4.

---

[*] The survey lives behind a paywall, but the company made an infographic available for free at https://tinyurl.com/mercerRPM.

[†] Run this Google search yourself at https://tinyurl.com/rpm-rwork.

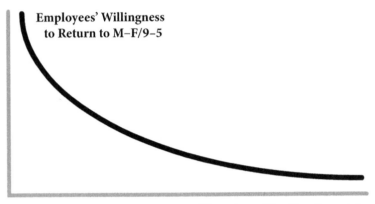

Figure 1.3: The Longer We Work Remotely, the Less We Want to Return to Pre-COVID Work Conditions

Figure 1.4: Percentage of Americans Who Are Choosing Not to Return to the Office (Source: Pew Research Center)

This begs the obvious question, Why? The reflexive answer: Because they can. After all, that's a sufficient reason for myriad employers to avoid offering paid parental leave to their workforces. Why wouldn't similar rationale hold here? What's good for the goose …

If this were *Family Feud,* then *personal choice* would be the top answer on the board. Figure 1.5 provides a more detailed window into why we're electing to work from home.

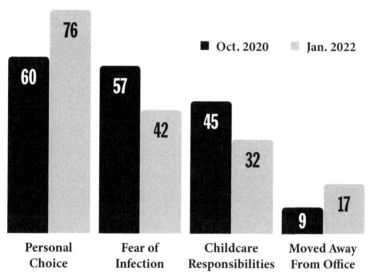

Figure 1.5: Why Americans Are Working From Home (Percentages) (Source: Pew Research Center)

There's a broader point here: COVID-19 gave employees time to rethink, spend time with loved ones, exercise, and take up a new hobby.

The pandemic made us realize the extent to which we've been subjugating our personal lives to our professional ones.

COVID-19 upended the status quo of work. As Figure 1.6 demonstrates, we've reexamined our relationship with work.

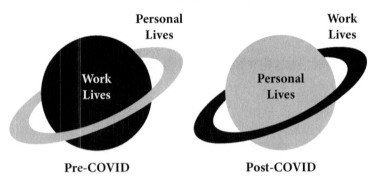

Figure 1.6: The Work Legacy of COVID-19

We're not keen on reverting to the prepandemic model, and hybrid and remote work are here to stay. The only question is how employers will attempt to accommodate their newly empowered, increasingly finicky employees.

> ### A Quick Note on Vaccine Mandates
>
> A clear majority of Americans supported President Biden's vaccine mandates for healthcare workers and large companies.[21] Despite this reality, it should surprise no one that US government's attempt to impose them on businesses ultimately failed.
>
> By way of comparison, dozens of countries passed similar—if not far more restrictive—legislation. A few examples include Germany, Ecuador, and Indonesia. The Latvian government banned unvaccinated lawmakers from voting and docked their pay.[22]

Chapter Summary

- As a group and for at least two decades, employees have never particularly felt engaged while on the clock. The reasons may stem from an especially pro-business environment in the United States.
- For decades, the business environment has been decidedly pro-business, especially in relation to other industrialized countries.
- COVID-19 caused the employer-employee pendulum to shift toward the latter. It won't be swinging back to the former anytime soon.
- Employees have spoken loud and clear: They want their work lives to revolve around their personal lives, not the other way around.

Chapter 2

NO SMALL CHALLENGE: MANAGING THE HYBRID WORKPLACE

"Tesla is restarting production today against Alameda County rules. I will be on the line with everyone else. If anyone is arrested, I ask that it only be me."[1]

—TWEET FROM ELON MUSK, MAY 11, 2020

It's hard to overstate how much we learned about ourselves during the early days of COVID-19.

For openers, not every CEO, mid-level manager, small-business owner, and rank-and-file employee welcomed this new era of employee empowerment and remote work with open arms. WeWork CEO Sandeep Mathrani justifiably took heat after saying that people who are most comfortable working from home are the "least engaged" with their jobs.[2] He had to walk it back.

For obvious reasons, some outfits needed to stay open for society to properly function during those dark days. Yes, it's time to use the *E*-word. Some businesses—and their workers—are essential. Hospitals, restaurants, police stations, post offices, pharmacies, and grocery stores qualify. Imagine a world without Amazon and Walmart. They had to press on. Elon Musk believed that carmakers qualified for that designation, too. Well, at least *his* carmaker did.

Barely two months into the pandemic, the petulant Tesla CEO took to Twitter, his social media outlet of choice. He aired his belief that government officials weren't easing their shelter-in-place restrictions fast enough for him.[3] As his earlier tweet demonstrated, his actions didn't belie his words. He was willing to walk the talk.

An ordinary, responsible business leader doesn't directly disobey the safety orders from a local government trying to navigate the early days of an unprecedented pandemic, much less so proudly and publicly. People familiar with Musk's history and antics, however, weren't surprised. Read Ashlee Vance's book *Elon Musk: Tesla, SpaceX, and the Quest for a Fantastic Future.* You'll learn that many adjectives describe Musk. *Law-abiding* and *ordinary* don't come close to making the cut.

Musk clearly viewed the spread of COVID-19 as a minor nuisance, one that need not disrupt the operations of his business or cause his company's stratospheric stock price to drop. With respect to both objectives, Musk wanted Tesla to continue as is.

In other words, he wanted Tesla to be more like Automattic, GitLab, Basecamp, and other distributed companies.

Business as Usual: The Exceptions That Proved the Rule

Employees at a small minority of firms didn't miss a beat when offices around the world closed for one simple reason: They'd never worked out of proper offices in the first place. The most prominent examples of these distributed companies include Automattic, Basecamp, and GitLab. To quote a popular meme, they were built for this.

I've got no shortage of theories about why work at these companies continued with minimal disruption, but I decided to ask someone with insider knowledge. Enter GitLab's head of remote, Darren Murph—aka, the Oracle of Remote Work. Here's what he told me:

> GitLab was all-remote from its inception. We use our own platform to collaborate across functions and time zones, easily capturing contributions from team members in more than 65 countries. Our company handbook serves as the single source of truth.[*] We don't rely upon a person or function. Our teams completed their projects with relative ease, especially compared to those at other organizations.[4]

Beyond increased continuity, I'd bet my house that distributed companies like these three have:

- Suffered far less employee turnover than stodgy firms struggling to navigate this starkly different world.
- Seen a deluge in new applicants.

People want to work remotely, and yes, they're willing to die on that hill. It's at this point in the story that we meet Jason Alvarez Schorr.

The Existential Employer Dilemma: When Employees Just Aren't That Into You

My favorite quote on returning to the office comes from Schorr, a 36-year-old software engineer based out of Manhattan. In January 2022, his then-current employer signaled that an office return

---

[*] Read it yourself at https://about.gitlab.com/handbook.

was imminent. Schorr promptly quit. When speaking to Callum Borchers of the *Wall Street Journal,* he said, "You're not going to get me on the train for two hours for free bagels."[5]

As someone who made the arduous commute to New York City more times than I can count, I couldn't help but laugh.

Schorr's hardly an outlier, but don't believe me. Read on.

Consider the research of Stanford economics professor Nicholas Bloom. Around the same time that Schorr was handing in his notice, Bloom's firm WFH Research surveyed people whose jobs allowed them to work from home. Figure 2.1 displays a histogram of their responses to a question regarding how many days they'd like to work in the office.

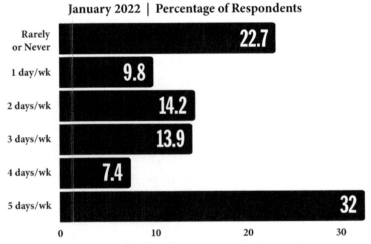

Figure 2.1: Number of Days/Week People Want to Work in the Office. (Data from WFH Research)*

---

* Data from 55,179 respondents reporting being able to work from home. Data re-weighted to match the US population. See https://tinyurl.com/RPMWTF.

The essential question isn't whether the future of work will be hybrid. As Bloom has said in subsequent interviews, "The battle is over. WFH won." The more intelligent query is, To what extent? WFH Research asked that question, too. Figure 2.2 presents the results.

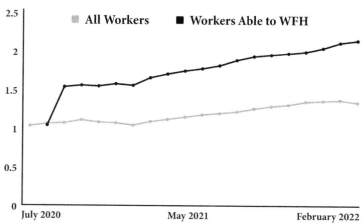

Figure 2.2: Employee Responses When Asked How Many Days Per Week Their Employers Will Let Them Work Remotely in 2022 and Beyond (Data from WFH Research)

Note the steadily upward trend. Employees claim that their managers are letting them work remotely more of the time—and not just in the United States.

Emerging evidence suggests that, a few reactionaries aside, the majority of employers have accepted the fact that M–F/9–5 is indeed a relic of the past. Derek Thompson of *The Atlantic* spoke with Bloom in February 2020. As the former wrote:

> In the next decade, U.S. workers will spend about 25 percent of their time working from home, Bloom says. That's 20

percentage points higher than the pre-pandemic figure, leaving companies with an important choice: sign for significantly less office space, or accept that significantly more of your space will go unused on a given day.

Bloom is betting strongly on the latter. "Office occupancy has plummeted, but corporate demand for office space is down only about 1 percent," he said. "That might sound shocking, but it's because so many companies planning for hybrid work are expecting most of the office to be in on some days of the week, so they can't shrink their space."[6]

Tara Sinclair, a professor at George Washington University, conducted an international survey on remote work as a senior fellow at Indeed. In her words:

We knew remote work was feasible, and we knew job seekers wanted it, but it was the pandemic that made it an actual day-to-day experience, and once it happened it stuck.[7]

The numbers bear this out. The compensation company Payscale found in its 2022 report that nearly two-thirds of employers now report offering remote work. See Figure 2.3.

Bloom and Sinclair are spot-on. Employers aren't just paying lip service to the idea of remote or hybrid work: In May 2021, LinkedIn reported that job postings containing the word *remote* rose a mind-boggling 457 percent, with technology and media companies leading the way.[8]

Supply, meet demand. It's not hard to understand why employees enjoy WFH as much as they do. Employers, maybe not so much.

Percentage of Companies Surveyed That Reported Offering Remote Work

Figure 2.3: Percentage of Companies Surveyed That Reported Offering Remote Work (Source: Payscale 2022 Compensation Best Practices Report)

In some cases, there's a fundamental trust issue. Consider James, a fifty-ish, old-school middle manager at a mature financial services shop who routinely struggles with technology. Remote and hybrid work worry him because he won't be able to watch his employees work anymore. Sadly, that's a genuine concern, but it's far from the only one.

Social Capital and Hybrid Hassles

In his bestselling 2000 book *Bowling Alone: The Collapse and Revival of American Community,* Robert Putnam laments the substantial decline of social capital, a term that he defines as follows:

> the connections among individuals' social networks and the norms of reciprocity and trustworthiness that arise from them.

Putnam adeptly demonstrates how high levels of social capital benefit all sorts of groups: individuals, businesses, communities, and even entire societies.

Everybody Wins

Think of social capital as a superpower of sorts. It can make:

1. Parties argue with one another less and with less vitriol. This facilitates solving thorny collective problems. As a result, our social environments improve. Our neighborhoods become safer and more productive.
2. Our mutual connectivity grows. Social capital can improve the quality of our civic and democratic institutions.
3. We can increase the flow of information, benefiting individuals and all sorts of institutions.
4. Our health and happiness can improve. After all, we're human beings. Our psychological and biological processes benefit from interacting with other humans.
5. Business transactions can go smoother. That is, social capital can serve as a lubricant. When employees trust each other, they're less likely to threaten each other.

Putnam published his book in 2001. As such, technology wasn't a central theme in the first edition of his book. In hindsight, it's hard to fault him for the omission.

Turn back the clock to the turn of the previous century. The World Wide Web was taking off. Amazon and eBay were already giants. Google was a mere three years old and still just a search engine. (No Android, Maps, Gmail, and the like.) Cellphones existed. No, they weren't the shoe-sized behemoths of the late 1980s, but they weren't anything close to *smart*. The iPhone wouldn't arrive for another seven years. If you wanted to connect with others, you certainly could. Facebook and Twitter didn't exist yet either. You'd have to use Six Degrees and classmates.com.[9] Even Friendster didn't launch until 2004.

Twenty Years Later

Fast-forward two decades, and the world is vastly different and even more politically polarized.[10] Thank social media, smartphones, user-generated content, cloud computing, powerful search engines, cyberattacks, the decline of newspapers, and a whole host of other factors.

The 20th anniversary edition of Putnam's book reflects these tectonic changes. It properly acknowledges the role of technology and social media in further eroding society and further disintegrating social capital. Pick it up, and you'll find twenty-three separate mentions of Facebook and thirteen of Twitter, but let's get back to the subject at hand.

Putnam surely wasn't writing primarily or directly about hybrid workplaces. Still, it's instructive to think about his ideas in the contexts of technology and hybrid and remote workplaces.

On Xerox Machines, Strangers, and Social Capital

When a complete stranger asks you to do something, will you do it?

The answer depends on myriad factors.

For one, consider the stranger's specific choice of words. In his bestseller *Influence: The Psychology of Persuasion,* Robert Cialdini describes a fascinating study by Harvard University's Ellen Langer and her colleagues:

> People simply like to have reasons for what they do. Langer demonstrated this unsurprising fact by asking a small favor of people waiting in line to use a library's copying machine: *Excuse me, I have five pages. May I use the Xerox machine, because I'm in a rush?* The effectiveness of this request-plus-reason was nearly total: 94 percent of people let her skip ahead of

them in line. Compare this success rate to the results when she made the request only: "Excuse me, I have five pages. May I use the Xerox machine?" Under those circumstances, only 60 percent complied.

At first glance, it appears the crucial difference between the two requests was the additional information provided by the words "because I'm in a rush." However, a third type of request showed this was not the case. It seems it was not the whole series of words but the first one, "because," that made the difference. Instead of including a real reason for compliance, Langer's third type of request used the word "because" and then, adding nothing new, merely restated the obvious: "Excuse me, I have five pages. May I use the Xerox machine because I have to make some copies?" The result was once again nearly all (93 percent) agreed, even though no real reason, no new information was added to justify their compliance.

All participants in the Langer study asked strangers for the same favor *in person*. This calls into question whether the medium matters.

In one 2017 study, researchers examined participants' willingness to comply with strangers' requests in person versus those sent via email. Two of its results are particularly instructive here:

- Requesters *overestimated* how frequently others would comply with their requests over email.
- Requesters *underestimated* how frequently others would comply with their requests when making them in person.[11]

Stitching together the two studies, the implications of social capital for remote and hybrid workplaces run deep. We usually ignore random messages from strangers, especially if they're poorly worded. Of course, our colleagues, partners, and bosses may not be complete strangers. When we've built social capital with them, all else being equal, we're more likely to do what they ask, and vice versa.

And there's the rub: It's more difficult to build social capital with people when they're out of sight and out of mind.

Proximity Bias

Psychologists use a more formal term to describe this phenomenon: *proximity bias*. A simple example will illustrate it in the workplace.

Brandt is a manager at a web design shop. He routinely sees Jeffrey in the office burning the midnight oil. Donnie works harder and smarter than his peer, but *invisibly.* That is, Donnie sits in the comforts of his home. Which one will Brandt probably remember when it's time to review employee performance and dole out raises and bonuses? This inclination doesn't make Brandt a bad person; *it just makes him human.*

Returning to the real world, let's meet London-based business anthropologist Simon Roberts. He's also the author of *The Power of Not Thinking: How Our Bodies Learn and Why We Should Trust Them.* Speaking to Kevin Delaney of Charter, Roberts opines:

> Hybrid work involves asymmetries. A simple example is a meeting where three people are in the room and two people aren't. It's very easy for the two people that aren't in the room to get crowded out of that conversation. Some of that can be addressed with clever hardware and software, and some of that needs to be addressed with behavioral norms being laid out. The grammar of a meeting or the grammar of how somebody takes a meeting needs to change a little bit to make sure that you are inclusive to the people being piped

in from over the internet. Those are very everyday things, but I think they're really important.[12]

Tru dat, as the kids say. I'm sold, but what if you're still a bit skeptical on the idea of proximity bias? What if it's too abstract? Say that you're not convinced that it's a real and burgeoning problem, or at least a problem that *your* company will have to confront. Time to bring out the big guns.

The Future Forum is a consortium with the stated aim to "help companies make the transformations necessary to thrive in the new economy." Its January 2022 Pulse Survey provides fascinating insights into many aspects of the post-COVID world of work.[13] For our purposes here, managers acknowledge the problematic gap between in-person and remote workers—one that may become a chasm, as Figure 2.4 demonstrates.

Percentage of Executives Who Cited the Potential for Inequities to Develop Between Remote and In-Office Employees as Their Top Concern

Figure 2.4: Percentage of Executives Who Cited the Potential for Inequities to Develop Between Remote and In-Office Employees as Their Top Concern (Source: Future Forum)

All hybrid workplaces suffer from some degree of proximity bias. The fleas come with the dog. Leaders will need to alter their pre-COVID management styles and establish new workplace norms.

Just remember that the hybrid workplace introduces proximity bias. Left unaddressed, a caste system will develop within any organization.

> ## Other Hassles
>
> One could write an entire book about the problems inherent in remote and hybrid work. This chapter touches on a bunch of issues, but I have to throw in one fascinating statistic.
>
> Project managers struggle when work takes place away from the office. In a 2019 survey, the software-comparison site GetApp found a mere 17 percent of PMs reported that they were fully able to manage their remote team members.[14]
>
> Here's one theory based upon my interactions with dedicated PMs over the years. They're responsible for different individuals' tasks and productivity as well as the status of a much larger project. Remote, distributed, or hybrid work makes this type of coordination more difficult.

Reports of the Death of the Office Are Greatly Exaggerated

There's one surefire way to eradicate proximity bias: Relevel the playing field, but not by mandating a butts-in-seats approach to work. Rather, take the opposite approach: Let everyone work remotely all the time and retire the office altogether.

It sure is a tempting idea. As Figure 2.5 shows, proximity bias effectively can't exist if everyone *always* works remotely or in person. In each case, the playing field is level.

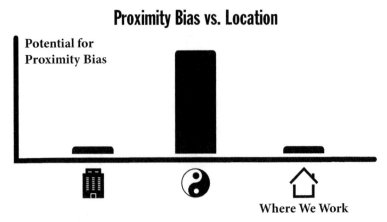

Figure 2.5: Proximity Bias vs. Location

Beyond placating newly empowered employees, the no-office approach confers added benefits. Real-estate and related costs (such as insurance) go *poof!*

Seemingly every day, high-profile companies bid *adieu* to their formal offices. The consulting firm PwC in October 2021 established a work-from-anywhere policy for its 40,000 US employees.[15] The advisory outfit Forrester Research followed suit a few months later.[*]

Did most employees at each company welcome the change? I have no doubt. The jury is still out, however, on whether the squeeze will be worth the juice. Although alluring, the move to an all-remote workplace is no logistical or management slam dunk. Also, employees represent just one of each company's key constituencies. What will their shareholders, partners, and clients think of the post-office world of work?

---

[*] Read the CEO's announcement at https://www.forrester.com/blogs/anywhere-work.

In Defense of the Office

Dunk on the office all you want, but it has traditionally served invaluable business functions, including:

- Giving a company its identity.
- Providing a secure and private space for client and employee meetings.
- Storing physical corporate assets.
- Allowing employees to participate in training.
- Building a sense of camaraderie among the staff.
- Promoting more collaborative work.
- Drinking, if your name is Don Draper or Roger Sterling.[*]

Five years from now, the PwC and Forrester bigwigs may regret the decision to go all in on remote work.

The Evolving Office

Less uncertain, however, is whether traditional corporate offices will remain constant. They won't. In fact, the idea of a single headquarters may go the way of the dodo. Employees may work in different, er, buildings. Suburban satellite offices are beginning to replace traditional corporate command posts.[16] WeWork is rebounding from its Adam Neumann debacle. As Melissa Kravitz Hoeffner writes for the *New York Times,* "smaller, resourceful co-working initiatives are cropping up everywhere, introducing new competition."[17] And *everywhere* includes Chandler, Arizona.

---

[*] I couldn't resist another *Mad Men* reference.

Coworking and COVID

In 2019, the Brazilian company Universo Online (UOL) flew me to its headquarters in Porto Alegre to record a two-day data visualization class. (I tell the story behind it in my previous book *Reimagining Collaboration*, so I won't repeat it here.)

UOL reached out to me again in mid-2021 to record an updated version of the course. Travel was still sketchy back then, and Brazilian COVID numbers were surging. Complicating matters further, Brazil's currency (the real) had dropped against the US dollar. As a result, my previous fee and travel costs had become prohibitively expensive. I understood, but preparing a six-hour course is no small endeavor.

It looked like we wouldn't be able to reach a deal.

A few months later, I recorded the class at Workuity, a slick coworking space near my home in Arizona. All things considered, it went well. UOL saved thousands on travel and lodging, and I didn't need to take six flights during a pandemic.

Now that we're two years past COVID-19's arrival, many employers understand that the office needs to evolve. Workers need a compelling reason to return to one. ("Because I'm your boss and I say so" no longer suffices, especially in this labor market.) Employees will walk. Many already have.

When employees do return to an office, they're likely to see significant changes in both its physical configuration and the expected behaviors in it. Myriad design firms boldly envision the future office as more of a clubhouse in which employees collaborate and bond.[18] As Chip Cutter writes in the *Wall Street Journal:*

> ... today's tech offices look different. Dropbox doesn't call its spaces offices anymore. Instead, it calls them studios: there are fewer desks and more meeting rooms and lounges for less formal team gatherings.[19]

Employees will be working with their heads up more often than down (read: checking email).

PwC and Forrester aside, not every company will abandon their offices altogether. So says Victor Coleman, CEO of the real estate investment group Hudson Pacific Properties. Speaking with Kellen Browning of the *New York Times* in February 2022, he said:

> I think there are a lot more companies that are saying, "You're coming back to work"—it's not "if," it's "when." The reality is that most companies are currently working from home but are wanting and planning to come back to the office."[20]

Coleman is no iconoclast. The same article quotes George Forristall, the Phoenix real estate director at Mortenson Development. He described the thinking on remote work "like a pendulum—it swung a little bit too far, and now it's come back a little bit." Figure 2.6 represents this pendulum.

Where will it ultimately settle? No one can be sure across the board, much less at any one company or in any industry. This much, however, I do know: For millions of people and companies, the pendulum won't be swinging back to its pre-COVID state.

Enough about offices. It's time to talk about compensation.

Understanding Traditional Labor Markets

In grad school, my two favorite classes were compensation and labor economics—two subjects that continue to intrigue me.

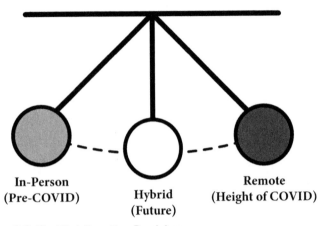

Figure 2.6: The Work/Location Pendulum

Fuse those two disciplines, and you understand why Miranda Priestly didn't need to pay her assistants all that much in *The Devil Wears Prada*. Despite her verbal abuse and the job's tortuous hours, hundreds of aspiring fashionistas would kill for that job.

That same cachet doesn't apply to open positions for nurses and security guards. People in those fields who work the night shift typically receive a shift differential. As a general rule, people who perform dangerous jobs effectively earn the equivalent of hazard pay. Coal miners and oil-rig workers[21] face significantly higher fatality rates than the servers who sling bang bang chicken at the local Cheesecake Factory.

Speaking of location, administrative assistants who live in Hawaii take home far more than their counterparts in Wyoming and Alabama. Turning to California, software engineers make more cheddar working out of San Francisco than they do if they call Temecula home.

Compensating Wage Differentials

All of this is to say that the specific attributes of jobs have always affected the wages that employers need to offer to attract employees. Economists observed this phenomenon long ago, coining the term *compensating wage differential.* Here's a simple, jargon-free definition:

> the additional amount of income that workers require to accept undesirable elements of jobs relative to the other jobs they can perform.

Companies that have ignored this economic orthodoxy have faced a difficult time finding qualified employees. Making $35,000/ year might satisfy a schoolteacher in Camden, New Jersey, but a Manhattan school district will have to pony up at least twice as much.

Makes sense, right? But what happens when employers decouple location from employee wages? That is, what if employees earn the same cabbage regardless of where they live and work?

We might be on the verge of finding out.

Zillow's Zany Experiment

Dan Spaulding serves as Zillow's chief people office. In September 2021, he took to LinkedIn to announce his company's new employee compensation policy. In his words, "When you work for Zillow, your long-term earning potential is determined by how you perform and will not be limited by where you live."[22]

In a word, *wow.*

Spaulding may believe that Zillow's new policy is fundamentally the right thing to do. (For all I know, he disagreed with his professors when they taught compensating wage differentials.)

Spaulding's timing is certainly propitious. He couldn't have tried this experiment fifteen years ago. Collaboration technologies have advanced considerably over the past decade. Context aside, however,

Zillow's shift doesn't stem from employer paternalism or benevolence. At least three factors are driving the company's decision:

- ☺ Promoting simplicity and transparency in its internal compensation policies.
- ☺ Minimizing employee attrition.
- ☺ Competing in a cut-throat war for talent.

Stay tuned. If more companies follow Zillow's lead, things will get very interesting—and not just for college professors teaching compensation and labor economics.

The Perfect Storm

What happens when a high-inflationary environment collides with woke employees and an unprecedented rise in remote/hybrid work? Quite a bit, as we're discovering.

For starters, employee pay rises. No shocker here. Payscale surveyed more than 5,000 employers in different industries.[*] Its report, *Refocusing Compensation's Role in the Great Reevaluation,* revealed that more than four in five organizations are planning to increase employee wages in 2022. Employers reported that those pay bumps are "significantly higher" than those from prior years. They still worry that those hikes may not keep pace with inflation.

History teaches us that high inflation eventually subsides. Its effects, however, are neither neutral nor ephemeral. Some of them tend to stick. In the words of Molly Kinder, a fellow at Brookings Metro:

> I don't think you're going to suddenly see the power shift back to employers. A good outcome would be if inflation cools, if

---

[*] Read it yourself at https://tinyurl.com/PSpayscale3.

2 No Small Challenge: Managing the Hybrid Workplace 59

some of these demand-and-supply issues modulate, and if workers continue to have some bargaining power.[23]

Adam Smith taught us that management will increase employee wages primarily out of their own enlightened self-interest: to thwart employee turnover and keep the lights on. In this case, however, there could be an added—and much needed—societal side benefit. Middle-class workers may finally see pay hikes after decades of stagnation.[24]

Attracting, retaining, and motivating employees are hardly new management challenges. In the post-COVID world, however, they've become Herculean ones.

When Technology Eats Geography

Depending on your vocation, where you live is less relevant now compared to three years ago. Thanks to the massive advances in collaboration technology over the past decade, geography no longer constrains employee job prospects, at least to the same degree as it did prior to the pandemic. To paraphrase an oft-repeated line from internet pioneer and prominent venture capitalist Marc Andreessen, software is eating geography.

The previous chapter illustrated that, as a general rule, American employers tend to enhance employee benefits only when they must. The same principle applies to worker compensation. And, as always, timing is everything.

The grass may have always been greener, but historically geography has constrained our employment prospects. Consider Esmeralda, a disgruntled 35-year-old architect living in Phoenix circa 2007. She could certainly conduct a national job search, but taking a position in Chicago would involve uprooting her family.

Fifteen years later, she can offer her talents to an increasingly global set of organizations without having to call U-Haul and finding a new school for her children. Put simply, labor markets have become much more fluid. Even if Esmeralda were relatively satisfied with her current gig, she could voyeuristically peruse available opportunities on her phone during lunch—the equivalent of an Airbnb vacation. By the same token, recruiters can easily take her temperature via LinkedIn.

Advantage: Workers.

Employee Stigmas and the Myth of the Company Man

Let's move Esmeralda back a decade to 1997. For different reasons, she's bounced around, working at five different companies. As a serial job-hopper, she would have faced a stigma when interviewing for new positions. I saw this play out firsthand during my brief career in HR in the mid-90s. Applicants who switched jobs every year had tough roads to hoe. We tried to fill our positions with stable candidates who'd be more likely to stick around.

Despite what our elders may claim over Thanksgiving dinner, however, they were not all loyal company men.

In August 2021, the US Bureau of Labor Statistics released a report finding that "individuals born in the latter years of the baby boom (1957–1964) held an average of 12.4 jobs from the ages of 18 to 54. Nearly half of these jobs were held from ages 18 to 24."[25] Stated differently, the average baby boomer held 6.4 different positions from the ages of 25 to 54. Boomers changed jobs just like members of Gens X and Y do.

Nietzsche was right. Time is a flat circle.

At a minimum, the stigma around employee movement has eroded. Ironically, in its place, an opposite stigma has developed in some cases. About ten years ago, I started hearing about recruiters

2 No Small Challenge: Managing the Hybrid Workplace

who refuse to hire people who have remained in the same company and in the same role for too long. The long-timers have been institutionalized. Questions include:

- Do they lack ambition?
- Will they be able to "unlearn" the bad habits they picked up from their previous employer or culture?
- Will they be open to new ways of doing things?
- Will their lack of disparate experiences ultimately hurt them?

People who make hiring decisions no longer view the right type of job-hopping as a liability; they consider it an asset.

Employees' Newfound Leverage

External labor markets have long moved faster than internal ones. As the pandemic progressed and the labor market tightened, employees discovered that putting in their notice often starts a conversation about their compensation and role. More than three in five Americans say that it's ethical to use another company's job offer to extract a salary increase from their current employer.[26]

A New Framework: The Tour of Duty

In 2012, LinkedIn cofounder and current investor Reid Hoffman and his chief-of-staff, Ben Casnocha, published a popular book. *The Start-up of You* makes the case that we need to reimagine the very idea of career. Rather than sticking with a company indefinitely, we should proactively manage our careers. If that means bobbing and weaving in and out of different organizations, so be it.

The authors advocate the adoption of a new employee-employer compact—one predicated on a *tour of duty*. As they explain in a piece for *Harvard Business Review:*

> The tour-of-duty approach works: The company gets an engaged employee who's striving to produce tangible achievements for the firm and who can be an important advocate and resource at the end of his tour or tours. The employee may not get lifetime employment, but he takes a significant step toward lifetime employability. A tour of duty also establishes a realistic zone of trust. Lifelong employment and loyalty are simply not part of today's world; pretending that they are decreases trust by forcing both sides to lie.
>
> Why two to four years? That time period seems to have nearly universal appeal. In the software business, it syncs with a typical product development cycle, allowing an employee to see a major project through. Consumer goods companies such as P&G rotate their brand managers so that each spends two to four years in a particular role. Investment banks and management consultancies have two- to four-year analyst programs. The cycle applies even outside the business world—think of U.S. presidential elections and the Olympics.[27]

Hoffman and Casnocha don't get all the credit, but the stigma behind job-hopping has at least partially eroded. (We can debate whether it was even justified in the first place.) Moreover, in historically tight labor markets, employers have had to take what they can get. Thanks to the rise of remote and hybrid work, expect these tours of duty to stick. Employers will have to take their medicine.

CEOs, small-business owners, and managers can choose to view more liquid labor markets as an opportunity. Benefits include access to a wider labor pool and the ability to bring in new blood.

Figure 2.7 summarizes the massive workplace changes that have taken place since March 2020. It's no overstatement to say that work became much more complicated in a relatively short period.

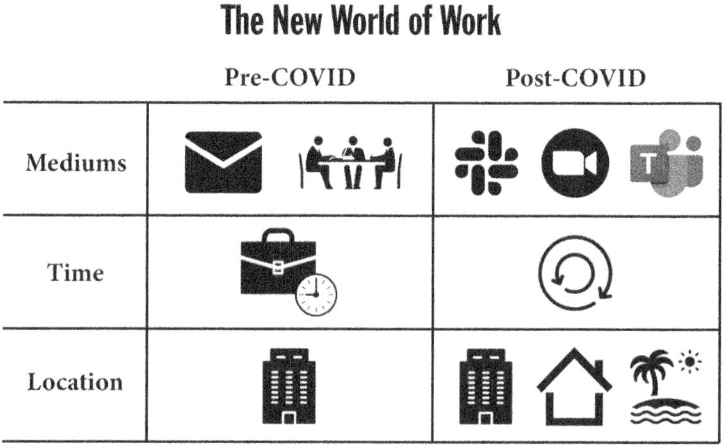

The New World of Work

Figure 2.7: The New World of Work

Hybrid Work and Project Management: The Bottom Line

Here's the good news. Bringing *all* employees back to the office on a full-time basis is neither required nor necessarily desirable. Certain jobs lend themselves to remote, asynchronous work more than others. The same holds true for certain types of work. As we'll see in Part II, project management doesn't fit this bill.

And there's the rub: Hybrid work is hard. Really, really hard.

Lynda Gratton is a professor at the London Business School and the author of *Redesigning Work: How to Transform Your Organization and Make Hybrid Work for Everyone.* In her book she writes the following about hybrid work: "There is no one-size-fits-all solution, no silver bullet, no list of best practices to copy."

When I read those words, I nodded my head so violently that I damn near gave myself whiplash. Gratton is absolutely right in recommending that organizations tailor their work based upon:

- Their own unique purposes and values.
- The specific capabilities and motivations of their employees.

Making hybrid workplaces work won't be easy, but organizations won't have a choice. Managers and leaders will need to determine their firms' own unique signature ways of working and embrace them.

Chapter Summary

- Elon Musk's audacious postpandemic behavior aside, certain types of work are much harder to pull off in remote and hybrid fashions.
- The process of navigating hybrid workplaces is especially tricky. Asymmetries abound, and proximity bias is a tough nut to crack.
- Thanks to massive advances in collaboration technologies and more relaxed views around remote work, employees can easily change jobs without uprooting their lives. The reduced friction in labor markets means more turnover, especially in today's high-inflation environment.

Chapter 3

REVISITING THE GREAT EFFICIENCY DEBATE: THE RETURN OF RESILIENCE

"Action expresses priorities."

—MAHATMA GANDHI

The last chapter described the tectonic employment-related shifts that employers faced in the months following the pandemic. Correction: *Continue to face.* If they'd been able to solve these prickly personnel problems, you wouldn't be reading this book.

For manufacturing firms, staffing issues aren't the half of it. Companies that build and ship physical goods have had to confront a separate set of unprecedented headaches—ones that are causing them to reevaluate their long-term approaches to making things.

This chapter delves into two critical and surprisingly similar fields: supply chain management and human capital management.

(I'll shorten them here to SCM and HCM, respectively.) No, the following pages don't represent a diversion from this book's main topic by a peripatetic author and his lax editor. Really. To fully appreciate the inherent challenges of project management in hybrid and remote workplaces, we need to understand a few core SCM and HCM pillars.

The Suddenly Sexy Status of SCM

For centuries, supply chain management has been an essential business discipline. No one ever would've labeled it *sexy,* however. As the pandemic progressed, SCM became kind of hip. Case in point: MBA students started declaring it as a concentration over strategy, finance, and other stalwarts.

Speaking with Matthew Boyle of *Bloomberg* in September 2021, Harvard Business School dean Srikant Datar summed it up as follows: "For years, we had sort of taken logistics for granted. The pandemic caused us to rethink it." Rutgers Business School professor Alok Baveja echoed Datar's assessment, saying, "Incoming business students who once defaulted to finance or marketing now want to explore supply chain management."[1]

If you're wondering whether a full-time grad student can devote the better part of two years studying SCM, the answer is an emphatic "Hells yeah." The global supply chain is enormously complex, fascinating, and dynamic. My favorite book on the subject is *Arriving Today: From Factory to Front Door—Why Everything Has Changed About How and What We Buy* by Christopher Mims of the *Wall Street Journal.* As far as I know, it's the only book ever written that features a pack of USB chargers as its protagonist.[*]

---

[*] In November 2021, Mims appeared on my pod *Conversations About Collaboration* to talk about it. Listen at https://tinyurl.com/mims-phil.

Like many folks, I didn't know much about SCM until a few years ago.

> *"If you want to learn something, read about it.*
> *If you want to understand something, write about it.*
> *If you want to master something, teach it."*
>
> —YOGI BHAJAN

SCM 101

During my four years as a full-time college professor, I taught six different courses. The most challenging was Introduction to Information Systems, a 200-level survey course far more wide than deep. It would be easier to list the topics that the course *didn't* cover. Put mildly, cramming 30 pounds of, er, stuff into a 10-pound bag was challenging. In total, I taught ten sections of that course. Today, I'm no Six Sigma Black Belt or expert on total quality management, but I can attest to the wisdom of Yogi Bhajan's profound words.

One lecture I gave in each section involved SCM. I'm going to assume that, like most college sophomores and even myself five years ago, you can't cite how SCM relates to information systems and vice versa.

It turns out that the link between the two disciplines is straightforward. Companies that manufacture physical products aren't simple enterprises. Sourcing raw materials, managing inventory, and shipping consumer products are all involved business processes that require sophisticated information systems. After all, it's 2022, not 1962.

So, everything's always all precise and scientific, right?

Nope.

Even applying the most advanced tech and analytics don't eliminate spoilage and human error. They can't control fickle consumer tastes, fiscal and monetary policy, geopolitical events, and overall uncertainty. Far from it. Ultimately, manufacturers, vendors, suppliers, and retail outlets all need to forecast consumer demand, and that can be tricky even under normal circumstances.

When in Doubt, Ask Homer

To illustrate the difficulty of predicting consumer demand during my lectures, I'd describe to students one of my favorite episodes of *The Simpsons*. (Added benefit: I was able to keep myself amused.)

"Duffless"—episode 16 of season 4—originally aired on February 18, 1993.[*] (Yes, I feel old writing that sentence.) In it, Homer loses his license after being cited for a DUI. Concerned about her husband's health, Marge pressures Homer to give up beer for a month. He concurs.

I asked the students, "How would this single action affect the supply chain?" (It was at this point that I would remind them that I don't condone underage drinking.)

Students would correctly point out that Homer would stop frequenting Moe's Tavern, his favorite drinking hole. This simple act would cause Moe to order less beer from his distributor. The distributor would, in turn, order less from its wholesaler. Eventually, the manufacturer would produce less beer. When Homer returned to Moe's and started downing Duffs again, the supply chain would need time to catch up.

---

[*] This episode features one of my favorite Homer Simpson quotes. Off the sauce while attending a baseball game, he laments, "I never realized how boring this game is without beer."

> (Stocking beer isn't as simple as reactivating your Netflix or YouTube Premium subscription.) Each step would take time to cascade throughout the chain.

And that, dear reader, is an example of *the bullwhip effect:* how small fluctuations in consumer demand at the retail level cause progressively larger fluctuations throughout the entire supply chain. See Figure 3.1 for a visual.

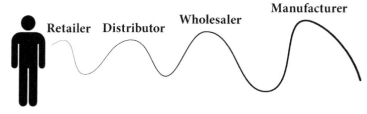

Figure 3.1: The Bullwhip Effect

Here are the two important things to remember about the bullwhip effect. First, it was alive and well in 2018 and 2019—that, is, before we started wearing masks. Second, it isn't a binary; there are degrees. Issues around fulfillment, sourcing, and distribution rattled the global economy in March 2020 and beyond for lots of reasons. The way in which many companies had configured their supply chains is arguably the most consequential.

Lean Manufacturing

Regardless of what they're selling, all companies that manufacture physical products need to make fundamental choices about how they'll optimize their supply chains. (Hulu, Twitter, and Spotify need not worry about their digital inventory.) Companies that don't probably won't last very long. This truism holds for giants such as General Motors and Apple and small businesses. Yes, even for Bongiorno Bagels near my home in Arizona.

Apple is particularly instructive because its CEO, Tim Cook, is an operations maestro. Here I'll focus on MacBook Pros, iPhones, iPads, Apple Watches, and the company's other physical products. I'll intentionally ignore iCloud, Apple Music, Apple Fitness+, Apple Books, Apple TV+, and the other offerings in its growing array of digital services.

Let's say that your five-year-old Beats by Dre headphones finally crapped out. A few of your friends are rocking the latest version of Apple's chic AirPods, and you decide to take the plunge. You visit your local Apple Store to purchase them because you can't envision even a single day without headphones. (How *did* we ever manage to do that, by the way?)

You find an Apple employee and explain that you'd like to purchase a pair of AirPods. At this point, the company's guiding philosophy and deliberate decisions around how it manages its supply chain intervene. Specifically, Apple could have done one of the following:

1. Stocked thousands of pairs of AirPods at every store, allowing you—and just about every customer that day or week—to walk out with a pair of them. Cha-ching.
2. Stocked zero pairs of them. In this case, you'd place the order in the store. Apple would then make you a "fresh" pair of AirPods.
3. Stocked a predetermined number of them at each store.

There are pros and cons to each approach, as Table 3.1 displays.

Approach	Advantages	Disadvantages
1. Store Thousands of Pairs	All customers will be able to purchase them and walk out with them.	High storage costs; less room for storing other products; unsold inventory sits and may need to be shipped to other stores or returned; risk of theft or fire; expensive recalls if defects are discovered.
2. Store Zero Pairs	Zero storage costs and risk of fire and theft; zero wasted inventory; more room for storing other products.	Customers won't be able to purchase them; they may decide to purchase the product from a different retailer or buy a different product altogether; customer frustration over making a futile trip.
3. Store a Reasonable Number of Pairs	Lower storage costs compared to the first option; some customers will be able to walk out of the store with them.	Estimates are imprecise; customers won't know for sure if they can purchase AirPods until they arrive at the store; frustrated customers may share memes on social media.

Table 3.1: Simple Stocking Options for AirPods at an Apple Store

Like any manufacturer, Apple can optimize its supply chain for efficiency *or* resilience, but not both. Alternatively, it can strike a balance between the two, as it does with the third approach. Figure 3.2 demonstrates this core trade-off.

Let's say that Apple's management has chosen the second option. That is, it emphasizes efficiency over resilience. At least it wouldn't be alone in this regard. Iconic companies such as Toyota, Intel, John Deere, and Nike have embraced lean manufacturing for decades. As such, they've optimized their supply chains for efficiency over resilience. You might say they've chosen "just-in-time" (JIT) over "just-in-case" (JIC)

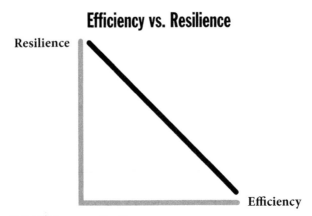

Figure 3.2: Efficiency vs. Resilience

.I'm vastly oversimplifying here, but proponents of lean manufacturing obsess over two intertwined goals: maximizing productivity and minimizing waste. Here are three concrete examples:

- Nike doesn't store extra four-month stashes of polyester, rubber, cotton, and leather in its factories.
- John Deere wants to avoid paying floor supervisors to sit on their keisters because customer orders *might* come in.
- Intel wants all its chip-making factories humming as much as possible. A plant with sufficient materials and insufficient labor is a problem.

These examples bring us to another essential manufacturing concept for our purposes: *work-in-progress,* or WIP. WIP represents the cost of unfinished goods in the manufacturing process. It consists of labor, raw materials, and overhead. Companies practicing lean manufacturing seek to minimize WIP at all costs.

> ## Kanban 101
>
> Kanban is a Japanese production system predicated on delivering what the process needs exactly when it needs it. Companies apply this philosophy to producing physical and digital products.
>
> A foundational Kanban concept is *throughput*: the amount of material or number of items passing through a system or process. Alternatively, consider it the amount of work delivered over a specified period. If you think that Kanban prizes efficiency and transparency, trust your judgment.

The Advantage Is the Disadvantage

I'll pick on Toyota here, but any automaker would do. Toyota can't manufacture and ship a single Camry without plastics, aluminum, steel, and cast iron. (Google makes me seem smarter than I am.) Because Toyota practices lean manufacturing, it doesn't need to hoard any of these materials. Lean manufacturing is glorious—until it isn't.

What happens when a massive shipment of steel and aluminum is delayed? As an adherent to lean manufacturing principles, Toyota would find this delay especially problematic because cars can't roll off the assembly line without, you know, engines. This critical delay would increase Toyota's WIP and its production would cease—a nightmare scenario for the carmaker. Workers would sit around with nothing to do. Losses would quickly pile up and would continue until more rubber arrived.

> ## Two Different Golf Philosophies
>
> The following analogy may come off as a forced joke, but what the hell … I'm rolling.
>
> JIT and JIC play a round of golf. JIT brings a single ball. If he loses it, he's in trouble. He'll have to buy a new one or borrow one from someone in his foursome. Golf is a tough sport with a ball, but it's impossible without one.
>
> JIC, however, would never dream of teeing off without at least a dozen spare balls in his bag. JIC abides by Franz Kafka's dictum, "Better to have and not need than to need and not have."
>
> So which method is better?
>
> It depends on the round, the course, and the quality of the golfer. If JIT doesn't put one in the drink or in the woods over the course of eighteen holes, then his approach is. If, like me, JIC routinely can't find his golf balls after he hits them, then his way is best.

A Fundamental Shift: The Future of the Supply Chain

As mentioned earlier, I'm anything but an SCM expert. By this point, however, I hope to have established at least a little credibility with you. In addition, accurate predictions often stem from nonexperts, as Philip Tetlock and Dan Gardner detail in their excellent book *Superforecasting: The Art and Science of Prediction.*

Prediction: Semiconductor companies, automakers, printers, and other manufacturers will trade some efficiency for resilience over the foreseeable future. No, they won't abandon the former entirely. Returning to the example from earlier in this chapter, Apple won't begin stocking 50,000 pairs of AirPods in every retail location.

Rather, manufacturers will tolerate a little more inefficiency than they have in the past. Shareholders and consumers will understand the shift in Figure 3.3

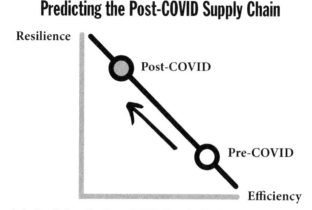

Figure 3.3: Predicting the Post-COVID Supply Chain

Substitute Goods

Here's a simple scenario: A manufacturer lacks an essential raw material or *physical* resource. Should it suspend production?

In a perverse way, that decision isn't that complicated, at least in the short term. The manufacturer should stop the line until it can purchase more of that critical input.

I know virtually nothing about how cars work but, last time I checked, they don't run so well without engines. There's no substitute.

What Will Eva Do?

Eva needs a car soon. She has her heart set on a slick new Avalon, but will she buy one if it won't arrive for at least a few months? (Engines aren't exactly floormats.) Employees can't "power through." Even Toyota CEO Akio Toyoda himself can't conjure up metals such as steel, aluminum, and cast iron out of thin air.

Will Eva wait for her new Avalon? I'm skeptical. Even if she lives in a relatively remote area, the rise of Uber and Lyft gives us all more options for getting around. Nothing against a Corolla, but consumers aren't going gaga for it like they are for Tesla's Model Y SUV and its Cybertruck. (Preorders for the latter are rumored to be 1.25 million.[2])

I don't know any billionaires, but I suspect that even the most narcissistic of them realizes that their custom-made Lamborghini won't arrive via next-day delivery.

The Metamorphosis of the Book

A more interesting scenario for our purposes involves physical books. During the pandemic, a number of publishers reluctantly pushed back the release dates for some of their titles. The culprit: paper shortages.[3] (Assume for the sake of simplicity that publishers print all their own books, although that's often not the case.) From what I've heard and read, the affected authors were displeased but understood. (I get the disappointment. I've damn near tackled UPS drivers as they've delivered the first boxes of my new books.)

Much like at Toyota, the top dog at HarperCollins, Brian Murray, may huff and puff, but he can't waive his magic wand and create paper. No matter how hard he prays, trees won't suddenly spring up from the ground. Unlike automakers short on rubber, though, publishers can still sell their books—sort of. There are other ways for publishers to get their products to the masses.

Say that a HarperCollins hardcover or paperback won't be available for a few months. The publisher could release the ebook and audiobook versions of its titles. After all, publishers own all the rights to the books. (Again, I'm simplifying here. The agents for A-list authors sometimes negotiate more restrictive publication and distribution terms for their clients.)

Let's leave aside the debate about which medium makes for a better experience. You may want to read the *Greenlights* hardcover by Matthew McConaughey, but you find the audiobook and ebook versions alright, alright, alright.

We've landed on what economists call *substitute goods:* two or more products that consumers can purchase to fulfill the same need. If this were 1990, then HarperCollins would be in the same boat as Toyota. Thanks to the advent of the ebook and audiobook formats, however, publishers facing a paper squeeze no longer need to punt. No paper? No problem. *Fuggedaboutit.*

Delays for Digital Doohickeys

With a digital product or service, we're not completely out of the woods. Production and purchasing snags can still occur; they're just different than those facing their physical counterparts. Once an ebook or audiobook hits the virtual shelves, there's no printing, packing, shipping, and delivery. Click a button, and it magically and instantly shows up on the Kindle or Audible app, right?

In theory, yes, barring any app glitches, billing problems, parental account locks, internet connectivity issues, or publisher spats with Amazon.[*]

Before the release of any digital good, production delays can still rear their ugly heads. In the case of ebooks or audiobooks, these hiccups may include:

1. The audiobook's narrator loses her voice.
2. The ebook-conversion specialist misplaces the manuscript.
3. The author misses a major deadline.
4. The publisher drops the author—as it has every right to do, by the way. (Although rare, it happens. Most recently, Simon & Schuster invoked the termination clause in Missouri Senator Josh Hawley's deal after the latter's behavior preceding the January 6 insurrection.[4])

In each of these scenarios, the loss of a critical human input or resource can compromise the delivery of the final good or service. HarperCollins can address its problems with relative ease, however, as Table 3.2 shows.

Problem	Possible Solution
The audiobook's assigned narrator loses her voice.	The publisher can hire a new narrator. At some point, artificial intelligence may even replace narrators altogether.[5]
The ebook conversion specialist misplaces the manuscript.	Two words: cloud computing. Beyond that, let's hope that the author has kept a copy of it.
The author misses a major deadline.	The publisher hires a ghostwriter. Expect the publisher to either take the fee out of the author's future royalties or withhold part of the advance.

Table 3.2: Sample Problems and Solutions for Digital Books

---

[*] Several times over the years, Amazon has earned the ire of traditional publishers by yanking its books from its site over pricing disputes.

As for the fourth scenario, don't throw a pity party for the author. Hawley quickly landed a new deal with a conservative publisher. The whole ordeal almost certainly helped him sell more books. (Next time you chat with Barbra Streisand, ask her if trying to prevent people from viewing something online works.[*])

To review, Toyota can't manufacture completed cars without different types of steels and aluminum alloy parts. Period. By contrast, a dearth of paper doesn't eradicate the ability for HarperCollins to produce a different type of book—one that many customers would prefer to purchase anyway. The lack of essential physical resources constrains the automaker, but not the publisher.

Thanks to Amazon, Apple, Samsung, and other hardware makers, publishers only need content to sell their books in digital formats. That is, they rely upon people far more than raw materials, and human resources are generally more fungible than physical ones. I repeat, *generally.*

The One and Only Bruce

Consider a lifelong Bruce Springsteen fan who drops $1,000 on a front-row ticket to see *Springsteen on Broadway.* He'd be livid if he showed up to find that an understudy had taken The Boss's place.

To state the obvious, Bruce, his management, and the folks at the Walter Kerr Theatre in NYC know as much. They'd never dream of pulling this kind of bait-and-switch. If The Boss were sick, ticketholders would receive refunds or tickets to alternate shows.

---

[*] Google "the Streisand effect."

HCM 101

A core tenet of SCM is that manufacturers need to make a fundamental trade-off between efficiency and resilience. When it comes to managing their *physical* resources, more of one necessarily means less of the other. That same tension applies to how an organization manages a different set of resources: its people.

Welcome to the field that consultants and academics call *human capital management.*

Think of HCM as the people equivalent of SCM. Toyota's management knows that steel and aluminum can't spontaneously turn themselves into car engines, and machines can only do so much by themselves. Our robot overlords haven't arrived just yet. Restaurants need chefs to cook meals and waitrons to serve them. And as I know all too well, colleges and universities need professors to teach their courses.

Allow me to mangle the Gandhi quote at the beginning of this chapter. Different organizations with different priorities adopt different HCM policies that result in different actions. Consider hospitals. They *could* opt for maximum HCM efficiency, but they don't, and for good reason. Forecasting the incorrect number of employees can directly result in patient deaths.

Most hospitals compensate nurses for being available—even if they're not working—in the form of on-call pay. To borrow some names from the Showtime series, Nurse Jackie works out of the All Saints Hospital in New York City. On specific days off, she still receives $10 per hour, but with one stipulation: She needs to be at the ready if the ER needs her to show up. She can't be kicking it in Bermuda. If the hospital rings her at 2 a.m., she'll have to report to work. For her trouble, she'll make her normal hourly wage plus the extra on-call rate. Figure 3.4 displays the hospital's balanced approach to HCM.

Figure 3.4: A Balanced Approach to HCM

Hospitals aren't alone. Other organizations have embraced contingent labor for decades. The NFL caps club roster sizes at 53 players, but teams can sign a maximum of 16 additional players to their practice squads. Publishers maintain long-term relationships with a cadre of independent contractors who index, design, and edit their books.

Unfortunately, not all outfits understand the need to embed a little slack into their workforces. Let's see what happens when one institution consistently tries to thread the labor needle.

The Perils of Extreme Efficiency: HCM Lessons From Academia

It's the end of the academic year. The weather has turned. Students will soon be celebrating, accepting job offers, and signing yearbooks. (Is that still even a thing?) Parents will tearfully snap pictures of their children in their graduation gowns. College and university presidents are preparing to give inspirational—if clichéd—speeches.

In between grading papers and final exams, hundreds of thousands of college professors are sitting down with their department chairs for their annual reviews. The process apes that of most corporate environments: Worker and boss discuss the former's performance over the past year and identify areas for improvement. You know the drill.

As is often the case in academia, however, there's a twist. The department chair also gives professors their temporary teaching schedules for the next academic year. In the spirit of keeping things simple, assume each of the following:

- There's no distinction between teaching and research professors. Everyone needs to teach a full course load every semester.
- Tenure doesn't exist. All professors work under nine-month appointments that the university can terminate at any time.
- No union represents faculty members. In this case, the American Association of University Professors can't advocate for its members.

The university and the department effectively dictate each of the following elements of professors' jobs:

- The number of courses they'll teach.
- The specific courses they'll teach.
- The number of students who can enroll in each course.
- The times and days of the week of those courses. A professor's schedule may be stacked or spread out over the course of the day or week. There are pros and cons to crammed and compressed ones.

- The locations of those courses. Depending on the school, they may take place in the same campus building, different buildings, or even different campuses.
- The modalities of these courses (read: in person, online, or hybrid).

In short, the university and department determine just about everything. It doesn't take a management professor to identify the power asymmetry.

This scenario isn't surprising. Employers tend to hold most of the cards, especially in nonunionized workplaces. As a lot, department chairs aren't inherently vindictive or incompetent when they assign courses for the upcoming year. A fundamental part of their job involves answering an ostensibly simple question: Who will be teaching the students next semester?

Optimization Obstacles

It might seem like an innocent or elementary query, but nothing could be further from the truth. Even at midsize colleges and universities, assigning professors is an elaborate optimization problem that requires an Excel workbook not for the faint of heart. The bigger the department, the greater the complexity. Specific constraints include:

- **Buildings and rooms:** Two classes can't take place at the same time in the same room. Seventy students can't sit in a classroom designed to fit fifty.
- **Budgets:** University presidents, school deans, and department chairs face financial restrictions, just like businessfolks who work outside academia's ivory towers.

- ☯ **Professor schedules and locations:** Professors can't strap on jetpacks and fly two miles across campus during the 15-minute break between in-person classes.
- ☯ **Boards of regents and trustees:** Depending on the university, these bodies establish the rules that govern how school faculty and administrators operate. For example, say that a department needs a professor to teach an additional class apart from her normal course load. For this extra work, she'll receive overload pay. The department can't just pile on additional classes.
- ☯ **School accreditation:** Departments want to obtain and maintain the imprimatur of the accreditation bodies that govern their disciplines.[*] (It's a strong selling point to 17-year-olds and their parents on the verge of making financial commitments that can tie them down for decades.) For better or worse, those bodies ding departments that rely too heavily upon adjunct faculty.
- ☯ **Professor egos:** They're not small.

Department chairs worth their salt try to build and maintain morale among their staff. They don't twist their mustaches and develop faculty schedules in a vacuum, especially at large institutions. Starting around March, many will survey their professors and solicit their preferences for the courses they'd prefer to teach for the upcoming year.

A professor's preferences, however, aren't binding. With so many logistical, financial, administrative, and human variables at play, a few profs are bound to be miffed upon receiving their schedules. Here are two of them.

---

[*] My alma mater Carnegie Mellon even employs a proper accreditation liaison officer.

Adventures in Academia

Emily wrote a book specifically for a course that she taught every semester. She also developed the online version of the course from scratch. Despite solid student evaluations, her department chair inexplicably deemed her no longer fit to teach that course during her review. Her successor kept using her book in the course. Evidently, she was qualified to write the book for the course, but not to teach it.

After a successful first year, Vernon learned that he'd no longer be teaching at his university's main campus for the next academic year. He'd have to schlep to the school's satellite campus twenty miles northwest of its main one. Because of when his classes started and where he lived, his one-way commute tripled from forty minutes to two hours thrice per week. He certainly hadn't signed up for this, and the extra travel wreaked havoc on his family life. When his colleagues finally saw him at his department's year-end meeting, he looked exhausted.

Regardless of a few bruised egos, the optimization process marches on, ultimately producing a *tentative* schedule for each professor. Much like a flight booked months in advance, any one person's itinerary may change for all sorts of reasons. For one, life happens. Professor Frick could win the lottery or get hit by a bus.

For their part, departments can cancel classes at the last minute due to insufficient student demand. The three freshmen who enrolled in an unpopular section of Econ 101 will have to make other arrangements. Conversely, student demand for a section can exceed the number of available seats in its designated classroom. What happens then?

You guessed it: The department will add another section. After all, universities are ultimately businesses. They're not in the habit of refusing additional revenue.

Think of each professor's tentative schedule as an individual block in a game of Jenga. After 20 moves, the tower is still standing, but it could easily topple at any point.

When the Jenga Tower Wobbles

All the following names are pseudonyms.

Colleges and universities typically offer teaching faculty nine-month appointments for the next academic year at the conclusion of the existing one. Unless faculty members opt to teach summer courses, they're under no obligation to go into the office or even check their email. Many professors use those three months to peace out, recharge their batteries, travel, write, or perform services for their clients.

In late June 2019, I was sitting in a hotel room in Porto Alegre, Brazil. I was there to teach a two-day dataviz class when I accidentally visited my work inbox. The department's second-in-command, Alice, had sent me an urgent message about my fall schedule. She wanted to know if I'd be willing to switch gears and teach a new slate of courses for the second time in two years.

I figured that an existing professor unexpectedly opted not to return in the fall. I wasn't wrong.

A single faculty member, Elizabeth, had decided to take a full-time industry gig, doubling her salary in the process. Alice was now scrambling to find replacements for each of

Elizabeth's four sections. The Jenga tower was wobbling and on the verge of toppling.

Alice wasn't picking on me; our interactions had always been amicable. She was just trying to solve a major problem. (A few of my friends told me later that she'd contacted them about the same issue.)

Replacing Elizabeth by recruiting and hiring a new faculty member was off the table for two reasons. First, existing professors from other schools had already committed to their employers for the next academic year. Second, let's say that Alice could magically identify a local candidate who could hit the ground running in the five weeks before the next semester began. Most of the department's existing professors and its chair weren't around to interview the candidate anyway.

I politely declined Alice's offer. I was already teaching two summer courses that were starting in a few days. My plate was full. Beyond that, I hadn't planned on spending the second half of my summer learning a new programming language. Although I didn't say it, I was thinking of Bob Carter's famous line, "Poor planning on your part does not necessitate an emergency on mine."

Saying no was a calculated gamble. Alice could have played hardball and threatened to rescind my appointment letter, although I'd already signed it. I didn't anticipate any resistance, though. If I said no, Alice would have to quickly fill eight sections in a few weeks, not just four.

Ultimately, Alice was able to fill those slots for the fall, but not without plenty of frantic juggling and a bit of pleading.

Scenarios such as these aren't uncommon when an organization, regardless of its industry, adopts an extremely efficient approach to staffing and HCM. Figure 3.5 displays this trade-off.

Figure 3.5: An Extremely Efficient Approach to HCM

As the following sidebar demonstrates, simple probability theory tells us that this approach will eventually result in a staffing crisis.

> ### Math Time, Part 1
>
> Let's say that the probability that any given professor returns from the summer to teach in the fall is 98 percent. Before the Great Resignation, that number may have seemed reasonable. What are the odds that every professor returns in mid-August?
>
> Time to bust out the calculator app.
>
> In a ten-professor department, that number is 81.7 percent (0.98^{10}.) In the case of our 50-professor department, that number plummets to 36.4 percent (0.98^{50}).

> Now, forget higher education and adjust your timeframe from 2019 to the present—and the level of employee turnover that we've seen over the past two years.
>
> If you decrease the probability that any individual employee returns to 0.95, the odds that *all of them* return quickly plunge. (For example, 0.95^{10} is 59.8 percent.) Bottom line: Regardless of their industry, organizations that adopt über-efficient staffing strategies will face an emergency at some point. It's a matter of when, not if.

Actions Express Priorities

In both the HCM and SCM worlds, the decision to emphasize efficiency over resilience is neither objectively good nor objectively bad. It is, however, an intentional and popular one. For decades, for-profit companies have sought to maximize productivity and minimize waste. Many university administrators don't want to pay professors to teach partial class loads in case one becomes sick or resigns to take a different job.

At this point, the parallels between SCM and HCM ought to be clear. They're more similar than dissimilar. Each involves managing resources—just different ones.

That wraps up Part I of the book. Having established a solid foundation, it's time to enter the intricate world of project management.

Chapter Summary

- Minor changes throughout the supply chain reverberate throughout it. The bullwhip effect causes major problems that no company can resolve overnight.
- The process of managing physical inventory and natural resources is often just as vexing as managing people.
- More efficiency means less resilience, and vice versa.
- Erring on the side of extreme efficiency makes any resource management system fragile.

PART II

Contemporary Project Management: Old Habits and New Challenges Collide

Chapter 4

PM 101: AN INSANELY BRIEF OVERVIEW OF CONTEMPORARY PROJECT MANAGEMENT

"They've done studies, you know.
Sixty percent of the time, it works ... every time."

—PAUL RUDD AS BRIAN FANTANA, *ANCHORMAN*

The existing commercial and scholarly canons around project management are substantial, as my agent reminded me when I pitched him this book. Still, it's silly to assume that everyone reading these pages understands the basics of contemporary PM.

To that end, let's hope that the title of this chapter tells you all you need to know. Even if you're a certified PMP or you've spent decades managing projects or launching products, I'd still give it a read.

Defining Our Terms

The world isn't exactly lacking for definitions of *project management*. As of this writing, a Google search of "definition of project management" yields 3.5 million results.[1]

As is the case with all Google searches, the top few results draw more water than all the rest combined.[2] Near the top of this search page's results is the entry from the venerable Project Management Institute. PMI defines the term as:

> the use of specific knowledge, skills, tools, and techniques to deliver something of value to people. The development of software for an improved business process, the construction of a building, the relief effort after a natural disaster, the expansion of sales into a new geographic market—these are all examples of projects.[3]

It's certainly a reasonable definition. I'll be the first to admit that I can be a bit persnickety when it comes to semantics, but PMI's mention of the term *business process* troubles me for two reasons.

Projects vs. Processes

First, it opens Pandora's box. Business process improvement, business process reengineering, and business process management are all separate management disciplines.[*] (Amazon lists plenty of books on each subject.) By design, this book ignores abstract philosophical questions, such as, Can the goal of a project be to refine an existing business process or create a new one? Answer: Probably, but my head is starting to hurt.

---

[*] If you think that explaining the differences among them to a bunch of disinterested 19-year-olds at 9:30 a.m. on a Monday is challenging, trust your judgment.

The typical goal of a project is to achieve one or more business outcomes; with a business process, the goal depends. A hospital that runs biweekly payroll isn't undertaking a project *per se,* at least in the traditional sense. A true project entails implementing a new system that yields a more efficient payroll process.

Alternatively, consider a typical organization that wants to secure itself against cyberattacks. This process should be ongoing; it generally doesn't yield a discrete outcome or event, such as the launch of a new product. A company can be secure now and vulnerable in ten minutes. And, in this scenario, the process ideally results in the *absence* of an undesirable event—specifically, a hack or ransomware attack.

In the spirit of avoiding semantic distinctions and maintaining a clear focus, let's keep things as simple as possible. Chapter 2 of my prior book *Reimagining Collaboration* distinguished collaboration from several adjacent terms, including project management. As I wrote in late 2020:

> I've seen plenty of people conflate collaboration and project management. For several reasons, don't make this mistake.
>
> First, the term project connotes defined starting and end dates. Maybe your organization is implementing a new customer relationship management system or running a marketing campaign for a client. At some point, those projects will come to an end.
>
> Second, project management doesn't necessarily need to be collaborative. For example, for years Google famously allowed its engineers one day per week to independently pursue their own projects. In theory, this policy would yield innovations.

This book defines *project management* simply and as follows:

Gathering and marshalling human, technological, or natural resources to do something with more than one person or organization.

Unpacking the Definition

I'll be the first to admit that the *to do something* in my definition is a large, amorphous category. After all, it could represent anything in Table 4.1.

Category	Description	Examples
Addition and creation	Building, activating, or launching a new physical or digital product, service, or feature.	An architect designs plans for a new house; Netflix releases a new feature that lets subscribers download and watch movies while not connected to the internet; Marillion drops its new album *An Hour Before It's Dark*.
Maintenance, change, and replacement	Revising an existing product, feature, or service.	A lawyer examines a client's employee-policy manual in light of sexual-harassment claims and recommends changes; two painters repaint a house; an automaker recalls cars to fix a known issue; a software company patches a security flaw in an operating system; an executive search firm finds a new chief marketing officer to replace the incumbent.
Subtraction, deactivation, destruction	Retiring or intentionally destroying a product, service, or other thing.	A software vendor retires or sunsets a legacy enterprise system; a city hires a company to implode an old sports stadium and make way for a new one.

Table 4.1: The Three General Project Categories

These distinctions are admittedly a bit arbitrary. Large projects may fuse one or more of these categories. What's more, organizations can split projects into phases.

4 PM 101: An Insanely Brief Overview of Contemporary Project Management   97

For the purposes of this book, assume that there's no such thing as a single-person project. Say that you're independently building a website or a custom standing desk for your office. I wish you the best of luck, but neither endeavor counts as a proper project here.

The Rudiments of Project Management

Now that we've defined project management, let's dig a little deeper. As the title of this chapter suggests, my goal is merely to acquaint you with a number of key concepts.

PMBOK

In the Introduction to this book, I briefly mentioned the PMP certification. If you ever see those letters displayed after someone's name, rest assured that this person has demonstrated a mastery of the Project Management Body of Knowledge. PMBOK consists of PMI's formal terminology and guidelines that, as you might expect, evolve over time.

V6: KNOWLEDGE AREAS

Version 6 of PMBOK arrived in September 2017. At the time, PMI powers-that-be felt that all certified PMPs needed to possess expertise in the ten PM knowledge areas presented in Table 4.2.

Integration Management	Resource Management
Scope Management	Communications Management
Time Management	Risk Management
Cost Management	Procurement Management
Quality Management	Stakeholder Management

Table 4:2: Ten PMBOK v6 Knowledge Areas

To be sure, the ideas behind these ten areas remain important, but version 6 exists for a reason: Five previous versions came before it.

At some point over the past few years, PMI recognized that PMBOK needed to better reflect the realities of today's world. Specifically, organizations need to complete projects and launch products faster than ever before. Agility and flexibility are essential. To that end, an overhaul of PMBOK was in order.

V7: PROJECT PERFORMANCE DOMAINS

In August 2021, PMBOK7 arrived. (Great name for an indie art-rock band, by the way.) At a high level, this most recent version focuses on performance, skills, project artifacts, principles, and outcomes. Beyond changes in nomenclature, *A Guide to the Project Management Body of Knowledge (PMBOK Guide)—Seventh Edition and The Standard for Project Management* is far more streamlined than its predecessor. (Don't let its length title and subtitle fool you.) The book clocks in at 250 pages, more than 500 pages shorter than its antecedent.

Jesse Fewell was one of the core writers on the recent PMBOK guide. In his words, the latest incarnation "represents the most disruptive redefinition of project management in my lifetime."[4] PMI retired its traditional knowledge areas and, in its stead, introduced *project performance domains.* PMI defines one as "a group of related activities that are critical for the effective delivery of project outcomes."[*]

Table 4.3 displays PMI's eight new project performance domains along with examples of what could—and far too often *does*—go wrong in each one during a project.

---

[*] For much more, see https://tinyurl.com/ps-pmbok7.

4 PM 101: An Insanely Brief Overview of Contemporary Project Management   99

Performance Domain	Examples of Potential Problems
Stakeholder	Senior employees disagreed with the decision to undertake the project from the get-go. As a result, they refused to engage with their colleagues and sign off on key milestones.
Team	A company's management didn't assign the right team members to the project from the onset. Beyond that, it never imbued in its employees a sense of ownership. As a result, team members didn't feel vested in the project's outcomes.
Life Cycle	The firm selected a methodology that just didn't fit the project. (Table 4.4 describes the differences between today's two main PM methodologies.)
Planning	A company lacked a backup plan in the event that essential developers left the company or the project. The search for adequate replacements and the coordination of schedules caused the project to miss early milestones. Compounding matters further, the PM didn't revise the project plan to reflect the time missed trying to locate and train new personnel.
Project Work	The instructions around the business requirements were often vague. Executives were never able to clarify what they really wanted from the new product. The PM never received formal approval to procure additional financial and human resources when delays began.
Delivery	The parties skimped on application testing and never agreed to a proper release schedule. Team members remained unsure about the process for fixing problems and the priority of doing so. Was it more important to fix existing bugs or to keep launching new features?
Measurement	The parties never agreed on a proper definition of *done*. This omission caused massive delays that compounded throughout the project.
Uncertainty	The stakeholders never agreed upon a formal process for resolving disagreements. To paraphrase former US Secretary of Defense Donald Rumsfeld, the team never identified known unknowns, much less unknown unknowns.

Table 4.3: PMI Performance Domains and Hypothetical Issues

Bottom line: PMI may have changed its preferred nomenclature in PMBOK7, but the underlying concepts behind successful project management didn't suddenly transform in August 2021 just because a prominent organization said so. Unclear goals, poor planning and risk management, dysfunctional team dynamics, and selecting the wrong methodology will still doom any project regardless of one body's official monikers and categories.

Keep these PMI domains in mind as you read the following chapters. At some level, they inform all of this book's examples, case studies, and prescriptions. No, I don't formally run every recommendation through each PMI performance domain, but they're lurking.

GOING DEEPER

College textbooks and PMP guides explore PMBOK in far deeper and broader ways than *Project Management in the Hybrid Workplace* does. (This shouldn't come as a surprise.) When you start to unpack PMBOK, you begin to understand why one would never refer to any PM textbook as a light read.

For starters, the 12th edition of *Project Management: A Systems Approach to Planning, Scheduling, and Controlling* clocks in at 848 pages.[*] Harold Kerzner's bible rivals the length of Stephen King's *The Stand*—the unabridged version. For its part, *Information Systems Project Management (version 1.1)* comes in at "only" 482 pages long—practically a Danielle Steel novel by comparison.

Again, this chapter serves only to highlight a few particularly salient and essential PM concepts. None is more important than one particular thesis.

---

[*] The previous version came in at—ready for this?—1,296 pages.

4 PM 101: An Insanely Brief Overview of Contemporary Project Management   101

The Theory of Constraints

Pretend for a moment that an organization possesses unlimited funds, a bevy of qualified and available personnel, and infinite time.* In this fantasy scenario, none of its projects could ever fail. By definition, it could never exceed its budget, miss its deadlines, or run out of people. *Every* project would be successful.

No entity exists in this make-believe universe. Not even Google.

Shit Gets Real at Google

In 2015, the search goliath reported $75 billion in revenue.† At the same time, though, the company's top brass realized that they had better learn some financial discipline—and soon. Wall Street was demanding it now that Google had been publicly traded for more than a decade. Free employee lunches could stay, but it needed to start reining in the profligate spending on moonshots and other wasteful internal projects.

In May that year, Google appointed ex-Morgan Stanley rock star Ruth Porat as its chief financial officer. A mere five months later, she became the CFO at Alphabet, Google's parent company. Her marching orders were clear: Tighten up the purse strings. And that's exactly what she accomplished.

As Max Chafkin and Mark Bergen of *Bloomberg* wrote in December 2016, "Porat's tenure has been controversial, earning her an unflattering nickname: Ruthless Ruth. 'She's a hatchet man,' says a former senior Alphabet executive. 'If Larry isn't excited about something,' the executive continues, referring to CEO Page, 'Ruth kills it.'"[5]

---

* "The Bizarro Jerry," to cite another *Seinfeld* reference.

† No, I'm not making it up. See https://tinyurl.com/rpm-google-rev.

All organizations face constraints. Every. Single. One.

From his grave, Eliyahu Goldratt was saying, "I told you so."

By way of background, Goldratt was a rare breed of cat. The prolific author and Israeli management wizard churned out business novels that have held up for decades. Perhaps his most important contribution is his 1984 effort *The Goal: A Process of Ongoing Improvement*. It has long been a staple in colleges and universities throughout the world. Of particular import here is his Theory of Constraints, or ToC, represented in Figure 4.1.

Figure 4.1: Goldratt's Theory of Constraints (Source: *The Goal*, by Eliyahu Goldratt | Figure: Author)

In the realm of project management, the implications of Goldratt's ToC are impossible to overstate. If a team needs to complete a project in less time, it can either reduce the scope or spend more money. If saving a few bucks is paramount, then dropping features or extending the project's duration needs to be on the table. Those who think they can have their cake and eat it too will invariably be disappointed with the quality of the final product. Something's gotta give.

More than a decade after his death, Goldratt's influence lives on. If there's a respected PM textbook that ignores his rich contributions to the field, I'm unaware of it. Outside of the classroom, you may have heard the colloquialism, "Fast, cheap, and good. Pick any two of the three." Mad props to Goldratt.

Parkinson's Law

C. Northcote Parkinson is another posthumous PM icon whose work warrants a brief mention here. The British naval historian penned 60 books over his lifetime. In his 1957 bestseller *Parkinson's Law,* he gave the world the following timeless gem: Work expands to fill the time available for its completion.

A project slotted for five months will take that long. If the team had allocated only four, it would have saved a month.[*]

PMOs

Small companies may engage in a single project or two at the same time. At larger ones, however, odds are that a dozen or more are taking place at any given point—and sometimes far more than that. To this end, they'll typically create a project management office, or a PMO. It is an internal or external group that:

> sets, maintains, and ensures standards for project management across that organization. They're the keepers of best practices, project status, and direction—all in one spot.[6]

PMOs can be a tad bureaucratic, and many of them don't last. One study found that three out of four of them will close within three years.[7] Still, the best ones provide high-level insights, visibility, and guidance that benefit individual PMs, teams, and projects.

---

[*] For more PM laws, see https://tinyurl.com/simon-pmhw-laws.

The IT-Business Divide

Finally, people who work in tech often speak of the IT-business divide. In lay terms, employees in HR, finance, marketing, and other functional business areas often don't understand technology all that well. For their part, IT peeps don't understand the nuances of their counterparts' core business functions and processes. This chasm has doomed plenty of projects over the decades.

PMI knows full well that employees in different departments often speak different languages. To attempt to mitigate this disconnect, it advocates a balanced PM approach called the Talent Triangle. Put simply, technical skills by themselves are insufficient for success when managing projects. Expertise in leadership, strategy, and business management are also essential if a project is going to hit its mark.

No argument here. Later in this chapter, we'll see if the Talent Triangle moves the needle.

Methodologies: How to Manage a Project or Launch a Product

It's certainly instructive to place projects into general buckets and introduce related concepts. That introductory text, however, ignores a critical question: How will we be conducting our project?

There's more than one answer to this question. Once again, thousands of books address this essential topic. As someone who's read more than a few of them—and implemented their principles on real-world engagements, I can say this: At a high level and regardless of what they're trying to accomplish, organizations today can employ several types of methodologies when managing projects and launching new products.

Here's a brief primer on each one.

The Waterfall Method

Boeing starts selling its aircraft. Around the same time, Pfizer launches a new drug.

Moving people around the world and improving human health may seem like apples and coconuts. As projects, however, the two endeavors are far more similar than outsiders think.

The aircraft needs to fly and land properly; the pharmaceutical shouldn't kill people. In both cases, fixing major post-launch problems is hardly ideal and über-expensive. To this end, each company should meticulously plan and forecast. To paraphrase Ron Burgundy, perfection from the get-go is kind of a big deal.

Enter the Waterfall method—aka a *Phase-Gate process* or *the Systems Development Life Cycle*.[*] Thanks to meticulous planning, we can decide who will be doing what and when throughout the duration of the project.

Participants on Waterfall projects have certainly seen Gantt charts like the one in Figure 4.2 from Asana.

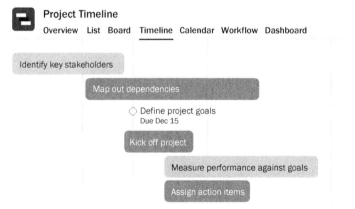

Figure 4.2: Generic Asana Gantt Chart

---
[*] For the sake of brevity, I'm going to ignore technical distinctions among these terms and the software development life cycle.

Don't let the relative simplicity of Figure 4.2 fool you; Gantt charts are rarely this straightforward. As a result, plenty of folks find them confusing, inflexible, and, on a practical level, tough to print. Gantt charts are tantamount to getting your teeth cleaned at the dentist. You deal with them not because you *want* to but because you *have* to.

Limitations aside, the Gantt chart embodies the essence of Waterfall projects: predictability and granularity. Want to see who's working on what now and even one year into the future? Just scroll right. All will go according to plan. When the project wraps up, the team will have created an error-free, fully functional product. Get your popcorn ready.

Well, at least that's the theory.

As I know from more than a decade working on these engagements, the same fundamental strength of the Waterfall method—predictions based on fastidious planning—often serves as its undoing. Even a minor omitted business requirement, specification, or problem can doom a Waterfall project, especially if someone discovers it after the initial planning phase. When you've already laid the concrete for a colonial, it's impractical to convert it to a ranch. Even increasing the size of the kitchen will be expensive, depending on when you want to do it.

I've seen this movie many times before. I penned *Why New Systems Fail* back in 2009. Back then, the world wasn't predicable. The subprime crisis and the Great Recession were rocking the world economy. Compared to then, however, we're currently living in downright chaotic times.

Agile Methodologies

If it's nearly impossible to predict the future, why bother trying?

That sentence, in a nutshell, represents the ethos behind Agile methods. Scrum, Extreme Programming, and their ilk recognize that the world can change. Don't fight it; lean into it.

Table 4.4 reveals some of the stark differences between these two approaches.

Bucket	Waterfall Approach	Agile Approaches
Approach	Sequential, fixed	Incremental, continuous
Team Attributes	Large, specialized	Small, cross-functional
Mindset	"We can control everything."	"We can't control anything. Let's not even try."
Planning	Long-term	Short-term
Building Blocks	Fixed business requirements	Flexible, constantly evolving user stories
Estimates	Absolute. "It will take 4.25 hours to mow Jerry's lawn."	Relative. "I'm not sure how low it will take to mow Elaine's lawn, but hers is bigger than Jerry's. I know that it will take longer."
Feedback	Takes place once when the team has completed the project	Occurs routinely at the end of each sprint
Loop Type	Open	Closed
Testing	At end of the development phase in a single phase	At end of every sprint
Batch	Large, delivered at end of project	Small, delivered on a regular basis

Table 4.4: How Mainstream Deployment Approaches Compare

For a far more detailed look at a popular Agile approach, check out *The Elements of Scrum* by Chris Sims and Hillary Louise Johnson.

Think of the Waterfall method as a marathon and Agile methods as the equivalent of appropriately named *sprints*. Typically one or two weeks long, sprints are decidedly shorter intervals in which teams complete a number of tasks (called *user stories*). After developing and presenting the new features, the team holds a retrospective to gather feedback, learn, and close the loop. Figure 4.3 displays a one-week sprint.

Figure 4.3: Simple One-Week Sprint (Gray Text Indicates Optional Meeting)

By now, it's natural to wonder which approach is better. Apologies in advance: I'm going to sound like a stereotypical management consultant. It depends on what the team, group, or company is attempting to accomplish. Projects following Agile methods don't have to ship with a flawless product. If the latest version of Minecraft doesn't work on your particular Samsung Galaxy Note, the Microsoft/Xbox folks can fix it next week. No one will die.

Another relevant question is, How do these types of approaches compare on a number of different dimensions? (Again, context.)

In his 2009 book *The Business Value of Agile Software Methods*, Dr. David Rico and his colleagues conducted a fascinating meta-nalysis comparing these two methods on software-development projects. In their words:

> We found 79 studies with quantitative data on the benefits of Agile methods. They cited an average of 26% improvements in

cost, 71% improvements in schedule, and 122% improvements in productivity performance. Quality improvements averaged 75% and customer satisfaction improvements averaged 70%.

As Larry David says, "Pretty, pretty, pretty good."

Horribly Named Half Measures

Any method of managing projects and launching products suffers from limitations. There's just no way around it. That grim reality, however, hasn't stopped some management consultants and organizations from trying to fuse Waterfall and Agile methods into one bastard creation. Think twice the calories with none of the nutrition.

The result is either the horribly monikered Agilefall or Wagile, depending on whose jargon you're using. Yes, my fingers hurt typing those two terms.

Imagine a method in which a team, group, or company handles part of the project in an Agile way, but others in the more traditional Waterfall manner. It's tantamount to a husband and wife practicing ethical nonmonogamy every other Saturday during even-numbered weeks except in March during leap years. The rest of the time, they're supposed to pretend they're in a conventional marriage. It's only a matter of time before one spouse unknowingly violates the rules of this convoluted arrangement.

As you've no doubt surmised, I'm not a fan of these half measures. Last year, my ex told me about an opportunity at her current employer to manage its Scaled Agile Framework efforts. From what she described, SAFe at this large financial institution sounded like a logistical and coordination nightmare that offered nothing but downside. I recommended that she pass. She took my advice and, a few months later, told me she was glad she did.

Note that the PMBOK 7 refers to Agilefall and their ilk as hybrid PM methods. I understand why, but I'll refrain from dropping the *h*-word here because of this book's emphasis on managing projects in hybrid workplaces. No sense in confusing you.

A Note on Lean Methods

In his bestselling 2011 book *The Lean Startup,* Eric Reis popularized the term *MVP*. Sports fans will be disappointed to know that it doesn't stand for *most valuable player.* Reis was referring to a *minimum viable product.*

Entrepreneurs don't know if their new product or service will ultimately find an audience. For every Netflix, Facebook, or Amazon, there are hundreds or thousands of others that die on the vine. As a result, Reis advocates building a no-frills, low-tech version, getting it out there, gathering data, refining it, and repeating the process. Build, measure, and learn. Figure 4.4 represents Reis's vision—one followed by countless startups.

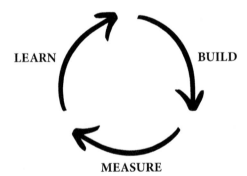

Figure 4.4: The Build-Measure-Learn Loop. (Concept: Eric Reis, *The Lean Startup* | Figure: Author)

The following sidebar illustrates the idea of an MVP in practice.

It's Gotta Be the Shoes

In 2006, entrepreneurs Nick Swinmurn and Tony Hsieh had a radical idea. They were convinced that people would buy shoes online.

This wasn't their first rodeo. The two knew that spending a ton of resources on a potentially flawed idea wasn't wise. Willing to put some money where their mouths were, they started Zappos in 2006.

Reis details the now-legendary story in his book. For now, suffice it to say that Zappos's methods were decidedly low-tech, especially at first. They'd buy shoes from existing shoe stores and resell them on their simple website at a loss. Losses aren't sustainable, but the founders quickly validated their core hypothesis without a massive investment. That experience increased their confidence and convinced them to proceed.

On a personal level, I was an early Zappos fanboy. Over the years, I've bought at least a dozen pairs of tennis shoes on the site, primarily because big-box retailers tend to skimp on stocking them. (Tennis has been a niche sport in the United States for decades.)

And I'm hardly alone. The company took off, reaching $1 billion in sales by 2008. Amazon acquired Zappos for roughly $1 billion in 2009.

Interestingly, CEO Hsieh eschewed remote work. He believed in the power of collisions, and employees weren't going to bump into each other unless they were in the office. He frequently and famously partied after hours with his Zappos peeps, and I met him a few times when I lived in Sin City.

> Hsieh retired in August 2020 and sadly died three months later at the age of 46.

For the purposes of this book, think of Lean methods as a cousin of Agile ones—and a close one at that. There's one major difference between the two. In the former, the product owner[*] analyzes user data to inform the features that the team will build next. Scrum and its ilk rely exclusively on the judgment of the product owner.

Common Project Artifacts

Regardless of the methodology, on formal projects it's common to encounter the following documents.

Statement of Work

Entrepreneurs famously bootstrap. Silicon Valley holds the mythical garage in high regard.[8] As a general rule, startup founders don't hire consultants for traditional client engagements. More mature firms do, typically signing legal statements of work that cover the following areas:

1. **Project activities and scope:** What each party will and won't deliver. (On fixed-bid projects, consultants aren't above yelling "Scope creep!" when a client demands something that the statement of work, or SOW, doesn't include or explicitly excludes.)
2. **Location:** Where the work will take place.
3. **Deadlines:** The dates by which each party will complete a single activity, phase, or milestone.

---

[*] There's more to it but, for our purposes, the product owner is the individual who selects the user stories that the team will complete during each sprint.

4. **Payment terms:** The amount of money that the client will pay the consultancy upon completing specific objectives, milestones, and project phases.
5. **Recourse:** Legalese around what will happen if one or more of the first four elements don't take place as promised.

You'd never call your garden-variety SOW easy reading. A humorous, one-page document it is not. Have SOWs evolved according to recent events—specifically, the move toward remote and hybrid work?

I posed that very question to respected industry analyst and consultant Brian Sommer:

> Statements of work have gotten more, not less, problematic in recent years. Service firms have fallen in love with the idea of phoning-in a stock arrangement letter without doing hardly any real scoping of what is and isn't required. The results: Customers who don't get what they want, lazy services and sales professionals, and poor reviews of service organizations.[9]

Despite their often prodigious length, many SOWs continue to omit or gloss over many elements that can sink a project today. Examples include:

- The communication and collaboration tools that participants will use on the project.
- When employees will work.
- Where employees will work.

Note that public sector projects frequently serve as an exception to this rule, especially when security clearance is an issue.

Project Charter

Prior to commencing an internal product or product launch, different departments, teams, or groups *from the same organization* don't sign formal contracts. That's not to say, however, that the suggestions in this chapter don't apply to internal projects. They most certainly do.

Rather, the groups create a project charter—or at least they should. This foundational document covers the project's scope, objectives, and participants.

Note that project charters can be just as valuable on engagements with outside parties.

RACI Matrix

Regardless of a project's complexity and where it takes place, it stands to benefit from conducting a remarkably simple and valuable exercise.

Formerly known as a *decision rights matrix*, the RACI matrix has provided project clarity since the 1950s. Not surprisingly, PMI has long recognized its considerable value. This simple document assigns one of four terms to each product task and goal:

- **Responsible:** Put simply, this label applies to the person who needs to complete an individual task. (Let's call her Rachel.)
- **Accountable:** Annie approves the work that Responsible Rachel completes.
- **Consulted:** Accountable Annie and Responsible Rachel seek input from Conrad.
- **Informed:** Rachel, Annie, and Conrad provide Ira status and progress updates. Ira doesn't weigh in on task- or project-related matters.[*]

---

[*] For much more on the evolution of the RACI matrix, see https://tinyurl.com/raci-ps.

4 PM 101: An Insanely Brief Overview of Contemporary Project Management   115

Before wrapping up this chapter, a few final points are in order.

Success Rates

At this point, it's natural to ask, What's the bottom line?

That is, at what rate do organizations successfully complete their projects and launch their products? Returning to the Theory of Constraints for a moment, how often do they achieve their time, scope, and cost goals?

At a high level and despite decades of research, not very often at all. Figure 4.5 displays 2016 project success rates—that is, ones that met their goals across three critical dimensions.

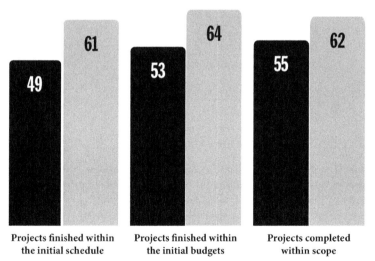

Figure 4.5: Project Success Percentages (Source: PMI 2016 Pulse of the Profession)

Even organizations that follow PMI's Talent Triangle don't report faring much better than those that don't follow it. Projects imbued with a combination of technical, leadership, and strategic expertise still come up short two times in five.

I deliberately selected the year 2016 for Figure 4.5. At that time, far fewer employees worked in remote or hybrid workforces compared to now.

In late March 2022, I conducted a highly unscientific poll in the popular LinkedIn group PMI Project, Program and Portfolio Management. I asked its members about the relative difficulty of managing hybrid and remote projects. Figure 4.6 displays the results of the 165-person poll.

Poll Results on Difficulty of Managing Projects in Remote and Hybrid Workplaces

I'm curious about managing projects in physical workspaces vs. remote and hybrid ones. Which ones are harder to manage?

Hybrid and remote are harder. ✓	39%
About the same.	47%
Hybrid and remote are easier.	15%

Figure 4.6: Poll Results on Difficulty of Managing Projects in Remote and Hybrid Workplaces (Source: LinkedIn Poll Conducted by Author)

For every person who said that managing projects in remote and hybrid environments was easier than doing so in person, nearly three people said it was harder.

Is there more to say about project management?

Nope. That's it. I've summarized everything in 30,000 books in this short chapter. I've got mad skillz.

I'm kidding.

This chapter never meant to cover every aspect of contemporary project management; it only served to establish a rudimentary background on the topic. (This should surprise no one. I tipped my hand in the Introduction.)

Now that we're on the same page, it's time to move on to the unique and formidable challenges that remote and hybrid workplaces pose to project management. Like many things, it's harder to complete the task when most of the people involved are on the outside looking in.

Chapter Summary

- ☉ Project management is a rich, vibrant, and multidimensional discipline.
- ☉ The type of methodology your team follows should reflect the project's ultimate goal. Don't try to fix a plane while it's in the air.
- ☉ Regardless of your approach on a given project, the trade-off among cost, scope, quality, and time is real. If someone suggests otherwise, run.
- ☉ Historically, projects have failed about two times in five—and that's when people largely worked in the same place at the same time.

Chapter 5

THE EXASPERATING SECOND-ORDER EFFECTS OF HYBRID WORK

"There's no such thing as a free lunch."

—ATTRIBUTED TO MULTIPLE INDIVIDUALS

Odds are that you associate this idiom with the economist Milton Friedman. I did until I started digging.

The genesis of this infamous quote harks back more than a century.[*] We've long used it metaphorically, but its lineage is decidedly literal. (Hint: It involves food, saloonkeepers, and whiskey.) Regardless of who originally uttered that eight-word line and why, its staying power has been remarkable.

We immediately embraced the accouterments of working from home. (And why wouldn't we?) First-order effects included 30-second

---

[*] Read about it yourself at https://tinyurl.com/RPM-no-free.

commutes to our kitchens or spare bedrooms, unprecedented flexibility, and more time to exercise and spend with loved ones. Once the initial excitement abated, however, we started to observe the second-order effects of WFH—as the kids call it. Put bluntly, we weren't as thrilled with them.

This chapter examines those second-order effects. It demonstrates how hybrid and remote workplaces exacerbate cognitive biases. They introduce new issues, complicate existing ones, add to our list of things to do, and augment our stress levels. And yes, returning to the subject of this book, all these problems can complicate projects and product launches. Left unchecked, these obstacles can cause new endeavors to fail outright.

Lessons From *Office Space*

Mike Judge's eminently quotable 1999 film *Office Space* centers on disgruntled corporate drone Peter Gibbons. The movie became a cult hit because so many of us can relate to its protagonist's plight.

Gibbons tolerates an onerous Monday through Friday commute, strict rules about TPS reports, an insufferable boss, annoying coworkers, and the general rigidity of office-based work. Without spoiling the flick for you, let's just say that he starts working on *his* terms. Gibbons's boss is displeased with the new arrangement.

Say what you will about the merits of 1990s offices such as Judge's fictitious company, Initech. On two dimensions, however, the stereotypical workplace was simpler back then. (Well, unless you wanted to print documents from your computer.) No, it wasn't idyllic, but just about everyone arrived at the same physical space at the same time. Work conditions were generally homogenous. This relative uniformity built a degree of social cohesion among colleagues and helped us get things done.

Employees have embraced remote and hybrid work arrangements. At the same time, however, this new reality has complicated different aspects of our jobs—and project and product management in particular. Compared to their in-person counterparts, remote and hybrid workplaces are more heterogenous in the following ways:

- **Where we work:** Some of us work in person, while others work remotely or in a hybrid fashion.
- **When we work:** Fewer people are working synchronously.

The results of these two changes are nothing short of seismic.

Of the two, WFH has received the lion's share of the attention in the business press. This second dimension, however, is arguably the more important one. Slack's Future Forum reported in January 2022 that three in four knowledge workers want greater choice over where they clock in.[1] As Figure 5.1 shows, more than nine in ten also want a flexible schedule.

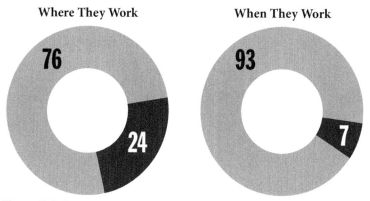

Figure 5.1: Employee Work Preferences: Time and Place (Source: Future Forum, June 2021 Pulse Survey)

There's no secret sauce for managing projects. Employee time and location preferences complicate project completion and product launches, regardless of the methodology that any one team is using. The best Gantt charts and sprints don't negate one simple fact: When our colleagues are working in different time zones, we can't tap them on the shoulder. It's more challenging to ask them quick questions. Our answers may come in minutes—or days—from people we've never met who've just joined the company.

The Human Condition at Work

When we don't get what we want when we want it from our peers, partners, clients, and managers, our cognitive biases instinctively kick in. (I'll leave family members, significant others, and the general public alone for the time being, but the same rule applies.) As a species, we suffer from dozens of these biases. At work, here are three biggies.

The Halo Effect

Whether you know it or not, you've experienced this effect at some point in your life.

Remote Bonding Over a 70s Concept Album

During an introductory Zoom call to kick off a new project, Natalie sees Nick's home office and spots a Pink Floyd poster on the wall. As a fellow fan of the legendary group, the two strike up a virtual bond and playfully debate the merits of classics like *Dark Side of the Moon* and underappreciated gems like *Obscured by Clouds*.[*] This bit of serendipity builds valuable social capital between

---

[*] Allegedly written and recorded in three weeks. Insane.

5 The Exasperating Second-Order Effects of Hybrid Work   123

the two of them—an essential element of hybrid and remote workplaces. All things being equal, this new rapport will make them more civil to each other. Great, but the newfound bond brings with it a potential downside as well. Each is more likely to exhibit additional confidence in the other's abilities, some of which may be unwarranted.

Natalie and Nick predictably give each other the benefit of the doubt. She assumes that he's dutifully completing his tasks and propelling the team and project forward. Unfortunately, he's not pulling his weight, but it's difficult for her to recognize that. After all, they both love the same band.

In this simple yet all-too-common scenario, Natalie let one of Nick's unrelated personal attributes positively influence her view of his professional capabilities. Doing so doesn't make Natalie incompetent or naïve. It just makes her human. As UCLA professor and award-winning social psychologist Matthew Lieberman explains:

> Unconscious cognition is essential to human functioning; it helps us to be efficient and responsive to the world around us. However, unconscious processes are also prone to errors—errors that remain unrecognized and uncorrected which can lead to flawed decision-making, significant bias and blinkered thinking.[2]

Researcher Edward Thorndike coined the term *halo effect* in a 1920 paper. More than a century later, it's as potent as ever. It affects all of us at home and at work—regardless of where and when we do it. (Yes, that means you.)

Confirmation Bias

Making an early first impression can pay off in spades. Unfortunately, the opposite holds true as well.

> ## Getting Off on the Wrong Foot
>
> David joins the project team, replacing Syd. Roger, a colleague, had interviewed David a few months ago but wasn't impressed. Something about David just rubbed Roger the wrong way, but his company hired him anyway.
>
> Over the first few months of working together, Roger keeps finding small issues with David's work. David didn't sign up for micromanagement and the incessant carping of a crusty peer. The problems compound, and David finally bolts after three months—not hard to do in a tight labor market rife with remote and hybrid opportunities.
>
> In truth, however, David's work was generally spot-on. Roger just never gave David a proper chance to succeed in his new role. Roger had formed a negative initial impression that at least partially preordained David's fate. Roger ignored all of David's positive contributions and focused on the latter's perceived limitations.

This little yarn demonstrates the power of confirmation bias, perhaps the most powerful and dangerous of our limitations as a species.

The Honeymoon Effect

In my days implementing enterprise systems, I sometimes picked up a client on the rebound. The organization had grown disenchanted with its previous consultants and given them the boot. When the payroll manager or head of HR asked me a question, I knew that it was my time to shine and make a good first impression.

I'd quickly and clearly provide an answer or my recommendation. When I didn't know the answer to an obscure query, I promised to research the issue and get back to them. (What can I say? I'm a giver.)

I could tell that my level of responsiveness and honesty pleased them, and the ensuing conversations with rebound clients would often go something like this:

> **Client:** "You seem much more experienced and knowledgeable than our previous consultant. We should have hired you months ago. We'll definitely turn this project around now!"
>
> **Me:** "Thank you, but please don't set the bar too high for me. I'll have nowhere to go but down, just like Pearl Jam's first album. Can we just agree that I'm competent for now? That way, I won't disappoint you."
>
> **Client (smiling):** "Gotcha. You're not terrible."

This is an example of the honeymoon effect: Early victories set unrealistic expectations that can come back to bite us in the ass—and not just in the office. Cognitive biases are *everywhere*. They pose formidable societal and political problems that are far outside the scope of this book. Staying on point, I'll examine how they complicate project management in remote and hybrid workplaces.

Hybrid Work: When Theory and Practice Collide

Let's return to Initech, the archetypical late-1990s workplace portrayed in *Office Space*. Assume that everyone works together in the same physical building. Employees occasionally take a little work home with them over the weekend, but all the important meetings, discussions, decisions, and collaborations take place IRL. Did cognitive biases exist back then?

One hundred percent. Here's a simple example.

While walking and gazing into his iPhone, Paul bumped into you on his first day at the coffee machine, staining your favorite shirt. Although he apologized, you never really forgave him. Damn millennials.

Three months later, and you still didn't like the cut of his jib. The coffee incident resulted in a kind of reverse-halo effect. The two of you got off on the wrong foot and struggled to complete projects when the other was involved.

Now let's examine a remote or hybrid workplace. Paul can't spill coffee on you over Zoom—at least not yet. (Maybe he'll be able to do that in the forthcoming metaverse.) Dustups will still happen, though. We've known for decades that modern collaboration and communication tools can gum up the works. All communication media aren't created equal.

Media Richness Theory

In 1986, researchers Richard Daft and Robert Lengel published an influential paper on what they called *media richness theory,* or MRT. In short, it examined how different communication mediums reproduce the information sent over them.[3] When it comes to transmitting information to others, the medium matters. Figure 5.2 illustrates their conceptual framework.

Daft and Lengel argued that we can only be so clear and effective when we send asynchronous text messages. To communicate with others as effectively as possible, we need to be in the same room with them at the same time. Period. Certain tools are fundamentally limited.

5 The Exasperating Second-Order Effects of Hybrid Work

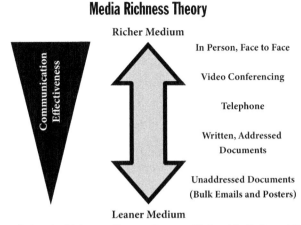

Figure 5.2: Media Richness Theory (Source: Richard L. Daft and Robert H. Lengel | Figure from Author)

At least, that's their theory.

Channel Expansion Theory

My four-year stint in academia was nothing if not instructive. The foray into the other side of higher education confirmed what I had long known: Professors are generally wicked smart. Not coincidentally, they're not exactly shy about criticizing each other. It should be no surprise, then, that MRT hasn't aged as well as an old Pinot. Criticisms abound.

Most relevant for our purposes is channel expansion theory, or CET. Academics John Carlson and Robert Zmud derided MRT as simplistic, flawed, and deterministic. (Oh, snap!) They postulated in their 1999 paper that the effectiveness of any communications medium is neither static nor absolute. Under CET, users' mileage with different mediums varies according to their prior experience with:

- ⊙ The specific medium being used.
- ⊙ The specific topic being discussed.

- The specific organization.
- The other people involved in the discussion.

For example, Steve communicates poorly across all mediums when discussing marketing matters. He meanders just as much in person as he does on Slack, email, and Zoom. To wit, email is not innately less effective than videoconferencing. Conversely, Ian's asynchronous marketing messages land better than Steve's in-person conversations on the same topic ever will. (These variations underscore the need for employee application training.)

Putting It All Together

Now let's put all these pieces together. Our colleagues' words and actions—or lack thereof—have *always* irked us from time to time.* Throw them under the bus if you like, but we shoulder some of the blame because of the cognitive biases discussed earlier.

Remote and hybrid workplaces trade old-fashioned, in-person communication for less personal *mediums*—plural. The nature and the sheer number of these tools can overwhelm even tech-savvy employees, never mind technophobes. We've learned the hard way that remote and hybrid workplaces often make it *more* difficult for us to perform what were once routine tasks and business processes.

The following three sidebars demonstrate this reality.

---

* Somebody's got a case of the Mondays. *Office Space* fans will appreciate the reference.

5 The Exasperating Second-Order Effects of Hybrid Work

When a Five-Minute Question Requires a Three-Day Response

—Gilfoyle, software engineer for a large communication company

I'm not bragging, but I know my way around my job as a full-stack engineer. After graduating college, I worked for four years at a small software-development firm. A friend told me I was woefully underpaid there—that I should be making twice as much cheddar based on my skillset.

So I finally started poking around for a new job. In late 2021, I landed a position at Pied Piper—a multi-billion-dollar communication company. The clincher: I could work remotely forever. My new employer even put that in writing.

I liked my new job, and I liked working at home. Still, sometimes I encountered delays that impeded my progress on certain projects. At one point, I was working on a product feature and needed a simple answer from my manager, Richard.

Now, if I worked in the same building as my boss, I could have just popped by, asked my question, and resumed development. Instead, I sent Richard a direct message in Slack and then … crickets. I followed up a day later when I didn't hear back. Finally, three full days after my initial query, Richard provided me the simple answer to my question.

Delays aren't the sole purview of developers looking for clarity on requirements. Try setting up a physical lab when you don't know where to find essential equipment.

What's in the Box?

—Tom Bardzell, technical specialist for a company that manages pharmacy benefits

I recently ran point on an office move under a tight timeline. Adding to the complexity, I had to build out the new site with used routers, switches, and equipment for technical troubleshooting.

If my colleagues were working in the office along with me, they would have helped me locate and configure the necessary equipment, as I'd done for them. Instead, my peers were working remotely. Further adding to the complexity, my colleagues had stopped receiving equipment orders at the company site. When I tried to find a critical component, they could only tell me that we "probably had it in a box somewhere in the lab."

As part of the move, I also had to reconfigure a few existing devices. Again, in the past, I could just approach my coworkers. With rare exception, they would stop what they were doing and make themselves available.

Not this time. I had to send a slew of emails and wait for their responses.

The project should have been a solid day or two of straightforward work. Instead, the on-again-off-again project took the better part of five frustrating days.

Over the last two years, we've encountered—and overcome—plenty of work-related challenges. Keeping the lights on has proven challenging but, as the next sidebar demonstrates, we're nothing if not resourceful.

5 The Exasperating Second-Order Effects of Hybrid Work

Houston, We Have a Problem ...

—Adom Asadourian, supply chain manager for a pharmaceutical company

From 2020 to 2021, I worked as an operations project manager for a medical device manufacturer in central New Jersey. With COVID-19 restrictions in place, I had to perform my duties remotely from my home in Chicago.

My client was ramping up test kit and assay[*] production over the next three years. We needed to store and package raw materials and finished goods pending quality release. Making space involved reconfiguring our temperature-controlled warehouse space.

Challenge #1: To manage an infrastructure-intensive program without any access to the physical work taking place. For example, it was critical to install new HVAC[†] and air-handling equipment on top of the warehouse roof. In reality, we needed a special crane for this scale of industrial installation. Unfortunately, only one was available in the New York/Philadelphia metropolitan area. In addition, a snowstorm had recently rocked the region. Finally, we could not impact order fulfillment operations during the regular workweek. This meant that all of us would have to do the work over the weekend.

I needed to understand how the work was progressing. If COVID hadn't happened, I would have just walked around the job site—no conference calls. Within a few minutes, I would have been able to understand the complexity and

---

[*] An assay is a laboratory test that finds and measures the amount of a specific substance.

[†] Short for *heating, ventilation,* and *air conditioning.*

scale of the installation. Since that was off the table, I needed feedback from the construction and engineering teams. The second challenge concerned the quality of remote communication—conference calls, Zoom meetings, and the like. Supply chain work is the sole purview of white-collar execs. It includes hourly manufacturing, warehousing, and distribution employees. When it comes to effectively operating in a decentralized, remote environment, the playing field is uneven. Some people have just never played this game before.

Mass meetings with everyone on the infrastructure team just weren't cutting it. We moved to one-on-one meetings. To understand the construction progress, we adopted a *cinema verité* approach. For example, the team was mounting Big-Ass Fans in the new warehouse space, and I needed to monitor the installation progress. The workers used their smartphone cameras and took up the virtual scissor lift to view their progress.

It took a while, but we landed on a creative way to get the job done. We were ultimately able to ascertain our progress and discover critical issues. We were then able to relay this information to the wider team.

A few different threads run through these three stories. In each, the diligent employee took pride in his job. In other words, the protagonist was no Peter Gibbons disciple. Second, the difficulties added to the employees' stress levels. When things took longer than expected, they naturally worried about what their bosses and colleagues would think. Most important in the context of this book, they needed to juggle more balls than before. And here we return to work-in-progress.

Work-in-Progress Revisited

Some surprising consequences can emanate from even small manufacturing hiccups. As we've seen throughout the pandemic, companies that followed a just-in-time inventory management philosophy have been particularly susceptible to production delays. In a nutshell, these delays add friction to a system's WIP.

Kanban afficionados in particular despise bottlenecks because they reduce *throughput*—the amount of stuff that moves through a system. Perhaps better than anyone, they understand that production in the physical world is identical to production in the digital world. It doesn't matter if you're building birdhouses or websites. In both cases, delays increase WIP, stress the system, create inventory headaches, slow production, and cause projects to miss their deadlines. You know, little things.

For a much deeper look at how WIP can grind a system to a halt and cripple employee productivity, read Gene Kim's *The Phoenix Project: A Novel about IT, DevOps, and Helping Your Business Win.*

Let's move from theory to practice.

The Big Impact of Small Delays

Automattic is the parent company of WordPress, the software that currently runs more than 43 percent of all websites.[4] In February 2022, CEO Matt Mullenweg sat down with Te-Ping Chen of the *Wall Street Journal* to discuss remote work. The journalist asked him, "What's the biggest challenge to operating asynchronously?" Here was his response:

> A strength of asynchronous work is that work can happen 24 hours a day. A downside is that it might take 24 hours to get five people to read and respond to something that they could do in a 30-minute synchronous meeting.[5]

As the sidebars in the previous section demonstrated, that 24-hour estimate might be generous. Still, Mullenweg knows of what he speaks. He's long helmed arguably the most successful distributed company in history.

Over the past two years, countless others have seen firsthand the delays that he describes in that interview. These bottlenecks:

- Exist in *all* three types of workplaces: in person, remote, and hybrid.
- Are more acute in the last two.
- Can become even more pronounced and frustrating when we work with people outside of our organization's physical or virtual walls.

Handoffs and Headaches: Working With Multiple Organizations

Depending on what we do, the move to hybrid and remote work has added friction to certain parts of our jobs. As we saw earlier, many tasks are much easier to accomplish when our colleagues sit in the same physical location and work the same hours as we do. But what about when our projects and products involve people who work at different *organizations* than we do?

A simple example will illustrate these all-too-common logistical difficulties and bottlenecks that stem from multiple masters.

Hooli is a large, California-based tech company that went fully remote in March 2020 and hasn't looked back. As a result, Monica can no longer pop by her colleague Richard's desk when she needs a clarification. She now has to ping him via Microsoft Teams. Communication and collaboration just became harder, but at least all Hooli employees use the same internal collaboration hub. Despite the additional friction, Monica and Richard are able to complete the project.

Now let's change the scenario. Monica still works at Hooli, but Richard quits and joins Pied Piper. The two companies embark on a joint project scheduled to last six months. After a few weeks, progress has stalled because of the following issues:

- Employees in the two companies typically work in different time zones, making in-person communication difficult.
- Vast generational, cultural, and gender differences persist. The two groups of employees exhibit vastly different levels of digital literacy.
- Execs in each company's IT department bicker over the tools that employees should use for the duration of the project. Hooli is still a Microsoft Teams shop. Its IT department has blacklisted Skype, Webex, and Zoom. Pied Piper, on the other hand, has gone all in on Slack and Zoom. Its IT department has blacklisted Teams, and employees simply won't use it.

In this scenario, who decides the rules of engagement? Which company accedes to the other? After all, Hooli and Pied Piper are theoretically partners, right? Which organization wins? And what if a third company—Raviga—enters into its partnership? Its management whitelists an entirely different set of communication and collaboration tools. Isn't remote work supposed to be easy?

As the next sidebar illustrates, even employees whose employers sanction the same software applications may be in for a bumpy ride. They often experience unforeseen difficulties when trying to do the simplest thing imaginable in 2022: hold a freakin' Zoom meeting.

Misadventures in Zoom Interoperability

Like you, I've been on hundreds of videoconferences over the past two-plus years. (Pro tip: Disable Self View to minimize Zoom fatigue.)

I've used Microsoft Teams, Slack, Zoom, Skype, RingCentral, Webex, and a few others. For podcasts, toss in Zencastr, Riverside.fm, and a few forgettable others. (My list is the technology equivalent of the cities that Johnny Cash names in his classic song "I've Been Everywhere," but I digress.)

As mentioned earlier, IT departments often—and for good reason—restrict their employees from using certain apps on their computers. You'd think that if everyone used the same sanctioned videoconferencing program, however, everything would always go smoothly.

And you'd be wrong.

As I learned while researching and writing *Zoom For Dummies*, IT departments can lock down specific Zoom features. Most relevant here, they can limit what their employees can do with people outside their organization during their Zoom meetings. These user restrictions include:

- Sharing their screens.
- Sending and receiving files.
- Giving call attendees remote control over their computers.
- Allowing only authenticated users to enter meetings.
- Restricting meeting guests to those accounts tied to a specific domain (such as microsoft.com).
- Sending text messages—aka, chatting.

- Talking about taboo subjects. (OK, I'm making that one up.)
- Accessing Zoom's annotation tools.
- Recording conversations.*

These are Zoom features, not bugs. Several times during Zoom calls over the past two years, I needed the meeting host to share their screens with me. Unfortunately, their IT departments had either disabled that feature or failed to enable it. In addition, the participants weren't Zoom admins. They'd have to submit formal requests to IT. (No, we weren't going to resolve the issue anytime soon, let alone during our scheduled time.)

Bottom line: A meeting with a new client, partner, vendor, or job applicant won't necessarily go seamlessly, even if the two of you are using the same videoconferencing software.

Collaboration Overload

Employees have overwhelmingly reported being as productive working from home as they were when they commuted to the office. For their part, managers have largely concurred with that assessment.

Rob Cross wouldn't disagree with either group. He's a professor at Babson College and the author of *Beyond Collaboration Overload: How to Work Smarter, Get Ahead, and Restore Your Well-Being.*[†] Speaking with McKinsey in December 2021, he described some of his research:

---

* That's why *Zoom For Dummies* came in at 400 pages.

† Cross appeared on my podcast to talk about the book in 2021. Check it out at https://tinyurl.com/rob-phil-pod.

Before the COVID-19 pandemic, people were spending about 85 percent of their time on the phone, on email, and in meetings. That number had progressively gone up over the past decade, about 50 percent or more. It has gone up again through the pandemic: people are working about five to eight hours more a week, and they're working earlier in the morning and deeper into the night.[6]

As the title of his book suggests, there's a chasm between working smarter and harder. Cross details ways in which people can collaborate better and get back a considerable chunk of their time. For now, let's address why employees burned the midnight oil during the early days of the pandemic—and, in many cases, continue to do so. Here are four theories.

Searching for Explanations

We may have learned about the Spanish flu, but we didn't live through it. COVID-19 was terra incognita. In March 2020, we were justifiably scared for our health and our livelihoods.

Companies began laying off employees *en masse*—actions that didn't exactly allay our fears. A record 20.5 million Americans lost their jobs in April 2020. The US unemployment ballooned to 14.7 percent.[7] Put simply, we needed the money. Case in point: At the end of 2021, 61 percent of the US population reported living paycheck to paycheck. The number actually dropped from a high of 65 percent in 2020.[8] Remember that, when it comes to societal safety nets, the US isn't Canada or Estonia.

Also, people who didn't receive pink slips were the lucky ones— and they damn well knew it. They felt compelled to prove to their bosses that they really *were* working at home and not watching Netflix. If that meant taking an extra meeting after dinner and

5 The Exasperating Second-Order Effects of Hybrid Work 139

working what some have termed the *second shift*, then so be it.[*]
Face time moved from the office to Slack, Zoom, Microsoft Teams,
and email.

Next, American business owners and managers aren't generally accustomed to asking their employees to work *less*. To be fair,
though, more companies have begun instituting no-meeting days
as the pandemic has progressed. Some have even temporarily shut
their doors to alleviate worker burnout. In August 2021, Nike
closed its corporate office for a week "to help its employees relax
and recharge."[9]

Finally, when we work remotely, we're in a sense playing with house
money. For example, Roland used to bolt at 5 p.m. to catch the 5:17
p.m. train every day. He'd arrive home around 6:45 p.m. and catch
a few hours with his kids before they went to bed. During lockdown,
Roland took meetings until 6 p.m. and still came out ahead.

Why We're Fried

At some point during late 2020 or early 2021, we moved from
Phase I of the pandemic to Phase II. We were no longer afraid
of losing our jobs—at least not to the same extent as we were in
March 2020.

Brass tacks: We're fried, and we have been for a while now. In
March 2021, two-thirds of workers reported that the pandemic
had worsened their feelings of burnout.[10] Sadly, only one in nine
managers is concerned about the topic.[11]

Can someone say *chasm?*

Now, I don't want to overstate things, and I need to stay in my
lane. But our heightened anxiety levels don't emanate exclusively
from Zoom fatigue or the increased workloads that Cross describes.

---

[*] Microsoft has termed this shift the *triple-peak day*. See https://tinyurl.
com/3peak-rpm.

School closings, supply chain issues, political polarization, the January 6 insurrection, mask and vaccine mandates, abortion restrictions, #BlackLivesMatter, social media, and the current war in Ukraine are all playing roles.

At a minimum, however, aspects of the contemporary workplace are increasing our collective agita. It's only natural to feel a little consternation in response to:

- Putting in more hours.
- Needing a week to complete a task that should take a day.
- Dealing with constantly shifting return-to-office dates.
- Being incessantly pinged from our colleagues.
- Watching inflation erode our wages.
- Seeing unprecedented numbers of our colleagues leave—either by their choice or our employer's.
- Having to pick up the slack when a colleague quits and management tries to backfill the position.

Searching for Solutions

In the short term, some of us are biting the bullet and toughing it out. Many are pining for the days of in-person work—at least a few days per week as Figure 2.1 demonstrated. But what if our work conditions don't materially improve a year or two from now?

Over the long term, employees are more likely to start perusing other opportunities. After all, the grass is always greener, and switching jobs these days doesn't necessarily require relocation.

And that's a wrap on Part II. It provided an overview of project management and the considerable challenges that remote and hybrid work pose to it. Fortunately, there are solutions. Part III gets prescriptive and provides them.

Chapter Summary

- Cognitive biases have always been problematic at work. They're even more vexing in hybrid and remote workplaces.
- The same delays that slow physical production lines slow human ones. The results are predictably similar.
- In their efforts to secure the enterprise, IT departments can complicate employees' efforts to communicate and collaborate, especially when working with outsiders.
- Employees have been working harder throughout the pandemic, but not necessarily smarter. Not surprisingly, they're exhausted. Something's gotta give.

PART III

Prescriptions for Success: How to Manage Projects in Hybrid Workplaces

Chapter 6

REEVALUATE YOUR VETTING CRITERIA

"Never above you. Never below you. Always beside you."

—WALTER WINCHELL

How do we pick our partners?

I'm not talking about our romantic mates. Rather, how do professionals choose their clients, employees, partners, and vendors? And, against a backdrop of remote and hybrid work, should they continue to rely upon prior methods when vetting others? If not, then which ones should we tweak?

Let those last two questions serve as this chapter's jumping-off point.

Questions ... So Many Questions

At some point during your career, you've interviewed for a job. It's also a safe bet that you've interviewed others, even informally. At a high level and regardless of who's doing the asking, all interview questions attempt to answer an overarching one: Can this person do the job?

That's not to say that we ask every question on our mind during the interview process. Some queries weigh on our minds, but we don't verbalize them. For instance, if we hire Derek:

- Will the decision make me look bad?
- Will my job become harder or easier?
- Does he possess the skills necessary to succeed in this role?
- Will he be able to pick up new skills as needed?
- Can he communicate clearly?
- Will he burn bridges with his clients and colleagues?
- Is he willing to put in long hours when needed?
- Will he stick around long enough to justify the company's investment in him? Or will I be interviewing to fill his position again in six months?

In short, we collect data. Companies have for decades used personality tests, behavior-based interviews, background and reference checks, and even algorithms to help them make better hiring decisions. Eventually, recruiters, hiring managers, and CEOs hopefully realize that the perfect candidate doesn't exist.[1] They make educated guesses about whether a particular applicant will pan out.

And you can make the same case for other types of voluntary business relationships. For instance, a company revising its internal policy on workplace discrimination hires an outside law firm. Its head of HR is wondering if we hire the new firm:

- Will it be able to complete the job on time and within budget?
- Does it possess the skills and experience to do the job right?
- Will the decision make me look bad?
- Could I lose my job if things don't go well?

6 Reevaluate Your Vetting Criteria   147

To be certain, these are all still valid questions to ask job applicants in an era of remote and hybrid work. We have to refine them, though. Returning to our friend Derek:

- Can he do the job *in a hybrid manner*?
- Is he willing to come to the office a certain number of times per week?
- Does he live close enough to our headquarters to do so? If not, is he willing to make the trip when necessary?
- Is he so fervently anti-office that he'll resist making the trip?
- Has he demonstrated both the willingness and the ability to learn new tools?
- Can he communicate clearly, both in person and in writing?

Asking these direct questions doesn't guarantee truthful applicant responses. Think of them as elimination questions. The mere fact that a recruiter asks them can scare off the wrong applicant. And isn't that an essential outcome of any interview process? Filling the position only to refill it three months later doesn't make anyone happy.

As it turns out, asking more refined questions is only one way to determine which applicants will succeed on remote and hybrid projects.

Try Before You Buy

When the chance of product or project failure is high, it behooves teams, departments, and even entire organizations to start small.

Recruiting Parallels

When interviewing certain types of applicants, kicking their tires has been standard recruiting practice for years. For example, software engineers routinely have to show their chops early in the application process. If you haven't heard of a *coding interview,* it works something like this.

Say that you apply for a position requiring expertise in the general-use programming language Python or structured query language—the underpinning of relational databases. Don't expect the hiring manager to accept your expertise sight unseen. Google, Airbnb, Dropbox, and countless other companies make coders demonstrate their skills in front of live audiences. If Dinesh can't write simple JavaScript code on the fly to determine if a number is prime, for example, he shouldn't expect a forthcoming offer. He's not as good as he claims as he is. Period.

Done properly, coding interviews can separate the wheat from the chaff. Great, but what about noncoders—people applying for positions in different fields? It's not hard to fathom comparable simulations for candidates seeking jobs in internal communications, employee compensation, marketing, analytics, and other business functions.

If coding interviews suffer from a chief limitation, it's that they can fail to reveal whether applicants play nice with others. A whip-smart developer might be a giant pain in the ass to work with—a brilliant jerk, in the parlance of Netflix CEO Reed Hastings.

What to do? A job-related or coding simulation during a single interview is one thing, but what about giving applicants actual projects to complete—ones that require them to work with their future colleagues?

From Theory to Practice

As we've seen throughout this book, Automattic is far ahead of the pack. Here, the company takes the try-before-you-buy idea one step further than most. Automattic *contracts* candidates before hiring them for full-time positions. (Yes, money exchanges hands.)

6 Reevaluate Your Vetting Criteria

That is, Automattic employees give job applicants small projects to complete before making formal offers to them. As the company explains on its website:

> All positions at Automattic involve a paid trial in the application process, which is a short project or set of tasks that will be assessed by our hiring teams. We've found that the best way to evaluate working with someone is to do just that!
>
> Trial projects vary depending on the role you are applying for, but they are based on very real areas of work within our teams. As in the code test, you will be assigned a Trial Guide who will provide feedback on your project and can help with any questions that come up while you're working.
>
> Depending on the role you are interested in and the time you're able to commit, the trial can last anywhere from a few hours to a few weeks. Most candidates complete the trial while working full-time and we know life is busy! Because of this, we encourage all candidates to determine their own working hours and schedule during this project. If you're curious about specific time requirements, check-in with your recruiter for additional information.[2]

The benefits of this project-oriented approach to interviewing are hard to overstate. At a minimum, it recognizes that any hiring process is fundamentally imperfect. Depending on the role, a single bad hire can weaken a team, a project, and even an entire company.

In addition, when applicants interact with their would-be peers, everyone involved gathers more information about how they'll work in the future. Automattic management can see for itself if Maude is as collaborative, chill, and knowledgeable as she claims.

In turn, Maude can glean necessary insights about Automattic's culture, internal processes, and other factors that will help her make a better decision about her future employment. The idea of employee-employer fit becomes less abstract for both parties. Beyond that, this type of dating minimizes the risks of marrying an incompatible spouse.

Later in the book we'll apply this same principle to projects involving multiple organizations. We'll see how a project pilot serves this same valuable vetting function, just on a larger scale. The paradox here is striking: An organization often won't hire a junior-level programmer without seeing if she's really up to snuff. At the same time, it starts a multi-million-dollar project with an outside entity without really kicking its tires.

Tips for Forging New Partnerships on Hybrid Projects

This chapter concludes with some practical tips to help you successfully vet future partners, clients, and vendors.

Research Your Partner's Preferred Tools

Say that you're evaluating prospective clients, vendors, or partners for a long-term project. Odds are that, prior to COVID-19, you asked yourself questions about:

- **Budget:** Can we afford to hire them? Can they afford to hire us?
- **Capability:** Does this organization possess the skills to complete the job?
- **Compatibility:** Will our culture mesh with theirs?
- **Policy and politics:** Will I take heat if I choose to do business with this entity? Is this service provider on our company's approved vendor list?

Are these still important ones to ask? Sure, but consider another one: Which tools does the company use to communicate, collaborate, and manage its projects?

In the past, essential stakeholders and decision-makers haven't asked that question as frequently as they should have—or they've pooh-poohed the eventual answer. In remote and hybrid workplaces, this is an essential one to ask.

And better yet, what if you don't have to ask that question because the company you're thinking of hiring has already answered it—and posted it for everyone to see?

Consider the webpage[*] shown in Figure 6.1 from Pearl Lemon, an international firm specializing in search engine optimization.

Pearl Lemon Website: Tools We Use

Figure 6.1: Pearl Lemon Website: Tools We Use (Source: Company Website)

This simple page provides an invaluable signal to prospective Pearl Lemon clients. It simultaneously accomplishes two goals.

---

[*] See www.pearllemon.com/tools-we-use-and-recommend.

First, it attracts clients who use these popular communication, collaboration, and project-management applications. Second and just as important, it potentially repels old-school clients whose employees insist upon "managing the project" via email attachments. (Remember the fictitious company mentioned in the Preface.) As we saw earlier, these projects are unlikely to succeed anyway.

Does the existence of this page guarantee a successful client engagement? Absolutely not, but it *can* weed out problematic clients from the get-go.

Prediction: More professional-service firms will publicize their choice of communication and collaboration tools and use them as points of differentiation à la Pearl Lemon.

Screen for Others' Digital Literacy

A company's preferred tools speak volumes about the way that it values its clients, vendors, and employees. No, not every organization needs to be on the bleeding edge with the latest version of everything. Still, one that relies on antediluvian tech sends an unequivocal message to its workforce: We don't value you.

When a new organization is courting your business or vice versa, consider the following questions:

- Is it using contemporary applications? For instance, is it sending you a document to sign as an email attachment as if it were 1998? Or is it using a better alternative, such as DocuSign or HelloSign?
- When you ask the organization to provide information, is it able to respond quickly? Or do its employees routinely struggle to find basic documents and correspondence?

6 Reevaluate Your Vetting Criteria 153

- ☻ When you try to share a Google Doc with your prospective partners, do they flat-out refuse to use it? Does the company's IT department ban employees from opening the links?
- ☻ When you send a scheduling link to your contact via YouCanBookMe or Calendly, does he guffaw?

The answers to these questions will help you suss out others' digital literacy. If your future corporate mates strike you as digitally illiterate, ask yourself this question: What are the odds you'll be able to successfully work together on a project or launch a product in a hybrid or remote fashion?

If you're not sold, keep looking.

Screen for Core Work Hours

As recently as the past decade, offshoring was all the rage among IT executives. From a 2010 CIO Insight article:

> A global CIO study from 2010 reveals that 90 percent of CIOs will be maintaining or increasing offshore outsourcing projects in 2010 and 2011. According to the UK-based IT staffing and managed services firm Harvey Nash, outsourcing has been greatly used during the recession and CIOs are inclined to continue using outsourced services.[3]

These days, not so much. More and companies are bringing their operations back or reshoring, a trend that some experts expect to continue.[4] It turns out that lower labor costs often don't justify the differences in time zones and other logistical issues, as the following sidebar illustrates.

Lesson Learned

A restaurant in San Francisco needed a new website and mobile app. Rather than pay a crosstown firm beaucoup bucks, it decided to go with a lower-cost shop in India.

As the owner of a small business hit particularly hard by COVID-19, his desire to save money was understandable. He also had to cope with the exodus of local residents.[5]

Was the decision to hire a distant partner a wise one? India is 12 hours and 30 minutes ahead of California. There's not much overlap, and the majority of the communication and work turned out to be asynchronous. The parties were unable to clearly communicate in writing. Simple requests took far longer to understand, much less complete. Work-in-progress increased, and the restaurant owner ultimately canceled the engagement.

I wasn't surprised that this project didn't succeed. Finding a partner in closer geographic proximity would have made more sense here—even if it meant spending a bit more.

Rather than selecting partners exclusively based on cost, it's best to also consider a prospective partner's *core work hours*. Writing for TechRepublic, Paul Gray defines the term as follows:

> Set aside a defined period each day that's open season for meetings, either scheduled or ad hoc. The rest of the day is open for employees to use for focus work, unconventional schedules, or travel. The primary expectation is that if you book a meeting, place an ad hoc call or chat, or send an email, your team will be available to respond during core hours. Generally, the core hour block is about half the workday and

is generally a three- to four-hour block that extends from late morning to early afternoon.[6]

Distributed companies like Automattic, Basecamp, and GitLab adopted this practice long ago. Go back a decade or more, and you can find passionate advocates for it—and for good reason.[7] Since lockdown, dozens more have jumped on board.[8]

Adherents have found that they can concurrently accommodate all types of employees, including early risers and night owls. (Remember: Employees value *when* they work more than *where* they work.) What's more, by obtaining real-time answers to their questions during a good chunk of their days, employees can reduce their WIP. Not needing to be constantly on-call also reduces worker stress levels.

In addition, companies that set boundaries around meeting times provide another, less obvious benefit: Their employees are no longer exclusively responsible for defending their schedules, to paraphrase Dropbox spokeswoman Jasmine Castro-Torres.[9]

Put all of these things together: All else being equal, companies that embrace core work hours stand to encounter fewer issues on hybrid and remote projects.

Factor in Partner Location

Related to core work hours, the willingness of your partner, client, or vendor to occasionally meet in person is paramount.

Company ABC is looking to remodel its office. Its management is considering two design firms—DFA and DFB. Table 6.1 displays a quick comparison of their attributes:

Attribute	DFA	DFB
Quote	Baseline	Baseline plus 10 percent.
Core Work Hours	No	Yes
Location	Across the country	30 miles away
Quality	Comparable	Comparable

Table 6.1: A Tale of Two Design Firms

Much like the restaurant example earlier in this chapter, the least expensive firm may not represent the best choice for a partner, especially when you factor in core work hours.

Chapter Summary

- Old standbys still matter, but it's imperative to add new questions when vetting prospective employees, vendors, clients, and partners for projects in hybrid workplaces.
- Consider the tools that a prospective partner uses to complete its projects. Generally speaking, the answer to that question will provide a valuable signal about whether you should walk down the aisle.
- Establishing core work hours can reduce employee stress, WIP, and turnover.

Chapter 7

COME TOGETHER

"The medium is the message."

—MARSHALL MCLUHAN

The combination of social capital and proximity bias in the workplace can be lethal. If we don't know our colleagues and can't see what they're doing, we're more prone to underestimate their contributions. Plenty of other counterproductive things can happen as well.

You may not have heard of social capital or proximity bias before reading this book. If that's the case, I'll bet each of them struck an intuitive chord with you.

This chapter explores the necessity of establishing social capital on projects that take place in remote and hybrid workplaces. Remote and hybrid product and project teams certainly face greater challenges in this regard than their in-person counterparts do. Still, it's not rocket surgery. With a little effort, colleagues can increase their cohesion, build valuable relationships, and increase their odds of success.

WFH Erodes Social Capital Among Employees

What have the pandemic and move to remote work done to our existing workplace relationships?

Over the past two years, Microsoft researchers have spent a great deal of effort answering that question. The verdict: The informal interactions that serve as the basis of social capital in the workplace have deteriorated. As researchers Nancy Baym, Jonathan Larson, and Ronnie Martin wrote for *Harvard Business Review* in March 2021:

> This year, teams across Microsoft (including ours) have conducted over 50 studies to understand how the nature of work itself has changed since early 2020. Microsoft's annual Work Trend Index is part of this initiative and includes an analysis of trillions of productivity signals—think emails, meetings, chats, and posts—across Microsoft and LinkedIn's user base. It also includes a survey of more than 30,000 people in 31 countries around the world.

> One of the biggest and most worrisome changes we saw across these studies was the significant impact that a year of full-time remote work had on organizational connections— the fundamental basis of social capital. People consistently report feeling disconnected, and in studying anonymized collaboration trends between billions of Outlook emails and Microsoft Teams meetings, we saw a clear trend: the shift to remote work shrunk people's networks.[1]

Existing employees have felt more and more disconnected from their peers, and their social networks have shrunk, but what about newly hired employees? The jury is still out, but many remote workers will *never* get a chance to develop proper workplace ties with their colleagues. That's a big deal. Writing for the *MIT Sloan Management Review,* Jennifer Deal and Alec Levenson argue that "figuring out social capital is critical for the future of hybrid work."[2]

Tsedal Neeley is a professor of business administration at Harvard Business School and the author *Remote Work Revolution: Succeeding from Anywhere.* Speaking with Paul Keegan of Bloomberg in March 2022, she estimated that roughly one in five workers are *remote natives.* These are people "who've joined companies during the pandemic and expect to continue working from home, even once COVID-19 becomes endemic."[3]

Remote natives joined their employers and started working without any in-person training and onboarding. They can't serendipitously bump into their new colleagues in the hallway or at the coffee machine. Against this backdrop, it's fair to wonder the following:

1. Will remote natives ever be able to establish any real bonds with their colleagues?
2. Will they be able to contribute as much as employees who had already built these bonds?
3. Will they find their jobs as fulfilling?
4. Will they quickly bolt if they can bump their salaries by 10 percent?
5. How will managers staunch the bleeding?

General questions such as these are interesting, but let's apply what we've learned about social capital to a specific hybrid project. What can happen on an objectively successful one when several colleagues fail to establish any bonds?

Funny you should ask.

Going Deep: A Detailed Case Study

The following case study provides valuable lessons for successfully managing hybrid projects. Before continuing, know that all the names are pseudonyms.* Although the case study takes place in higher education, its issues and internal politics mirror similar projects endemic to other industries.

Project Background

Waystar Royco is a small consultancy that specializes in shipping international commodities. Over the years, its management had worked jointly with NRPU, a large research university based in the United States. The two organizations had completed a number of small projects over that time.

As Waystar Royco's business evolved and grew, its management realized that it needed to begin systematically tracking logistics data for its clients. (In 1978, FedEx founder Fred Smith famously said, "The information about the package is just as important as the package itself.") Unfortunately, Waystar Royco didn't know where to start.

To that end, the company's top brass, Tom and Shiv, contacted NRPU's Department of Strategic Alliances about taking on another potential engagement. Ultimately, two DSA executives, Roman and Gerri, inked the deal with Waystar Royco to build a simple database prototype for $25,000 in June 2017.

After the deal closed, Roman and Gerri contacted Logan, the chair of NRPU's Department of Information Systems. Roman and Gerri suspected that Logan would be able to find a suitable professor to oversee the project.

---

* For giggles, I based them on *Succession* characters.

As it turned out, Logan knew the perfect candidate: a new professor with nearly two decades of real-world experience named Josh whom he'd held in high regard. Josh had done well in his first year, handling every curveball the department had thrown at him with aplomb.

Logan emailed Josh and asked if he had time to chat for a few minutes. It wasn't a big ask. After all, neither one of them was off galivanting in exotic locales at the time. Josh was teaching two in-person summer courses down the hall from his boss's expansive office. He popped by one day after his classes ended.

Logan explained the project to Josh, who immediately expressed interest. Eager to get into his boss's good graces and earn some extra cheddar, Josh agreed to come on board and manage the hybrid project. The team's marching orders were clear: to present a working prototype of the database by early December, which marked the end of the semester.

Logan was pleased. He told Josh to expect an invitation to a forthcoming exploratory conference call.

Getting to Know You

A few weeks later, the group held that call. Logan, Josh, Tom, and Shiv from Waystar Royco, and Roman and Gerri from the DSA all dialed in. The discussion was productive and, from Josh's perspective, Tom and Shiv seemed solid.

Josh suggested that the Waystar Royco folks come to campus in mid-August for a full-day, in-person kickoff meeting. They agreed. (Josh wasn't averse to travel, but his hands were tied. The university's rule prohibiting professors from missing classes severely restricted his ability to travel during the week.)

Beyond wanting to shake their hands, Josh wanted Tom and Shiv to meet Kendall and Connor, the two mature and talented students who would be building the database if Josh had his druthers. (Josh would soon hire them both through proper university channels.)

Apart from their cursory introductions, Roman and Gerri barely said boo. Soon after the call began, Josh had forgotten that the DSA folks were even participating on it. (It's not like they were using Zoom, Skype, or Webex.)

Formally Kicking Off the Project

In-mid August, soon after the fall semester commenced, Tom and Shiv flew cross-country to attend the day-long kickoff meeting. Josh reserved a sizeable conference room for the day, equipped with whiteboard, projector, food, and beverages.

As the project manager, Josh's main goals for the day-long meeting included, in no particular order:

1. To build a sense of community—at least to the extent that a one-day get-together would allow. Josh wanted everyone on the team to get to know each other a little bit, including Kendall and Connor. The two student-workers participated to the extent that their schedules allowed. Curiously, while Tom and Shiv made the five-hour flight, Roman and Gerri didn't make the five-minute drive. Neither stakeholder even bothered to RSVP.

2. To decide on the type of database that the team would be building. (There are many different ways to do this, and one size never fits all.)

3. To agree upon the project-management methodology that they'd be following for the next four months. As a proponent of Agile methods, Josh suggested Scrum. After a brief explanation, Tom and Shiv concurred.

4. To shore up project roles and responsibilities in the form of a RACI matrix. No methodology exists on an island. Assigning formal roles is imperative if the project's got a snowball's chance in hell of succeeding.
5. To review the reasons that the project could fail.
6. To codify the tools that everyone would use during the engagement. Relying upon email for internal communication and project management is never wise. Double that when key project participants often travel to different continents.

Yeah, it would be a full day.

The first five goals don't exactly qualify as revelations—or at least they shouldn't to any experienced and self-respecting PM. These are essential elements for any project, regardless of where and when it takes place. People all too often gloss over the sixth. This is a critical error on all projects, especially remote and hybrid ones.

Agreeing on the Tech

Fortunately, Tom and Shiv understood this critical point. Josh suggested that they use the following applications during the project:

- ☺ Slack for communication and collaboration.
- ☺ Trello for project management.
- ☺ Contemporary database-development tools that don't matter much for the purposes of this book.

Tom and Shiv had never used Slack and Trello before, but they seemed open to learning these new tools. Josh spent about 15 minutes demonstrating each of them on the room's projector. They were impressed, but each wondered if their extensive travel schedules would impede their progress. After all, they could go days without being in an area with adequate Wi-Fi. How would they know the status of any one task or issue without being able to use a proper computer?

At that point, Josh whipped out his iPhone and showed them the Slack and Trello mobile apps. Everything they did on one device would seamlessly sync with any others. Tom and Shiv were sold.

Josh wouldn't have to convince Kendall and Connor. He had chosen these two rock stars based upon his previous interactions with them. Each had excelled when taking one of Josh's classes. Beyond possessing impressive technical chops, the two students knew how their professor rolled: Josh was allergic to email and preferred Slack. They did, too. Beyond that, they'd followed Scrum and used Trello on their semester-long capstone projects.

Thanks to the in-person meeting, Josh was able to build trust and social capital with Tom and Shiv. Josh had already worked with Logan, Kendall, and Connor; they weren't starting at ground zero. As stakeholders, Roman and Gerri were essentially ghosts, but Josh paid it no mind at the time. They weren't responsible for any project tasks. #foreshadowing

Figure 7.1 displays the approximate social capital that Josh had built with the people involved in the Waystar Royco project.

Everything seemed to be falling into place. The kickoff meeting had built a solid foundation for the rest of the project. The tried-and-true question remained: Would it hold up?

They were about to find out.

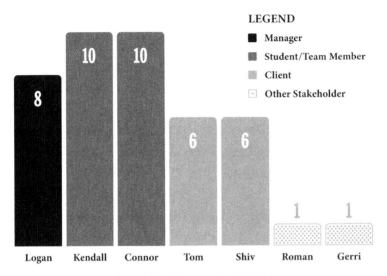

Figure 7.1: Trust and Social Capital on a Hybrid Project

Sticking the Landing

Over the course of the next three-plus months, the group faced its fair share of challenges, but the project was an unequivocal home run. Josh met in person with Kendall and Connor and virtually with Tom and Shiv. Everyone used Slack and Trello, and Josh could easily determine the status of any issue. Not coincidentally, the team accomplished all the project's goals—and then some.

Kendall, Connor, and Josh delivered a far more powerful and extensible database than the contract required. The minutiae isn't important here. Suffice it to say, however, that the team used superior technologies that allowed Waystar Royco employees to access the database via their mobile phones. Oh, and the team came in on time and 40 percent *under* budget, both of which are black swans on these types of projects.

Josh also documented the entire project in a 120-page final report. This documentation would help Waystar Royco in future phases of database development, regardless of who ultimately took the reins.

The results left Tom and Shiv ecstatic. Waystar Royco had gotten more than its money's worth, and they both knew it. They immediately wanted to commence the next phase of the project with Josh reprising his role. Tom and Shiv jokingly asked if they could start a local chapter of the Josh Fan Club. (As further proof of the project's unqualified success, a year later the team's work won an industry innovation award.)

Roman and Gerri had remained invisible stakeholders since the kickoff call. Along with managing the project, Josh tended to his professor responsibilities and other professional commitments. He had forgotten that these stakeholders were even tangentially involved.

Early December arrived. It was time to put a bow on the first phase of the project. Josh reminded Kendall and Connor in Slack to submit their final weekly hours so they'd get paid. As a final step, Josh dotted his i's and crossed his t's. He emailed everyone involved that the team had completed the project. He thanked the team and included a link to the master project document that contained all database credentials.

Time to clink the champagne glasses.

Failing by Succeeding

If only the story ended there ...

Upon receiving Josh's email, Roman and Gerri responded with their own. By including Outlook's ominous red exclamation point, they were throwing down the gauntlet: They were suddenly no longer invisible and ostensibly disinterested stakeholders. They wanted to chat with him *pronto.* Josh expected a gold star for the team's efforts or, at the very least, plaudits for a job well done.

7 Come Together   167

Boy, was he wrong.

By way of background, Roman and Gerri were mere administrators. Both lacked anything remotely resembling a technical background. Neither that omission nor their invisibility over the past four months, however, prevented them from tearing into Josh on the conference call a few hours later. Both of them asserted that Josh's team hadn't met the terms specified in the statement of work.

Gerri was particularly caustic. In her remarkably uninformed view, no team could have possibly accomplished what Josh said it did for only $15,000 (60 cents on the dollar).[*] Gerri made it clear that the client's utter delight with the project's results was irrelevant. Something *had* to be off—and it certainly wasn't DSA's original estimate. In so many words, she was calling Josh a liar.

At any point during the project, Roman and Gerri could have viewed the group's steady progress and burn rate by doing one or more of the following things:

- ☺ Logging in to the Slack workspace.
- ☺ Viewing the project's Trello board.
- ☺ Viewing the students' weekly timesheets by requesting a report from the university's payroll department.
- ☺ Simply asking Josh for a quick update.

Any one of these actions would have quickly manifested that the team had *always* been working efficiently.

Josh suspected that their motives were far from benevolent. Although Roman and Gerri tried to couch their complaints under the aegis of vague "technical issues," Josh saw through their ruse. One of three things was clearly happening, if not all three:

---

[*] Gerri telling Josh that the database "couldn't possibly work" was risible. To paraphrase a classic Bill Burr joke, it was akin to Josh telling her what it was like to be pregnant. How the hell would he know?

1. The savings that Josh's team had generated for Waystar Royco had effectively "cost" DSA $10,000. (Josh had seen similar unprofessional behavior among bickering partners at consulting firms over his career.)
2. Roman and Gerri had already booked the sale and DSA had received payment in full. They would now have to refund Waystar Royco the overage or apply it to the project's second phase. Josh suspected that their annual bonuses were tied to their bookings.
3. Although they wouldn't admit as much, the fact that Josh's team came in 40 percent under budget would make Roman and Gerri look bad in the eyes of their peers. Maybe NRPU internal auditors would start poking around. On what other projects had they been so wrong?

If that tense phone call was the gasoline, then their subsequent emails—copying Logan, of course—represented the match that caused the situation to explode. Accusatory messages started flying back and forth. Other senior NRPU employees started getting involved. Josh was justifiably furious. Although Logan was out of the country, he needed to intervene and make peace.

When the dust finally settled, Josh passed on working on phase two of the project—leaving Tom and Shiv disappointed. For Josh, the game wasn't remotely worth the candle. Roman and Gerri had questioned his integrity when they were the ones who had acted unethically; the idea of even talking to either person again sent chills down Josh's spine.[*]

---

[*] Adding salt to the wound, it took another three months for Josh's department to include the project stipend in his paycheck.

Lessons

Here are the three morals of the story. First, if at all possible, get everyone together at the start of a project—especially a hybrid one. It's difficult to build trust and social capital when you've never met someone. Second, sometimes you can fail by succeeding, particularly when organizational politics run deep.

Third, stakeholders with hidden agendas exist no matter where a project takes place. It's typically more difficult to identify them, though, in hybrid and remote workplaces. Project enemies and detractors can more easily sit on the sidelines in stealth mode and, when they spot an opportunity, suddenly pounce.

Simon's Law of Slamming Others

Once the database project began in earnest, Roman and Gerri never deigned to engage with any team members. Not once. It's hardly a coincidence, then, that they turned out to be the project's only two detractors. Both would have been less apt to castigate Josh and the team if they'd all sat down for a cup of coffee. Their use of email as their cudgel of choice is also instructive.

The NRPU example demonstrates that employees, colleagues, partners, managers, subordinates, and vendors don't always get along. Generally speaking, our propensity to throw shade at others is a function of several factors, including:

1. Whether we've ever met them in real life.
2. Our proximity to them at the time.
3. The medium that we're using.

Few of us would even dream of confronting our peers in the hallway and start belittling them, especially since workplaces have become more woke. Rather, we tend to be more passive-aggressive.

We channel our inner Marshall McLuhan. Our chosen medium informs—*and often becomes*—our message.

While hardly scientific, our colleagues seem *less likely* to disparage us after we've met them and established at least a little rapport. Figure 7.2 demonstrates this relationship.

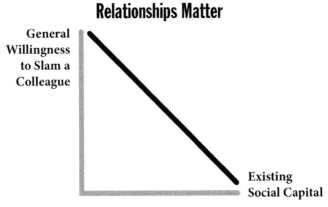

Figure 7.2: Relationships Matter

Generally speaking, it's easier to demonize our colleagues when we view them only as impersonal avatars or email addresses. It's tougher after we've broken bread with them. That doesn't mean, however, that a crusty colleague won't throw you under the bus just because you both ate paninis at Panera three months ago. As proof, allow me to take a quick, semi-painful trip down memory lane.

Yeah. This Happened.

In the early aughts, I was working as a consultant for a software company on a project for a large utility close to my home. Around 5 p.m. one day, I received a scathing email from Melissa, a colleague one rung up from me who'd also worked on that project. In it, she misrepresented and criticized my work for our client. To put salt in the wound, she cc'd my boss and hers.

Ho hum. Just another day in the life of a consultant, right? Isn't that why I earned the big bucks?

There's just one catch: I was sitting in a cubicle adjacent to hers when she hit the Send button.

I read the email, took a deep breath, stood up, turned around, and looked Melissa dead in the eyes. As diplomatically as possible, I posed the following question to her:

"What the *fuck*?"[*]

Now, Melissa didn't *need* to blindside me. She could have taken me aside to chat about what I did—or, in her eyes, *failed to do*—that day. It's not like I was hard to find.

I was peeved, but I understood what she was doing. After all, many of us try to avoid face-to-face workplace conflict if we can. Change the medium, and you almost always change the message.

Driving home that night, I was in a pensive mood. Yes, Melissa had thrown me under the bus a few hours earlier. At the same time, though, I couldn't help but wonder what she

---

[*] Although I wasn't nearly as funny, my tone resembled that of John Malkovich in a hysterical scene in the classic flick *Burn After Reading*. See https://tinyurl.com/malk-wtf.

> would have been done if we'd never met. What if I'd been working in another time zone?
>
> Maybe I got off easy.

Note Melissa's preferred communications weapon in attacking Roderick: email. Unless your name is Will Smith (too soon?), we're more likely to use some mediums more than others when we take our colleagues to the woodshed. Figure 7.3 demonstrates this relationship.

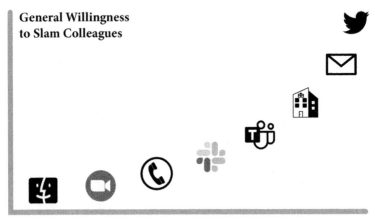

Figure 7.3: Slamming Colleagues: The Medium Matters

How to Build Social Capital on Hybrid Projects

The Waystar Royco case study in this chapter manifested the general importance of in-person get-togethers. They can help colleagues build invaluable social capital, especially when the team members have never previously met. The social cohesion that can stem from in-person interactions, however, is especially important on complicated projects and product launches. See Figure 7.4.

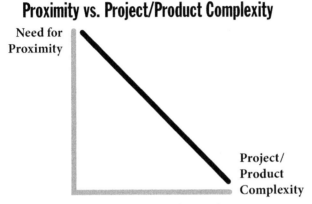

Figure 7.4: Proximity vs. Project/Product Complexity

Think of Figure 7.4 as a general construct, not an iron law. For instance, two companies start a project with a formal, one-week in-person kickoff. In the following months, the team members enjoy regular in-person interaction.

Does this fact by itself mean that the project is a lock to be successful?

Of course not. Remember that project management is tough even under the best of circumstances. Team A can convene for a proper in-person kickoff, meet regularly, and still botch a relatively simple project. Conversely, Team B can opt not to meet and still hit a complex product launch out of the park. Both scenarios, however, are unlikely. And there are myriad examples that lie between these two extremes.

The benefits of regular in-person employee interactions can be significant, especially on hybrid projects. Rather than hit you with more stats and studies, though, here's a story from someone whose company routinely brings its employees together.

Employee Playtime at Playfair Data

—Amy Leonard, senior director of operations at Playfair Data

As the world shifts to more remote and hybrid workplaces, we have to remember the value of human connection. Sharing a meal or a memorable experience with our colleagues can help us be more thoughtful, efficient, and committed to each other and our work.

Since forming Playfair Data, we've understood the importance of getting people together. The company employs about 20 people, split between its Kansas City and Orlando offices. To build team camaraderie, we host semi-annual team summits—one each in both cities. Agendas include:

- A welcome dinner.
- Two days of learning opportunities and working sessions.
- A half- or full day of fun. One summit included a private trolley tour ending at a local beer hall. Another time, we took a trip to the Kennedy Space Center and the Space Coast.
- A closing reception.

The summits enable our team members to build upon the connections they've already established online. They give everyone an intentional yet casual opportunity to get to know their peers in a more meaningful way. Team members better understand their colleagues' work styles, personalities, and preferences. They build a familiarity with each other that fosters better communication and collaboration when they return to their home offices.

> Building team camaraderie is just one way in which the summits more than justify their expense. They give Playfair leadership an opportunity to learn more about everyone's personal values, individual strengths, and professional goals. When we listen to our team members, they feel more engaged.
>
> Beyond that, this knowledge helps leadership select the projects that each employee is best suited to accomplish and the ones that they'll find most rewarding. In the end, employees are more likely to successfully manage and complete their projects.

In the spirit of maximizing the chances of success on new projects and products, here are a few tips on building social capital to conclude this chapter.

Where to Get Together

Traditional headquarters with individual employee offices don't lend themselves to true team building. Beyond that, the vibe is usually pretty corporate and uninspiring. Marie Kondo wouldn't say that gray cubicles spark joy. It's best to find a proper collaboration space.

While the scale is much larger than most companies can afford, learn from Salesforce. In February 2022, the company procured a 75-acre retreat set in the California redwoods.[4] The new campus will provide its employees with a much-needed respite after nearly two years of Zoom meetings. From its website:

> Trailblazer Ranch is an exciting new gathering place where employees can forge trusted relationships with their colleagues, learn from one another, get inspired, grow in their career, get

trained on the company, and give back to the community in a fun and safe environment. It is a place where we can share and strengthen the Salesforce culture ...[5]

A bit salesy? Sure. But founder CEO Marc Benioff recognizes that employees need to build social capital, and he's spending serious cabbage to make that happen.

When and How Long to Get Together

There are no hard-and-fast rules here. Employees at the distributed company Automattic get together once a year in an exotic locale.[*] Other teams and partners regularly meet on weekly, monthly, quarterly, or semi-annual bases.

As the main example in this chapter demonstrated, kickoff meetings should take place when projects start, not six months later. Also, if a project is going poorly in February, holding an additional in-person gathering makes more sense than waiting five months until the next scheduled one in July. By then, the project or product may well be DOA.

Take the same approach with meeting duration. For an annual gala, one solid week together represents time and money well spent. The team that comes together monthly can probably get away with a day or two each time. Team members who see each other two or three times a week may not need to take *as many* big trips, but don't ignore them completely.

Remember that hybrid work isn't a binary; there are degrees. Also, experiment, tweak, and experiment some more. There's no universal playbook for remote or hybrid work in general or for project and product teams. What works for one may not work for another.

---

[*] Look at some of the employee photos at https://tinyurl.com/autom-phot.

What to Do

I'll try not to be too preachy here, but consider the following advice:

- Embrace collaborative, deep work. Be present. Turn off devices. No checking email, Slack, or Microsoft Teams.
- Spend your time getting to know your new colleagues, partners, clients, and vendors.
- Take advantage of the time. If you can do it remotely and in front of your computer, don't do it now.
- Think face up, not face down.
- Learn from Playfair Data and have fun. The new relationships that everyone will forge and the memories they'll create can bear fruit six months down the road when project pressures mount.

Chapter Summary

- Millions of employees have accepted jobs during the pandemic. As a result, they have yet to meet their peers and have struggled to build valuable social capital with them.
- Through in-person meetings and project kickoffs, employees can build invaluable relationships and social capital. The benefits can be significant on complicated projects as problems manifest themselves.
- When getting together, think face up, not face down.

Chapter 8

SETTLE EARLY ON THE TECH

"Technology is wonderful when it isn't in the way."
—MARILLION, "MONTREAL," WORDS BY STEVE HOGARTH

This chapter is all about tech.

It's indeed wonderful, but it's also very much in the way.

Workplace tech is everywhere these days. Rare is the employee who uses only a handful of applications while on the job. Rather, pervasive tech is generally overwhelming employees, adversely affecting their ability to effectively complete projects and launch new products.

As we'll see in this chapter, when two or more entities begin work on a new endeavor, it's essential to involve IT early in the process. The parties involved need to discuss, agree upon, and codify the tools that employees will use throughout the project.

Those who want to "move fast and break things" may scoff at what they perceive as additional bureaucracy. Pay them no mind.

This is time well spent for all concerned that can nip all sorts of potential project- and product-related problems in the bud.

The Current, Dizzying State of Enterprise-Tech

Think about the last time you worked on a significant project or your company launched a new product. What application(s) did your teams—and others, for that matter—use to track the project's progress, identify and resolve its issues, and track its overall status?

If I'd asked you that question in 1998, you'd have probably answered *Microsoft Project*. Originally launched in 1984, for years it was the PM white whale. It's still around today, but it's far from the only game in town. Exhibit A: The software-comparison site GetApp conducted a 2019 survey and found that 97 percent of PMs reported using two or more tools to manage their projects.[1]

One particularly popular tool today is Asana. Since 2008, the company's web-based software has helped teams organize, track, and manage their work. As of this writing, it sports more than 114,000 paying customers.[2] Asana faces stiff competition from monday.com, Wrike,* Microsoft Project, Smartsheet, Basecamp, Trello, and many more. And let's not forget the growing cadre of flexible no-code/low-code tools like Airtable, Notion, and Coda. No, these aren't PM tools *per se,* but these flexible and extensible applications challenge the notion of a traditional digital document.

So. Many. Tools.

Let's say that your team recently used a proper PM application to manage its project or launch its product. I'll go with Asana here, but any one of them would do for our purposes. The choice of Asana doesn't mean that all project-related work will take place inside of it. Team members still need to use a slew of other applications.

---

* Now part of Citrix thanks to a $2.25 billion deal.

Think about the other employees in your organization—and not necessarily your colleagues. Which tools do they use? Again, the answer depends on their specific role. Some will use Zendesk but not Workday. Designers may use the Adobe Creative Suite or Figma, but not necessarily a code repository like GitHub.

Even employees in the same department often use different tools for similar purposes. For instance, hard-core finance wonks use Microsoft Excel. They build intricate models in multi-spreadsheet workbooks that run meticulous macros. For quickly sharing data, however, Excel is overkill. Why not use Google Sheets? A Mac user might be more comfortable with Apple's program Numbers.

How many different websites, applications, frameworks, enterprise systems, and other technologies do you use in your current job? I'd bet that the number exceeds 20. If it does, you've got plenty of company.

Was it always this way? No. The following sidebar provides a short explanation of how we arrived at this point of tech saturation.

In Brief: How Enterprise Tech Fragmented

For decades, corporate IT was far more centralized than it is today.

In the olden days, a department or group within an organization that wanted to purchase software licenses had to follow proper channels (read: bureaucracy). Centralized procurement meant that one department—IT in this case—controlled technology for the entire organization. Large one-time capital expenditures ruled the day, and no VP was going to sneak one past the goalie.

Over the past twenty-five years, the move toward decentralized tech has gained speed. The movement was already afoot.

The ascensions of cloud computing, software-as-a-service, open-source software, and mobile devices only accelerated it.

As a general rule, it's easier to slip one past the goalie now because the net is so wide. In other words, IT may still serve as the *de facto* gatekeeper of all things tech. On the finance side, capital expenditures (CAPEX) have given way to much smaller monthly or quarterly operational expenditures (OPEX).

For example, an impatient VP of sales is dissatisfied with her company's legacy customer relationship management system and makes gradual plans to replace it. She might now be able to quickly move her team to Salesforce while flying under IT's radar. Thirty years ago, she would have been hard-pressed to pull off this move.

This shift toward decentralization and fragmentation means that different parts of an organization can use different applications and technologies that serve the same business goal. In 1996, the idea that a firm in need of a new enterprise resource planning (ERP) system would intentionally purchase both an SAP and a PeopleSoft license was absurd. (It still is, by the way.) The CIO suggesting as much wouldn't last the week. The same holds true for purchasing Oracle, IBM, *and* Microsoft SQL Server databases. In 2014, however, that same firm might have used both AWS and Microsoft Azure. Sales might have used Webex while marketing paid for a Zoom license.

We can debate the merits of each approach all day long. At least some people, however, are clamoring for the good ol' days—a return to a more structured tech environment. As Lizzy Lawrence writes in February 2022 for *Protocol,* "A workplace where everyone uses a separate tool stack sounds hellish."[3]

8 Settle Early on the Tech

Don't assume that your potential colleagues, partners, clients, and vendors will use "whatever." As Lizzy Lawrence writes in the aforementioned *Protocol* piece:

> Alex Torres just couldn't envision spending his entire work day in Microsoft Teams.
>
> He was close to scoring a six-figure job at an enterprise software company. The workload seemed manageable, the people seemed smart. But the first round of interviews took place on Teams. Torres, a San Francisco-based writer with experience in the tech industry, likes to be delighted by his workplace tools. And Teams doesn't spark joy. When the recruiter asked for his writing portfolio, he said no.
>
> "I literally told the recruiter: 'I'm sorry, using Microsoft Teams is not for me,'" Torres said. "I never thought I would be passionate about this. But I am."[4]

At least it's better to find out ahead of time if someone's going to resist using a core enterprise technology.

It's Not Just You

Okta makes software that helps more than 14,000 organizations securely manage their applications.[5] Single sign-on might not sound all that sexy, but it sure is useful. User authentication prevents myriad employee password resets and help desk tickets every day. Because of the nature of its business, Okta is privy to a veritable treasure trove of data on the different applications that its customers use.

In 2021, the company published its annual "Businesses at Work" report. Among its findings, its *average* customer uses 88 different business technologies throughout its organization. Among the most popular are Microsoft 365, Amazon Web Services, Salesforce, Google Workspace, and Zoom. Some larger organizations report using twice as many—and that number omits employees who use their own tools under the radar. Thanks to smartphones, we long ago entered the era of Shadow IT in which you could bring your own devices to work—aka *BYOD.*

Employee Responses to Increasingly Taxing Tech

Organizations generally don't pay for systems and applications unless at least a few of their employees actually use them. (Industry insiders use the term *shelfware.**) So how are people coping with workplaces that rely upon an increasing number of technologies and applications?

In an attempt to address that very question, Asana conducted research with the researchers from the University of California, Berkeley. The former released its Anatomy of Work Index 2021. Among its findings:

> With the evolution of the physical office environment, we now face new collaboration challenges due to a lack of clarity around work practices. Despite organizations' best efforts to recreate what worked in the office in a remote setting, "work about work" continues to rise.

> Organizations of every size, and across all industries, are losing countless hours to work about work. As a result, 60% of time is spent on work coordination, rather than the skilled, strategic jobs we've been hired to do.[6]

Here are some more nuggets from this fascinating report:

---

* This is the moniker for unused applications that sit on the virtual shelf.

8 Settle Early on the Tech   185

- 31 percent of office workers say they frequently struggle to find documents they need during a tense moment at work.
- 81 percent of office pros have had a hard time finding an important doc when a boss or client has them in the hot seat.

Even finding simple messages and information can be time-consuming and stressful, as the following sidebar illustrates.

Apps Galore

"We use Slack in some parts of the organization, but Teams in others. Oh, and I communicate with my salespeople in WhatsApp and, of course, there's still email to deal with."

These are the words of a CEO of a staffing company, Kirk, whom I met in September 2021 over lunch. I was there to speak on an in-person panel at the Collaboration in the Gig Economy conference in Phoenix, Arizona. (Yes, I attended an actual real-world conference during a pandemic. Weird.)

I asked Kirk and his colleagues if they typically spent a great deal of time trying to find messages and documents. "Oh, you have no idea," he lamented. "It's a real problem." Everyone at the table nodded their heads and looked to me for answers. After all, my badge did read *speaker*.

I asked them about the impact of all these apps on the company's ability to complete projects on time. They all chuckled, and Kirk said, "What do *you* think?"

The Anatomy of Work Index is nothing if not eye-opening. More than ever, employees are juggling an increasing number of disjointed apps. As a result, workers often become confused and overwhelmed. To be sure, the problem exists in in-person workplaces, but it's arguably more pronounced in remote and hybrid ones. (All the more reason to stitch them together, as I recommend in my previous book, but I digress.)

Time out. Isn't tech supposed to make our personal and work lives *easier?*

Donald Norman has been ringing this bell for decades.

The Paradox of Technology

Norman is a design guru and the current director of The Design Lab at University of California, San Diego. In 1990, he penned *The Design of Everyday Things*. From the book:

> The same technology that simplifies life by providing more functions in each device also complicates life by making the device harder to learn, harder to use. This is the paradox of technology.

Norman was describing hardware back then, but the parallels to today's powerful *software* applications are self-evident.

Taken together, though, the Asana and Okta reports reveal what far too many of us already know all too well: It's not just you. The proliferation of workplace applications is real and out of control. Today's average knowledge worker is struggling to keep up with an increasing number and variety of technologies. Employee burnout and stress[7] are pervasive. In the process, our tchotchkes are causing the following workplace problems—and exacerbating them when they already exist:

- ☺ Confusion and anxiety.
- ☺ Duplicate work.
- ☺ Rework.

With all the applications running rampant, we're more prone to simple errors and incorrect business decisions stemming from multiple versions of the truth.

To be fair, these problems have existed for a decades; they've just intensified over the past fifteen years—and particularly since we started working less in person.

Making matters worse, employees who routinely work with external organizations not only have to learn *their* employer's tools, but often their clients', partners', and vendors' applications as well. Managing a project or launching a product often entails adding even more tech into the fray.

Now that we better understand the multidimensional problem around workplace tech, it's time to offer some solutions. The next sections explore how we can minimize the technological friction, problems, and agita that cause so many projects and products to struggle, especially in hybrid workplaces.

The Necessity of Using a Proper PM Tool

I'll cut to the chase: Any major project or product launch requires a proper, dedicated application. But which one?

Answering Key Questions

The good news is that just about every decent PM application these days ships with robust reports, dashboards, data visualizations, and custom calculations and fields. Taken together, this functionality allows users to answer easily just about any question related to projects, teams, and individuals. Examples include the following:

- Which employees aren't pulling their weight?
- Which tasks are behind, and who's responsible for them?
- How far behind is each task?

- Which tasks, goals, and milestones are likely to miss their due dates?
- Which human resources appear to be overextended?
- What are the resources allocated to each task?
- And much, much more.

Equipped with these powerful tools, PMs, teams, and organizations can quickly identify project bottlenecks, make necessary changes, and see improvements. The following sidebar illustrates a simple example.

He Shoots. He Scores.

For years, the National Hockey League, or NHL, struggled to launch custom apps for its thirty different business units.[8] Although significant, the NHL's problems certainly weren't unique. They included:

- Organizational silos, exacerbated by the distance between the different offices.
- Incomplete product specifications that confused and frustrated developers.
- Unclear task and priority guidance from internal clients.
- Inadequate resource allocations.

By implementing monday.com and making some internal process changes, the NHL significantly decreased the time it needed to launch new apps. Vice president of information technology Carol Dann reported that her team shaved an average of four full weeks off its development cycle.

Say that you use a popular PM tool, but it lacks specific functionality common with its competitors. Fret not. Odds are that the feature is coming soon. Software vendors frequently, er, borrow from each other. Case in point: Trello lacked native dashboard functionality until adding it in February 2021.[9] And what if you want to use your favorite dashboard, reporting, or dataviz tool? It's never been easier to do so. For example, want to connect Asana to Tableau? Have at it.*

If a PM, product owner, or other responsible party cannot easily pull accurate information addressing these issues, then either one or more of the following statements is true:

- The PM application really does suck—and it's time for a new one.
- The PM isn't using the current application properly. (Ahem, the employees need training.)
- Users aren't entering updates accurately or in a timely manner. Garbage in, garbage out.

Disclaimers

First, I don't want to overstate the power of today's PM applications. The diligent use of Smartsheet, Asana, or Basecamp by itself doesn't guarantee a successful project. Think necessary, not sufficient—especially on large projects. You might be able to effectively manage a small project with one other person via email and memory, but this approach quickly breaks down. It's only a matter of time before something falls between the cracks. Figure 8.1 demonstrates this relationship.

---

* See https://asana.com/apps/tableau.

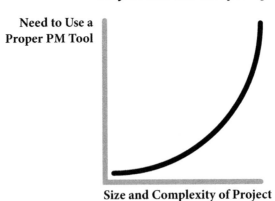

Figure 8.1: The Need for a Proper PM Application vs. Project Size and Complexity

Second, any application is only as good as the data inside of it. As the following sidebar illustrates, even best-of-breed PM applications can't overcome suspect or missing data.

> ### Missing Due Dates
>
> A while back, I worked with an independent publisher on a small book project. At first glance, this one seemed to have its act together.
>
> Soon after joining the project, I received an Asana invitation. Boom. I signed in and quickly saw the tasks assigned to me, but one omission became readily apparent. My tasks lacked due dates, and no one had granted me permission to add them myself.
>
> I spoke with the PM about fixing the issue, but he never did resolve it or grant me access to do the same. This lack of

critical data compromised the utility of Asana throughout the project. I wondered why the publisher even purchased a license for a tool that it used so sporadically.

Finally, one need not use proper PM tools to evaluate *every* type of job, employee, group, and department. All sorts of automated systems provide basic reporting and analytics for more routine work.

Consider employees who answer calls, process insurance claims, or perform other routine tasks. In these instances, sophisticated systems automatically provide managers with reports; the employees need not solicit status updates from them. There's no proper project to track or manage.

Handling the Haters

If I had a nickel for every time I heard someone utter either of the following pithy three-word assessments, I'd have more than a few bucks:

- ☺ "This application sucks."
- ☺ "This system sucks."

In some cases, that's unequivocally true. Technology can outlive its usefulness. (Don't get me started.)

More often than not, however, we're wrong. We love to blame technology because it can't blame us back. If a system could talk, maybe it would explain the source of our frustration à la the classic article from *The Onion.* Maybe the conversation would go something like this:

---

* See https://tinyurl.com/ps-dell-onion. You're welcome.

Person: "Why don't you do what I want? You're killing me, Smalls."

System: "I'm sorry that you're struggling. It looks like you don't know how to use me properly. Did your company send you to a proper training class, as Phil Simon's new book advocates?"

Perhaps we've picked up disjointed tips on the fly without taking the time to understand the technology's fundamentals. Alternatively, consultants can take a good system and screw it up. I've seen it happen.

Tech Prescriptions for Potential Partners

As a starting point, recognize that personal, group, and organizational professional preferences vary. Some like learning new tchotchkes more than others do. (I'm raising my hand here.) It's foolish to pretend otherwise. To that end, get it all out in the open.

Second, expect differences—even major ones. (See the sidebar "In Brief: How Enterprise Tech Fragmented" from earlier in this chapter.) The odds that everyone uses the same set of applications and technologies are remote. All things being equal, the more people and the more organizations involved on a product launch or project, the greater the tech heterogeneity. See Figure 8.2 on the next page.

Even on an internal, cross-departmental project, don't assume that all your colleagues use the same tools as you do. That's a big mistake, especially at large firms.

8 Settle Early on the Tech

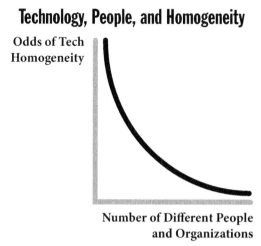

Figure 8.2: Technology, People, and Homogeneity

When it comes to collaboration tools, a large percentage of organizations aren't exactly monogamous. As Matthew Finnegan writes in *ComputerWorld* in July 2019:

> Slack and Microsoft may be battling for dominance in the booming team collaboration market, but most organizations rely on both applications—and some companies use even more.
>
> Those are some of the results of a survey by Mio, an Austin, Texas-based startup that sells software to enable communication between different messaging tools. Mio polled 200 IT decision-makers at organizations ranging in size from hundreds to hundreds of thousands of employees.
>
> The company found that 91% of businesses use at least two messaging apps and Slack and Microsoft Teams are present in 66% of the organizations surveyed.

"Remarkably, we are also seeing the same companies that are now using Microsoft Teams increase Slack use in parallel," said Mio CEO Tom Hadfield.[10]

Beyond collaboration applications, employees in myriad organizations use different design, content-creation, PM, and coding tools. It's not 1998.

Selection Scenarios

We've seen how organizations can choose to work with partners, clients, and vendors based *in part* upon their use of specific tools. It's time to review some common scenarios that we're likely to encounter when selecting our potential partners.

#1: THE TECH SOULMATE

Sometimes we get lucky right out of the gate. Call it love at first sight.

For example, say that everyone at your firm loves Basecamp, Slack, Google Docs, WordPress, and Photoshop. (All solid choices, by the way.) To help you launch a new digital product or service, you find a vendor whose choice of tools precisely mirrors your own. Boom. What are the odds?

This brings us to Simon's Law of Tool Overlap: All things being equal, the greater the similarity between the parties' preferred applications and technologies, the greater the chance for the project's ultimate success. See Figure 8.3.

In this case, each company has found its tech soulmate. The project may well still crash and burn, but this initial—and essential—degree of alignment alleviates potential future conflicts over whose tools will ultimately prevail.

Figure 8.3: Simon's Law of Tool Overlap

Although idyllic, however, this scenario is unlikely. Like all romantic relationships, professional ones take work. You have to negotiate. It's time to talk about dealbreakers.

#2: SHE'S OUT OF MY LEAGUE

Same scenario as above, but there a hitch: That vendor charges twice as much as your allocated budget for the project.

That dog won't hunt.

You may be understandably disappointed. At least you know from the get-go that you're fundamentally incompatible.

#3: REALLY CLOSE

A prospective partner uses all your group's preferred tools except one. In addition, the company charges 10 percent more than your desired budget. In this case, the extra effort is probably worth it. Maybe there's a creative way to get the deal done, unlike the next scenario.

#4: OIL AND WATER

While dancing, the two of you are constantly stepping on each other's toes. Every time you mention a preferred application, your potential project-mate mockingly dismisses it. For instance, you profess your love for Asana; your snobbish counterpart lives in Microsoft Project and would never consider using anything else. The two organizations rely upon wildly different sets of tools, as Figure 8.4 demonstrates.

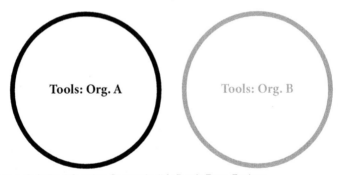

Figure 8.4: Tool Overlap Scenario #4: Don't Even Bother

Returning to our example, fret not. By having this conversation early, you've both saved significant time and effort. Much like the second scenario, there's no sense in making the partnership Instagram Official.

#5: WE CAN MAKE THIS WORK

Despite some differences, preferred tools generally overlap. In other words, the two parties are in the same park, as Figure 8.5 demonstrates.

Tool Overlap Scenario #5: We Can Make This Work

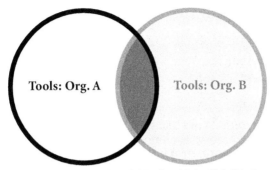

Figure 8.5: Tool Overlap Scenario #5: We Can Make This Work

Here the two parties can probably work it out, so it's time to start negotiating. To that end, consider the following advice.

Avoid the Temptation to Ignore an Essential Application

Remember that employees, teams, departments, and entire organizations use a more diverse set of technologies than ever in the workplace. Because of that, it might be tempting to ignore specific differences or kick these cans down the road.

Don't.

For example, one of the most important decisions for the project or product team to make involves its choice of an internal collaboration hub. (We saw earlier how the sheer number of tools overwhelms employees.)

By way of background, during the pandemic, we started to change how we sent electronic messages. Oodles of employees began using email less frequently for internal communication and collaboration. In its place, they gravitated more toward the internal hubs that I described in *Reimagining Collaboration*. (Called it.) In January 2022, Microsoft Teams surpassed 270 million *monthly* active users.[11] Roughly 90 percent of the hundred largest US companies reported using it in some capacity.[12]

But don't equate Microsoft's gaudy Teams numbers to its mid-1990s dominance of operating systems.[13] When it comes to collaboration tools, individual employees, groups, departments, and even entire companies often dig in. As a result, it's tempting to revert to an old standby.

The conversation goes like this:

Jack (from Company A): "We're a proud Slack shop. We hate Teams."

Jill (from Company B): "Funny. We love Teams and hate Slack."

Jack: "Screw it. We'll just use email instead for this product. Everyone knows how to do that."

Jill: "Fine."

This type of decision is understandable, and it *seems* expedient.

Don't take the bait: It's a recipe for disaster. Today's collaboration hubs are so much more powerful than email. Unlike with inboxes, when employees leave using today's collaboration hubs, all their valuable information, documents, and decisions remain in a centralized knowledge repository for their replacements to view easily.

The same principle applies for other applications. Exhibit B: Companies that punt on selecting a proper PM application, opting instead for a general-use application such as Microsoft Excel or Google Sheets. No, no, no.

Embrace Early Disagreements

You and your prospective partner are butting heads over tech from the start. Think of it as a valuable opportunity. The law firm

8 Settle Early on the Tech

or consultancy that won't budge now is showing its cards. If its management is being this rigid during the courting phase, will it suddenly soften up in six months? Maybe, but is the risk worth taking?

Early relationship issues serve as an invaluable litmus test for how the rest of the project is likely to go. (Much like personal relationships, the intelligent question isn't, Do you fight? Rather, it's, Do you fight well?)

Regarding the choice of a particular technology or application, try to find a compromise. Consider the following hypothetical exchange:

> **Ringo (from Company A):** "We use Adobe XD* for design and Trello for project management."
>
> **Paul (from Company A):** "Hmm ... We use Figma for the former and Wrike for the latter."
>
> **Ringo:** "Let's meet halfway. We'll buy a license for Figma and learn to use it if you do the same with Wrike."
>
> **Paul:** "Done and done."

Equipped with no other information, I'd bet on this project succeeding—no matter when and where employees are working.

Open Your Mind

Your team or company prefers Trello and Slack based upon its years of experience with them. Your future bedmate, however, isn't down with either. You attempt to reach compromises like the previous one, but you can't come to an agreement.

Should you immediately walk away?

---

* Short for *Adobe Experience Designer.*

Not necessarily.

For all sorts of reasons, it might be wise to bite the bullet and adopt one or more of your new partner's applications. Perhaps you've been looking for an excuse to pick up a new tool. Maybe your current ones are a little long in the tooth. Even if that's not the case, if you absolutely had to use Smartsheet, Google Workspace, or a similar tool, would it be *that* difficult to pick it up?

As a parallel, say that you speak fluent Spanish. If you traveled to Italy, you'd get the hang of the language pretty quicky. (The masculine word for *friend* is *amigo* in Spanish and *amico* in Italian; the feminine counterparts are *amiga* and *amica,* respectively.) It's not like you'd be learning a fundamentally different language like Korean. Beyond that, working with another popular application never hurts. View it as another arrow in the quiver—one that might prove useful if you decide to seek greener pastures.

Walking Down the Aisle

Before signing contracts, it's high time for each organization's leadership to formalize the tech arrangement. Think of it as the business equivalent of saying, "I do."

In a real wedding, you might hear the officiant, rabbi, or priest ask attendees, "If anyone objects to this marriage, speak now or forever hold your peace." (For better or worse, I've never seen anyone chime in here.) In keeping with this analogy, however, each company's IT department should act as the cynical future in-law who wants to prevent her loved one from making a life-altering mistake.

The advantages of asking the "if anyone objects" question are both mutual and significant. By obtaining IT's blessing, the project and product teams err on the side of caution. Employees won't have to fly under the radar with their applications once the project begins. For its part, by sanctioning the union, each IT department

8 Settle Early on the Tech

effectively acknowledges that, for the duration of the project, employees from their respective companies won't encounter any problems regarding application:

- Whitelists.
- Blacklists.
- Technology costs.
- Issues around application permissions.
- Security issues.

Bottom line: Involving IT from the start means asking for permission as opposed to forgiveness. Sure, it takes some extra time and effort, but all parties can then proceed at Godspeed without fearing tech-related problems down the road.

Sealing the Deal

You've hashed things out with your prospective partner. The independent contractor, design firm, consultancy, or other third party can clearly do the job. Its reputation checks out, and its estimate falls within your price range. Still, you want to avoid becoming one of the cautionary tales covered earlier—much less the upcoming doozy in the next chapter.

Enter the statement of work, or the SOW.

Traditional SOWs have typically omitted or intentionally ignored a number of PMBOK areas. These omissions have included the tools used during the engagement, the core work hours, and other borderline-squishy areas about how everyone will perform the duties expected of them.

To be fair, these omissions weren't necessarily oversights. During countless pre-COVID projects, teams and employees worked mostly in person and synchronously. As a result, the applications that everyone used to communicate and collaborate didn't necessarily need to be uniform. Ergo, the need to codify them wasn't as acute. The Lucky Strike folks could usually ask Don, Roger, or Peggy questions by calling them during business hours or popping by their offices.

The *Mad Men* model of work is long behind us. In remote and hybrid workplaces, project participants often lack essential clarity around who's doing what and when. A RACI matrix can certainly help in this regard but, by itself, it's not enough to completely solve the problem. Formalizing the tools that employees will use on a project has become as important as formalizing each party's role in the project, the budget, and the end product.

Before putting your John Hancock on the contract, make sure that it lists all the tools that the parties will use on the engagement to do the following:

- Collaborate and communicate.
- Manage the project.
- Build the actual thing. (The applications, frameworks, and materials will vary wildly based upon what the parties are building together.)

Think of this final step before walking down the aisle with your soon-to-be external partner. (Different groups within the same organization should consider adopting formal project charters.) In either case, this last step shouldn't be a chore; both parties should *demand* this level of transparency. If your counterpart doesn't, reevaluate whether you want to proceed.

Now that the parties have settled on the tech, it's time to war-game everything that could go wrong once the project commences.

It's not a short list.

Chapter Summary

- Employees use a greater array of tools than ever. Their willingness and ability to use those tools well—and possibly learn new ones—can determine if a project or product will succeed or fail.
- As soon as possible, talk tech with your would-be partners. Discuss and agree upon the tools that the team will use. And, for God's sake, involve IT early.
- Use a proper PM tool from the get-go. If you start a new project with a simple spreadsheet, it's unlikely that you'll think of everything you ultimately need from day one.
- For years, it's been dangerous to assume that another department within the same company uses the same tools—never mind an entirely different company altogether.

Chapter 9

PERFORM A PROJECT PREMORTEM

"The answer to a feasibility study is almost always yes."

—ROBERT L. GLASS

By now, we know that organizations have generally sported mediocre to abysmal batting averages on all sorts of projects and product launches. I suspect that very few of them, however, *suddenly* fail. When a disappointing project is veering toward the abyss, the decision to pull the plug usually comes after repeated attempts to salvage it. Google "project remediation plan template" if you're skeptical.

For those of you unfamiliar with the drill, the key players usually hold tense meetings in an attempt to right the ship. Before long, things become testy, and the blame game begins. Friends become enemies. The meeting ends, the CYA game begins, and emails with *Urgent* in the subject start flying.

PMs adjust schedules, tweak dates, alert their PMOs, massage earlier estimates, and occasionally consolidate project phases—usually to disastrous effect. They rattle off status reports and document the hell out of everything. Managers reassign under-performers and bring in fresh blood or supplemental resources. Maybe there's even a change in project leadership. For their part, employees bunker down for late nights and weekend work. A few start polishing their resumes.

While well intentioned, these half measures rarely work, and the flailing project continues its descent and inevitable collapse. In the extreme, lawsuits sometimes result.

But what if the parties take a different tact from the start? What if they examine all the factors that caused the project to go belly-up? What if they assume from the onset that the new website or office redesign had *already* failed?

Premortem: Definition and Benefits

As its name suggests, a *premortem* takes place *before* the autopsy. The idea behind it is neither complicated nor new. A team convenes before the project has started in earnest. Over the course of a day or a week, team members war-game how their forthcoming project or product launch *missed* its mark. (Note the crucial past tense here. Everyone pretends that the catastrophe has already happened.)

The team then works backward to determine what caused this hypothetical failure. Based on this analysis, participants make recommendations and establish informal norms and formal policies to prevent that very failure from happening when it's go-time.

---

* I just can't bring myself to type in all caps, much less to add four exclamation points.

9 Perform a Project Premortem

Writing for *Harvard Business Review* fifteen years ago, noted research psychologist Gary Klein explained how premortems help avert project failure:

> Although many project teams engage in prelaunch risk analysis, the pre-mortem's prospective hindsight approach offers benefits that other methods don't. Indeed, the pre-mortem doesn't just help teams to identify potential problems early on. It also reduces the kind of damn-the-torpedoes attitude often assumed by people who are overinvested in a project. Moreover, in describing weaknesses that no one else has mentioned, team members feel valued for their intelligence and experience, and others learn from them. The exercise also sensitizes the team to pick up early signs of trouble once the project gets under way. In the end, a pre-mortem may be the best way to circumvent any need for a painful postmortem.[1]

Read that last sentence again. Embroider it on a pillow and place it on your sofa.

Despite the compelling benefits of premortems, rare is the organization, team, or party that conducts one before any project begins, let alone a significant one. I couldn't find definitive statistics on the frequency of project premortems, so I'll offer the following anecdotes as evidence.

First, in my career, the premortem has been a veritable *Bahama nuthatch*—the rarest of birds. In my days implementing enterprise systems, nary a one performed anything close to a proper premortem. (On rare occasion, a team would hold a less formal, one-hour risk-assessment meeting.) Second, I interviewed four dozen experienced PMs, consultants, executives, and academics in researching this book. Just about every time I broached the subject of a *premortem,* the interviewee thought I'd misspoken and meant to say *post*mortem. A friend of mine who spent nine years at Microsoft was the lone exception.

Why Should We Conduct Premortems?

The short answer is that, as humans, we absolutely suck at planning, estimating, and doing many other things that successful projects require. For the longer and more scientific answer, we need to access the big brain of Nobel Prize winner Daniel Kahneman.[*]

In his seminal 2011 book *Thinking, Fast and Slow,* Kahneman demonstrates how a slew of cognitive biases hinders our ability to make accurate estimates. With respect to projects, he cites optimism bias as a major problem:

> When forecasting the outcomes of risky projects, executives too easily fall victim to the planning fallacy. In its grip, they make decisions based on delusional optimism, rather than on a rational weighting of gains, losses, and probabilities. They overestimate benefits and underestimate costs. They spin scenarios of success while overlooking the potential for mistakes and miscalculations. As a result, they pursue initiatives that are unlikely to come in on budget or on time or to deliver the expected returns—or even to be completed.

When applied to projects, we routinely and mistakenly:

- ⊙ View circumstances through rose-colored glasses.
- ⊙ Overstate our own attributes and associated skill levels. As the late, great George Carlin once joked, "Anybody driving slower than you is an idiot, and anyone going faster than

---

[*] Fun fact: I met the man himself at a speaking gig in late 2011 in Washington, DC.

you is a maniac." Miraculously, we all think that we drive at the perfect speed all the time and that our children are smarter than average. This is the Lake Wobegon effect.

- ⊙ Attribute our success to skill and hard work and our failures to bad luck. We do the opposite for others. This is the fundamental attribution error.
- ⊙ Set unrealistic timeframes. To overcome this limitation, Agile methods prescribe relative estimates over the absolute ones of Waterfall projects.
- ⊙ Exude overconfidence in our ability to predict the future.

I could keep going, but you get my point. We often can't accurately forecast *our own* timelines and the effort involved to complete tasks. How can we reliably do the same with *others* involved in a project—many of whom we've just met?

That's a big ask—even if we actively observe what others are doing in the office.

Even if all people on a project exhibited zero cognitive biases, you could still make the case that premortems are essential. Projects in remote and hybrid workplaces face even greater obstacles than those that take place in person. The premortem is one of the most effective ways for organizations to identify those issues and address them at their roots. They should represent the rule on projects, not the exception.

Stir the halo effect with the other cognitive biases mentioned in this book. Add a pinch of the hybrid workplace. Some key ingredients arrived two weeks ago. Oh, and the chef just joined the company during the Great Resignation.

Let's cook.

Only Emeril Lagasse could make the case that the ensuing meal will taste good. I'd bet that some employees will experience allergic reactions at the table.

If you've got a disease, it's better to know as soon as possible.

Math Time, Part 2

Let's return to PMBOK for a moment. Assume that a project can succeed only when a team or company successfully navigates each and every one of PMI's eight project performance domains. For example, a company selected the right development approach. That's great, but that decision alone isn't going to suffice when major stakeholders refuse to participate and there's no way for the PM or PMO to measure the progress of the project.

For the sake of argument, let's generously assume that the probability of checking each box is an independent 95 percent—that is, successfully performing in one domain results in doing the same in all the others. (In reality, this assumption is flawed, but we're keeping it simple here.[*])

What are the odds that *all* eight independent events take place? A smidge over 66 percent (0.95^8). Interestingly, the number jibes with PMI's figures on successful project completion rates displayed way back in Figure 4.5.

If all this seems a bit abstract, allow an expert on the topic with decades of experience to make it more concrete.

---

[*] Welcome to the world of dependent probabilities and Bayes' theorem.

Doomed From the Start

—Bruce F. Webster, corporate IT consultant and adjunct professor of computer science at Brigham Young University

Any technology project faces significant probability of exceeding its schedule and budget or failing altogether. The bigger the project, the bigger the chance of failure.

Yet in my experience, very few leaders sit down at the start of such projects and ask themselves the following questions:

- What are the odds of this project failing?
- What would the likely causes be?
- How can we detect these factors and, if possible, eliminate or at least minimize them?
- What will we do if we see that the project is, in fact, failing?

I have spent twenty-five years reviewing large-scale technology projects, both as an outside consultant and as an expert witness. During that time, I have found repeatedly that clear indications of a given project's eventual troubles or failure existed at the very beginning. Unfortunately, people routinely ignored or glossed over them, as this anonymized example illustrates.

A manufacturer (Baker) needed to replace its legacy enterprise system and solicited bids from system integrators. Eager to win the business, a consulting firm (Able) put in a fixed-price bid for the job. Able wanted to configure and implement a customized third-party enterprise resource planning system (CAIN) for Baker. Internal Able documents and testimony indicated that:

- Able lacked any domain experience with Baker's line of business.
- Able lacked internal expertise on essential aspects of CAIN that Baker considered critical.
- Able lacked in-house staff sufficient for the project. As a result, it had to find, hire, and manage remote contractors scattered around the world.
- Able's fixed-price estimate lacked any actual foundation in project analysis. For some reason, though, Baker considered it. Able subsequently lowered its bid to win the contract. Able's management prioritized the future client reference over making a profit.

The Able/CAIN project launched but repeatedly slipped. Baker finally canceled it and filed lawsuits to recover funds spent.

At the trial, I testified that the project was doomed from the start. Able would have been far better off walking away from this opportunity, reminding me of what I wrote 30 years earlier: "There are products that you shouldn't develop, companies you shouldn't challenge, customers you shouldn't win, markets you shouldn't enter, and recommendations from the board of directors you shouldn't follow."[2]

Webster's vast expertise lies in large-scale IT projects, but make no mistake: These types of troubles thwart all sorts and sizes of projects in every industry. *Every* project these days requires a healthy dose of technology—no matter where the team(s) may be working. As I'm fond of saying, "All companies are tech companies. Some just haven't realized it yet."

Conducting a Premortem: The Struggle Is Real

In the Preface, I described the red flags that I'd spotted and attempted to address on a small writing engagement. Getting everyone to use Microsoft Teams in lieu of email was a struggle, and even that minor change didn't stick. If I'd had the minerals to, er, suggest conducting even a cursory project premortem, the publisher would have selected another writer who was lower maintenance.

Unfortunately, there's no secret sauce to overcoming others' resistance to performing premortems for the very reasons mentioned earlier. We consistently overestimate our ability to stick the landing. Suggesting that the project won't be successful runs the risk of labeling yourself as a Negative Nelly. (I get it. A few times during consulting projects, my colleagues or clients have told me that I don't exactly exude positivity.)

In addition, many lean outfits refuse to allocate the requisite human or financial resources for a project as is—and that's sans a proper premortem.

All hope isn't lost, though. Here are a few ideas to convince others to do a premortem for your next project.

Quantify the Scenario

Conservatively assume that the project sports a 25 percent chance of failure. Say that the premortem reduces that probability to 15 percent on a relatively modest $200,000 project. Do some math. Compare the cost of a few days of everyone's salary to that reduction in project risk. Wouldn't that decrease justify a solid week of forecasting, war-gaming, communicating, and looking at potential changes to the project's timeline, personnel, and methodology?

Size Matters

There's a world of difference between a massive project such as the Able/Baker one and the modest, relatively straightforward ones that I've detailed in this book. Still, even the relatively small endeavors stand to benefit from the rigor of a proper premortem. As a general rule, the greater the size and complexity of the project, the greater the need for a proper project premortem. Figure 9.1 demonstrates this critical relationship.

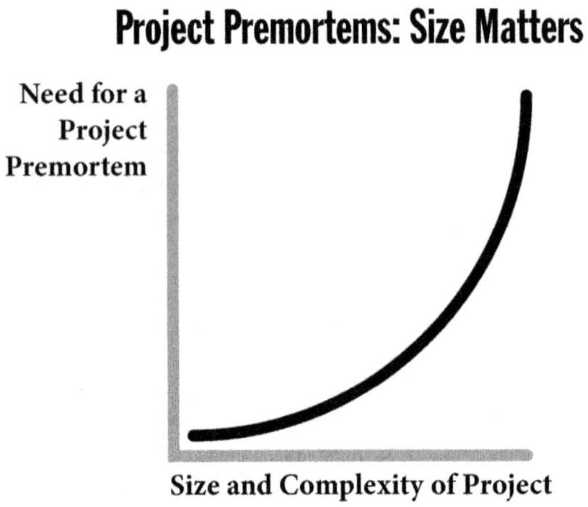

Project Premortems: Size Matters

Need for a
Project
Premortem

Size and Complexity of Project

Figure 9.1: Project Premortems: Size Matters

It's tempting to pooh-pooh the importance of a premortem on a simple project. There's a good chance, though, that you'll regret it afterward if you skip it. For colossal, multimillion-dollar, year-plus-long endeavors, skipping the premortem is tantamount to buying a house sight unseen. Don't be surprised when the home inspection reveals a leaky roof, rampant mold, and a cracked foundation.

Use the Premortem as a Litmus Test

Carefully vetting potential clients, partners, and vendors is critical. Say that one of these parties refuses to perform or participate in a project premortem. Feel free to ignore that tidbit, but the reason behind that rejection is worth exploring. Ask yourself the following questions:

- Is the organization properly staffed?
- Are its execs a tad overanxious about closing the deal? Are they afraid that the results of the premortem will make them think twice about committing to the project?
- Is its process or methodology so rigid that it can't accommodate an important change?
- Are its leaders overly confident that it will succeed?
- Are these folks incapable of envisioning scenarios in which their projects fail to deliver the goods?

Food for thought ...

Chapter Summary

- Conducting a project premortem reduces the chance that an organization will have to perform an autopsy down the road.
- An array of human biases prevents us from accurately assessing our ability to successfully plan and complete projects.
- Odds are that you'll face resistance when suggesting a project premortem, but the pros of doing one typically outweigh its cons.

Chapter 10

CONDUCT A PROJECT PILOT

"Every battle is won before it's ever fought."

—SUN TZU, *THE ART OF WAR*

By way of review, new projects and products often fail—and they are arguably more likely to disappoint when the people involved work in hybrid and remote workplaces. In addition, the premortem covered in the previous chapter is a useful exercise to determine what *could* go wrong on any given project or product launch. Still, to some, it might seem a smidge theoretical. As it turns out, though, there's a way to move from theory to practice and make project risks more concrete.

If you're like me, the word *pilot* is indelibly etched in your mind. For that, I blame—and by *blame,* I mean *thank*—Quentin Tarantino for his 1994 classic *Pulp Fiction.* In the movie, a pilot serves as the centerpiece of one of the many colorful exchanges between the characters played by John Travolta and Samuel L. Jackson.[*]

---

[*] Watch it at https://tinyurl.com/pilot-rpm.

Tarantino's tour de force dropped in 1994, but the idea behind a pilot predates his amazing movie by decades. (Fun fact: The wizards behind *Gilligan's Island* filmed the pilot episode "Marooned" in November 1963.)

This chapter is all about the pilot, but in a different context: launching new projects and products. We'll see how they can serve as invaluable magnifying glasses on complicated endeavors that are about to begin in earnest.

Lessons From Netflix

Traditional TV networks are a risk-averse lot. They're in the business of saying no to new ideas and projects. For decades, all execs followed the same basic and cautious playbook around new shows:

1. Hear the pitch from the showrunner(s).
2. If the pitch is good, then read the script.
3. If the script's good, then commission a pilot.
4. Offer notes.
5. Film the pilot.
6. Air the pilot.
7. Look at viewer ratings.
8. Decide on whether to order a full or a partial season of the show.

By dipping their toes in the pool first, execs at NBC, TNT, CBS, and their brethren have historically been able to determine if the water was too cold before jumping in. Less metaphorically, this understandable, conservative approach *usually* prevents them from making expensive flops. The downside is that they miss out on *Mad Men, Breaking Bad,*[*] and other genre-defining series that don't fit

---

[*] Readers of my blog and books know that I'm contractually obligated to reference the show in each of my books. (Yes, I'm kidding, but not really.)

10 Conduct a Project Pilot

neatly into existing categories. Don't throw a pity party for HBO, but its top brass famously passed on these two seminal shows that have come to define *prestige television*.

No one would ever accuse Netflix of being risk averse. Launched in 1997, the whole idea behind the company was audacious from the get-go, as Gina Keating details in her excellent book *Netflixed: The Epic Battle for America's Eyeballs*.

Exhibit A: the eye-popping 2012 decision to drop $100 million for two 13-episode seasons of *House of Cards* sight unseen. Translation: Go big or go home. Back then, the economics behind the bet seemed baffling, even irresponsible.[1] Industry types laughed.

They weren't laughing for long.

Nearly a decade later, we look back at the company's decision to greenlight *House of Cards* as bold and prescient. Winning seven Primetime Emmys, two Golden Globes, and two Screen Actors Guild awards tends to do that.

When you swing for the fences and connect with the ball, the ball's going to travel a long way. No one bats 1.000, though; even entertainment juggernauts like Netflix occasionally whiff. *Marco Polo* was one of those misses—and an expensive one at that.

On the heels of HBO's über-successful *Game of Thrones,* Netflix dropped a cool $90 million for the inaugural 10-episode season of *Marco Polo* according to the *New York Times*.[2] Put mildly, the results didn't approach Netflix's lofty expectations. Not even close. The streaming giant pulled the plug on the series after only two seasons, although then-content chief and current co-CEO Ted Sarandos claimed that the show had "done what it was supposed to do."[3] Sounds like spin to me.

It's never been easy to predict which series, comedy specials, and flicks are going to pop, find an audience, make critics fawn, and take home hardware at award ceremonies. Despite a massive trove of data on user habits and preferences, Netflix has learned that ponying up tens of millions of dollars doesn't guarantee a successful program or outcome.

No one needs to remind Hertz's leadership of that painful lesson. They've seen this movie before (pun intended).

Hertz Is Hurting

Let me paint a scenario.

Say that you know nothing about large companies, consulting firms, websites, and managing large-scale IT projects. It's 2016, and you're the CEO of a multi-billion-dollar car rental company. Its website and mobile app are long in the tooth. You know that it's high time to swap out these clunky ones for slicker, more contemporary versions. After a careful vetting process, you land on a reputable Fortune Global 500 firm that specializes in information technology services and consulting. Your budget is $32 million.

Equipped with no other information, what do you think will happen?

I'll wait.

Lags and Lawyers

I'm guessing that your answer didn't include the words *attorneys* and *lawsuit*, but you can't properly tell the Hertz tale *without* including them. As Kieren McCarthy writes in *The Register*:

> The US corporation hired monster management consultancy firm Accenture in August 2016 to completely revamp its online presence. The new site was due to go live in December 2017. But a failure to get on top of things led to a delay to January 2018, and then a second delay to April 2018 which was then also missed, we're told.

As Hertz endured the delays, it found itself immersed in a nightmare: a product and design that apparently didn't do half of what was specified and still wasn't finished. "By that point, Hertz no longer had any confidence that Accenture was capable of completing the project, and Hertz terminated Accenture," the car rental company complained in a lawsuit lodged against Accenture in New York this month.

Hertz is suing for the $32m it paid Accenture in fees to get to that aborted stage, and it wants more millions to cover the cost of fixing the mess. "Accenture never delivered a functional website or mobile app," Hertz claimed.[4]

Let's unpack that last sentence. For the sake of argument, assume that it's accurate: Accenture never delivered the goods. Explaining *what* didn't happen necessitates a brief discussion of *why* it didn't happen. And that brings us to Henrico Dolfing, an executive who provides interim management services to financial firms. Like me, he knows a thing or six about working with prestigious consulting firms, project failures, and website design.

Lessons From the Postmortem

On his website, Dolfing penned an extensive postmortem on the Hertz project. A few of his observations are particularly instructive. First, Hertz and Accenture followed Agile software-development practices—and still failed. Sure, the benefits of delivering small batches are considerable, but foolish is the soul who believes that any PM methodology guarantees a successful outcome. (Hello, Agilefall folks.)

Next, when it comes to talent, the Hertz folks weren't exactly smitten with the consultants that Accenture provided. In recounting the project's timeline and subsequent events, Dolfing writes:

> On June 20, 2019, Hertz files an amended lawsuit against Accenture and lays out their case on their claim of deceptive and unfair practices. In doing so, Hertz takes aim at Accenture talent and trashes the team that had worked on the Hertz program.[5]

Now, I'm not privy to any inside information on this project's implosion. If Accenture sent its B-team, however, it wouldn't be the first time that a prominent consultancy did as much. I've seen it happen on these types of engagements. A firm's management places green consultants in no-win situations because they're available and less expensive, never mind the fact that they aren't qualified to perform the work.

This example proves that old adage "nobody gets fired for buying IBM" is alive and well. Hertz management was able to justify Accenture's hefty price tag because the latter's brand provided sufficient cover. In reality, dozens of capable but lesser known firms could have met Hertz's technology and business needs at a fraction of the cost. No, those relatively anonymous firms wouldn't have come with Accenture's cache, but ultimately the quality of the product supersedes who built it. The decision to hire Accenture has CYA and internal Hertz politics written all over it.

The idea of a shit show of this magnitude may shock you, but grizzled industry veterans aren't surprised. People who've worked on these types of projects don't blink an eye upon hearing these tales. I told a friend of mine with an eerily similar background to mine about the Hertz debacle. He tersely replied, "$32 million? That's *it*?"

Project Pilots: Real-World Scrimmages

In the acclaimed Amazon Prime movie *Brittany Runs a Marathon*, Jillian Bell plays the eponymous protagonist who's making big changes in her life. Before she attempts to complete her 26.2-mile journey, she starts training. No sense in trying to run anywhere near that distance when you can't make it down the block.

Think of a project pilot as a similar type of test run. Specific objectives include:

- ⊙ To identify and attempt to fix nascent process, technology, data, and personnel issues—or course-correct, to use a spaceship analogy.
- ⊙ To revisit the premortem. Are any of our worst fears coming true? What things did we miss when we speculated about how this project would implode?
- ⊙ To determine specific in-person and logistical requirements. Perhaps the team needs to establish core working hours, such as 12 p.m. to 4 p.m. EST.
- ⊙ To assess stakeholders' general confidence that the product launch or project will go well.
- ⊙ If necessary, to pull the plug before it becomes the next *Marco Polo*.

In keeping with the previous metaphor, I would bet my house that Hertz and Accenture didn't run a 5k. As we saw with Netflix, skipping a pilot is a risky gambit. On one hand, it can result in *House of Cards*. On the other, it might yield *Marco Polo*. Despite hiring a safe partner, Hertz wound up with the latter.

What would a pilot project at Hertz have looked like?

If Woody Had Gone Straight to the Police: A Hypothetical Pilot at Hertz

Accenture could have built a few components of the new Hertz website or its desired mobile app with only a minimal number of features. Let's go with the app here.

A small group of internal testers could have used a simulated version of the iPhone app[6] to reserve one type of vehicle at a single airport or at a single location. Forget Android users for the time being. Remember that we're sticking with the basics out of the gate. In this piloted version of the app, customers could *not* perform any of the following tasks:

- Cancel or change existing reservations.
- Easily share their reservations with others.
- Log in to their Hertz accounts via Facebook.
- Pay with PayPal.
- Split reservation payments, like you can with rides in the Uber app.
- Find the nearest Hertz via Google Maps.

Accenture would not have tried to boil the ocean, to use a common expression in the IT world. Had the parties conducted a pilot, the issues that ultimately and publicly doomed the project would almost certainly have manifested themselves—and fast.

Let's assume that the Hertz claims are valid. Its management would have realized each of the following:

1. The consultants that Accenture assigned to the project lacked the experience and knowledge that the Hertz folks expected. (Whether those expectations were realistic in the first place, who's to say? To be fair, when a company hires Accenture, its management expects its partner's A-team.)
2. The Agile methodology was not delivering the expected results.
3. The cultural fit between the organizations was off. As a result, the project was never going to end well, regardless of why and which party was to blame. Sun Tzu was right.

Turning to Accenture, a pilot would have provided it with equally valuable information on its new bedfellow. Perhaps Hertz stakeholders couldn't clearly articulate their specific business needs or couldn't make key design decisions in a timely manner. (There are myriad ways to build websites and mobile apps.)

Accenture could have exited the project without the stain and expense of a high-profile lawsuit. As someone who used to work for a large consultancy, I'd lay odds that the partner who signed the Hertz deal intentionally minimized any red flags. After all, Accenture is a publicly traded company. (The NRPU case study in Chapter 7 shows that larger organizations tend to accept projects first and ask questions later—if at all.)

Think of a pilot as a way of doing additional due diligence or, if you like, a way of dating before getting married.

On Pilots and Dating

Regardless of where and how you met your significant other, eventually you have to tell your friends and family that story. In 2013, if the two of you had met on match.com, you'd sheepishly admit it to others or bend the facts so the tale came across as less … weird.

At some point over the past decade, though, *weird* gave way to *normal*. Even before the pandemic, meeting online had become the most popular way to meet a significant other.[7]

Think of online dating as a funnel: You both swipe right and, after a few in-app messages, exchange phone numbers and chat for 30 minutes. If the guy won't let you get a word in edgewise in that time, you're probably not going to meet him at happy hour for drinks and light appetizers. If you do and he eats with his mouth open, keeps talking about his ex, and asks you to split the bill, it's unlikely that you'll want to see him again.

At the risk of being overly clinical, each step represented a hurdle for the other to clear. You could have disqualified him at any point—and vice versa for that matter. A woman wouldn't go on a two-week trip to Europe with a complete stranger, never mind take his ring.

So why do companies embark on the equivalent of long-term relationships with their new partners after the equivalent of a few drinks? To complete the analogy, at least spend the weekend together first.

A 2014 study of 3,000 couples found that those who dated for at least three years before their engagement were nearly 40 percent less likely to get divorced than couples who dated less than a year before getting engaged.[8]

Managing Expectations

Let's play revisionist history for a moment. Assume that Hertz and Accenture began the project by conducting a project pilot.[*] For the sake of argument, it went swimmingly well. Nothing but smooth sailing ahead for both parties, right? See you in the champagne room.

Let's not overdo it.

Writing for HBR, Ron Ashkenas and Nadim Matta wisely—if a little clunkily—caution against reading too much into a pilot's initial success:

---

[*] I don't definitively know that they didn't. I just find it impossible to believe that a project could break this bad after having conducted a successful pilot.

10 Conduct a Project Pilot

... there are many reasons that a pilot project can look good. The people chosen to participate are often particularly receptive to trying new things, they often feel they're "special" for being chosen and therefore work particularly hard (a variation of the Hawthorne effect[*]), extra staff provide training and support, managers are incentivized to make the pilot work, and the usual cultural and administrative barriers to change are temporarily suspended.[9]

Although valuable, a pilot is neither necessary nor sufficient for a successful outcome—in this case, effectively completing a project or launching a new product. The pilot doesn't guarantee victory, and *not* conducting one won't necessarily lead to defeat and court depositions.

It's best to view a pilot project as an informative litmus test. If it disappoints, then what are the odds that the full-blown project will magically hit its mark? If a team struggles while doing the pilot project, why should it expect a materially different outcome on a larger one?

It's reductive to claim that teams should conduct a pilot for every conceivable type of project. When making the pilot decision, it's essential to consider a number of factors. Table 10.1 displays these general rules of thumb.

Project Characteristic	Lower Need for Pilot	Higher Need for Pilot
Size, Cost, and Scope	Small	Large
Complexity	Simple	Complicated
Relative Product/ Technology Maturity	Established	Cutting Edge

---

* Individuals know that others are observing them as part of a study. As a result, they modify their behavior and compromise the results of the study.

Project Characteristic	Lower Need for Pilot	Higher Need for Pilot
Organization Size(s)	Small	Large
Importance to Organization's Mission or Future	Low	High
Team Member Existing Familiarity	High	Low
Methodology	Agile	Waterfall
Workplace(s)	In Person	Hybrid, Remote

Table 10.1: Factors to Consider When Deciding to Conduct a Project Pilot

Note that the project characteristics in Table 10.1 are both subjective and dynamic. If there's a universally accepted gauge of team familiarity and cohesion, I'm unaware of it. (To be fair, Bruce Tuckman's five-stage framework of group development is a valuable construct.[10]) Also, a cutting-edge technology today may become old hat in five years.

Table 10.1 shines a light on the types of projects and teams that would benefit from proper pilots. For instance, a tightly knit web design team has worked with the same client for ten years. Over that time, the two parties have developed a solid rapport and a mutual admiration. In this case, a proper pilot is not (as) necessary.

At the other end of the spectrum lies the Hertz project.

It's not like Hertz's management was going out on a limb in 2016 by wanting to launch a modern website and mobile app. iPhones were nine years old at that point. The fiasco proves that even reasonable, well-conceived projects and products fail all the time.

A Few Parting Words on Pilots

Sometimes conducting a project or product pilot simply isn't practical. The global design and architecture firm Gensler won't build a single story of a skyscraper to see how it goes. The home

10 Conduct a Project Pilot   229

construction company Pulte won't just lay the concrete for the kitchen of your family's future home. Top-shelf criminal-defense firms won't represent their clients for a week to see if things go well.

Even the most promising pilot doesn't guarantee a successful outcome, nor does the wise early decision to use a RACI matrix. (Amazon routinely relies upon them both internally and externally,[11] but that didn't change the fate of its Fire Phone.[12]) Rather, a pilot and a RACI matrix—and the mindset behind them—only increase the odds that a product or project will ultimately bear fruit.

Finally, plenty of ambitious products and services never find their footing—and pilots wouldn't have necessarily changed their fates:

- ☺ **Facebook:** The embattled social network's cryptocurrency Diem represented the very definition of *tone deaf* and now resides in a graveyard.[13]
- ☺ **Microsoft:** An entire Pinterest board is dedicated to its product morgue. RIP, Zune. We hardly knew ye.[*]
- ☺ **Google:** The company has launched and retired a slew of social networks. Wave, Orkut, Google+, and Buzz most readily come to mind.
- ☺ **Quibi:** Watching short videos on your phone is all the rage today. You've doubtless heard of TikTok, but what about Quibi? The ill-fated app let users stream short-form entertainment from some of Hollywood's biggest creators. It raised close to $2 billion in March 2020.[14] Upon launch, it was essentially DOA. Roku bought its assets for pennies on the dollar.[15]

Pilots are invaluable in the following regard: They allow organizations to fail fast on products and projects that ultimately won't

---

[*] Check it out at https://tinyurl.com/ms-morgue-rpm.

succeed. Leaders can then direct their efforts to more suitable uses of their organizations' resources.

Chapter Summary

- ⊘ Project and product pilots aren't novel ideas. In hybrid and remote workplaces, however, they're more important to conduct than ever.
- ⊘ As Hertz's management learned the hard way, hiring a venerated consultancy doesn't guarantee a successful outcome—no matter which party was ultimately culpable for the $32-million disaster.
- ⊘ Pilots can snuff out all sorts of project issues before a team or company gets in too deep. Potential problems may stem from employee skill levels, communication styles, partner compatibility, and logistics.

Chapter 11

PROVIDE FORMAL EMPLOYEE APPLICATION TRAINING

If you think education is expensive,
try estimating the cost of ignorance.

—HOWARD GARDNER

We know by now that project management is a multidisciplinary field that, for oodles of reasons, often fails to deliver the goods. This chapter examines an oft-overlooked reason that has become even more essential in remote and hybrid environments: a lack of formal employee application training.

We'll see that employers tend to minimize the importance of formal, structured learning on company time. In so doing, they place the onus on employees to learn key applications on their own time and dime. When they don't, a project typically suffers—and, in lockstep, so does its internal communication, collaboration, and organizational performance.

In Search of Easy Answers

Say that a project, a department, a project team, or even an entire organization is performing poorly. It's tempting to blame the nominal person in charge of it: the VP, the PM, the chief product officer, or the CEO, respectively. After all, isn't that why they make the big bucks? Replace the leader, and everything else will magically fall into place, right?

As Bart Simpson famously said when campaigning for school class president against his erudite opponent Martin Prince, "My opponent says there are no easy answers. I say he's not looking hard enough!"[1] (No, I never tire of *Simpsons'* references.)

It's an understandable mindset. Unfortunately, it's also a misplaced one.

Back in the real world, plenty of organizations have heeded Bart's advice over the years. Case in point: On January 22, 2016, the Cleveland Cavaliers of the National Basketball Association were riding high. A year after making the NBA Finals, the Cavs sported the Eastern Conference's best record with 30 wins against a mere 11 losses.

On that day, the team unceremoniously fired head coach David Blatt. As Dave McMenamin and Ian Begley wrote for ESPN:

> [in] discussing the coaching change during a news conference late Friday afternoon, [Cavs' general manager David] Griffin cited "a lack of fit with our personnel and our vision."[2]

11 Provide Formal Employee Application Training   233

Translation: Generational talent and *de facto* GM LeBron James wanted then-assistant coach Tyronn Lue to run the show. And what LBJ wants, he typically gets.[*]

Normally, coaching changes such as these don't pay immediate dividends, at least not to the extent that players, fans, or the team's ownership demand.

In this case, however, it *sort of* did. The Cavs once again made the NBA Finals. The team rallied from a 3-1 deficit against Steph Curry and the historically great Golden State Warriors to claim its first and only championship. Cleveland fans went nuts and would have elected James governor of Ohio that night.[†] For my money, Game 7 in San Francisco was one of the most exciting contests in the history of sports. I watched every minute of it with some friends.

It's impossible to know what would have happened if Blatt had remained in charge. Again, the Cavs were already in first place in their division. Perhaps the team would have won the title with him at the helm—and in fewer games to boot.

Counterfactuals aside, giving Blatt the boot was yet another example of an exception that proved the rule. Ask the Browns, the Cavs' crosstown counterparts, if coaching changes lead to post-season glory. Since 1989, no fewer than fifteen different men have held the title of head coach for that hapless NFL franchise.[‡] (The job of Spinal Tap drummer is arguably safer by comparison.)

---

[*] To be fair, other star athletes have done the same thing. Magic Johnson let it be known that he didn't care much for the Lakers coach Paul Westhead. Ditto for Michael Jordan with Doug Collins.

[†] James's clutch fourth-quarter chase-down block of Andre Iguodala's layup attempt may go down as his career-defining play.

[‡] I created a Tableau dataviz comparing the wildly different coaching histories of the Browns and the New England Patriots. Check it out at https://tinyurl.com/ps-browns.

The Browns have made the playoffs a mere four times during that span—abysmal in a league based upon parity.

Outside of the sports world, a carousel of CEOs couldn't steer the horse at internet trailblazer Yahoo! after its precipitous fall from glory. Perhaps its most embarrassing stain: Newly appointed Scott Thompson only lasted five months after word leaked that he misrepresented his college degree on his resume.[*]

More broadly, changing the occupant of the corner office *can* improve a company's long-term financial performance, but it's complicated. For example, in 2020, a group of researchers published the results of a sophisticated analysis on corporate performance.[3] Firms that hired a certain type of CEO—a leader—performed better than their peers, all things being equal. Oh, and don't expect immediate results. It typically takes a full three years for a new captain to really make a difference.

Providing adequate training to employees isn't as splashy as handing the reins to a leader with a bold new vision to fix things.

Application Training: Essential but Often Neglected

Go back to the 1970s for a moment—an era in which office and knowledge work barely resemble their modern-day counterparts. Interoffice memos were all the rage. (Google it.)

Yes, computers existed, but they were decidedly *impersonal.* IBM and Control Data Corporation—the *other* CDC—built massive mainframes the size of entire rooms. Even during the era of computer punch cards, employee training was paramount. Fun fact: The popular tech and data maxim "garbage in, garbage out" harks back to 1957. US Army mathematicians used it to describe their work with early computers.[4]

---

[*] See https://tinyurl.com/ps2-yahoo.

11 Provide Formal Employee Application Training 235

Application or "computer" training has *always* mattered. To be fair, employers spend gobs of money on it every year. In 2016, that number was $359 billion.[5] Unfortunately, as a general rule, on-the-job training usually misses the mark.

A McKinsey survey revealed that only 25 percent of respondents believed that the training they received from their employers measurably improved their performance.[6] Ouch. I'll keep piling on. Tech research and consulting firm Gartner found in April 2019 that 70 percent of employees reported that they lacked the skills to perform their jobs effectively.[7] Most organizations don't even bother to track their training investments.[8] Accountants shudder when reading these words.

Statistics certainly help frame the problem, but they often lack the pizzazz of a detailed example. The following sidebar illustrates how inadequate employee training compounded a massive IT mistake. The affected firm, not surprisingly, no longer exists.

Enterprise Systems and Shoemaker's Children

Pittsburgh-based Education Management Corporation (EDMC) had managed post-secondary educational institutions since 1962. In the early aughts, the for-profit company purchased and implemented a new enterprise resource planning system.

EDMC employees and consultants possessed significant application expertise on the financial and technical sides. On the HR, benefits, and payroll sides, however, no such acumen existed. (Not the first time that HR got the short end of the stick.) The ERP's HR and financial modules were certainly integrated, but the former operated in a fundamentally different manner than the latter did.

This dearth of domain-specific application knowledge caused EDMC to make a rookie configuration mistake: Each of its eighteen departments was effectively its own independent legal entity.

In the abstract, that fact may not sound significant. Let me make it real. Here are a few concrete examples of the cumbersome daily administration that its employees would now face from the minute that the company activated its new system:

- The payroll manager Debbie would have to run each of the ten different payroll programs eighteen different times every two weeks.
- EDMC employees frequently transferred from one department to another. To process one of these transfers, an HR clerk would have to create an entirely new employee record from scratch. An action that should take two minutes would now take at least an hour—and the chance of error would multiply.
- HR, payroll, and benefits users would have to navigate multiple screens and consolidate multiple reports to do their jobs and provide simple information. Again, manual errors would skyrocket.

At this point, it's natural to wonder how the company found itself in this state. Three scenarios come to mind:

- Management never held employee training sessions.
- Management held training sessions, but employees never bothered to attend them—and management shrugged it off.

- Employees attended the sessions but clearly didn't pay attention. Management either didn't notice or didn't care.

Regardless of what did or didn't happen at EDMC, someone should have realized that they would soon be entering a world of pain. Within minutes, their managers would have demanded that the company push the ERP's looming go-live date.

Playing this out, this wake-up call would have allowed the company to rebuild the HR modules before going live. (The new configuration would benefit everyone. For instance, Debbie would be able to run biweekly payroll once for all EDMC employees.)

None of that happened. For whatever reason, EDMC turned the keys of its new system over to people who didn't know how to drive. With playtime over, HR and payroll folks soon realized that the new system would complicate their jobs by an order of magnitude. Because EDMC had already "sunset" its prior enterprise system, it had long passed the point of no return.

Fixing this data-intensive issue involved a hell of a lot more work than merely checking a few boxes. On the contrary, EDMC eventually hired a team of consultants to perform the complicated data-migration work—and I was one of them. Total project cost: Upward of $1 million.

The irony is rich: An education company failed to educate its own employees before it launched an enterprise-wide system that would affect everyone in the organization. The old saying comes to mind: The shoemaker's children always go barefoot.

Today, EDMC is long gone. In 2018, it declared Chapter 7 bankruptcy and began to liquidate its assets.

Two final notes on EDMC. First, all employees were colocated, and training *still* missed its mark. Imagine how much worse it would have gone if people had worked remotely or in a hybrid fashion. Yikes. Second, although its snafu was certainly a whopper, it's hardly the only time that a company has fumbled efforts to provide its employees with necessary training.

Before continuing and by way of background, I've dutifully attended training classes when my employer required me. Beyond that, I've been training corporate courses on and off for nearly a quarter-century. During that time, my seminars and classes have run the gamut: different software applications, sexual harassment, and book-related ones over the years. Most of them have gone very well—a few, not so much.

When I reflect upon the most successful in-person application classes I've led and attended, a number of commonalities strike me:

1. Ample time for the class.
2. Committed and focused attendees.
3. Adequate physical space and audiovisual equipment.
4. Good tech and internet connectivity.
5. Mid-morning and -afternoon breaks that allow attendees to clear their heads.

Each of these elements matters, but the first one is downright essential: A class simply can't be successful without a dedicated block of time. Put differently, a sufficient window is necessary but insufficient for true learning to take place. As the following sidebar illustrates, however, some people unfortunately fail to appreciate this simple fact.

Why Bother?

Dave is a VP at a midsize hospital in the midwestern United States. As the pandemic progressed, he suspected that the nurses in his department weren't using the company's new collaboration and productivity applications as well as they could.

And, really, who could blame them? They were pulling stressful twelve-hour shifts at the height of COVID. Many were working overtime. The idea that they would lack the time and motivation to independently teach themselves the inner workings of Zoom, Microsoft Teams, and Microsoft OneNote isn't exactly farfetched. In LinkedIn's 2018 Workplace Learning Report, employees cited a lack of time to learn the skills they need as the biggest reason that they feel held back from learning.[9]

In April 2021, Dave had had enough. He knew that I'd written *Zoom For Dummies* and contacted me about creating a custom online training class. Dave wanted me to teach nurses how to effectively use each of these three robust applications.

I could certainly do that. It's not like I'd be hurting for material. It wouldn't be a stretch to spend three eight-hour days on either Zoom or Microsoft Teams. Even if we just skimmed the surface on each of them, I envisioned a solid one-day class with breaks.

Dave's vision was starkly different. Specifically, he expected a trainer to cover all three applications in one hour. Not each. Total. And, oh, by the way, he asked me without the slightest hint of humor, "With the remaining time, could you also show attendees how computers work?"

You just can't make this stuff up.

As diplomatically as I could, I urged Dave to reconsider. He paid me no heed and was adamant: Did I want the training gig on his terms or not? (How he ever attained the rank of VP is beyond me. Nepotism?)

Needless to say, I declined the opportunity—quickly. I told him that no trainer could effectively cover that much material in such a short period of time. In fact, it would be a challenge to give anything more than the briefest of overviews of *any* of those applications in an hour, especially Microsoft Teams and Zoom. Dave ended our chat by saying that he'd buy some copies of *Zoom For Dummies* for his staff instead.

Yeah, that's a reasonable substitute.

Envision the following scenario: Nurses work long, stressful shifts plus overtime in a pandemic. They finally arrive home, exhausted. Rather than kicking off their shoes, putting on some music, pouring a glass of white, they read ... a book about Zoom.

And, scene.

Let's just say, though, that I had accepted the gig. I then presented and rushed through all of the material that Dave wanted me to cover. Bad idea.

Class attendees would have quickly become frustrated because they didn't really learn anything. I would have wasted their time. On a personal level, regardless of the planning that took place behind the scenes, attendees are going to blame the trainer.

11 Provide Formal Employee Application Training

At least the EDMC folks and a healthcare VP aren't alone. They aren't the only people to fundamentally misunderstand the core functionality of a system or an application.

It's time to meet Professor Cal Newport.

Even Intelligent Folks Misunderstand Today's Tools

Newport dropped his new book *A World Without Email: Reimagining Work in an Age of Communication Overload* in March 2021. Like most academics, he's not lacking for opinions—and he doesn't disappoint.

If you don't feel like reading the entire book, check out his December 2020 article in *The New Yorker* "Slack Is the Right Tool for the Wrong Way to Work."[10] In Newport's view, Slack and email are equal scourges that distract us and, by extension, prevent us from doing our best work. From the piece:

> We're simply not wired to monitor an ongoing stream of unpredictable communication at the same time that we're trying to also finish actual work. Email introduced this problem of communication-driven distraction, but Slack pushed it to a new extreme.[*]

Time to unpack.

Newport is spot-on about the impact of being interrupted while we're working. *(Flow: The Psychology of Optimal Experience* by Mihaly Csikszentmihalyi is worth its weight in gold.) TL;DR: Letting ourselves be interrupted hinders both our productivity and the quality of our work.

---

[*] For more of Newport's thoughts, give his pod with Ezra Klein a listen at https://tinyurl.com/1cal-ezra.

But equating email to Slack? Sorry, professor. Louis Brandeis said, "Behind every argument is someone's ignorance." He couldn't be more right. Let's start with the small issue first.

One quick note about the next few sections: If your organization uses Microsoft Teams, Google Workspace, Zoom, or another internal collaboration hub, just swap out Slack for your tool of choice.

Misconception #1: The Binary Nature of In-App Notifications

In a way, Newport is right: Slack is a relatively new communications tchotchke. New communication mediums have arguably caused as many problems as they've solved. In another, more accurate way, however, Newport is way off. He treats the idea of Slack notifications as a binary. That is, users either get all of them or none of them. To him, there's no middle ground.

There's just one flaw with this criticism: Nothing could be further from the truth.

There are at least half a dozen simple ways in which Slack users can control which messages and notifications they receive—*and, critically, when and how they receive them.*[*]

And Slack is hardly the only internal collaboration hub to offer bells and whistles that let people avoid distractions while on the job. Zoom, Microsoft Teams, Google Workspace, and others provide similar functionality that allows users to easily customize their in-app notifications. These software vendors have long realized that, when it comes to alerts, one size doesn't fit all.

Returning to Newport's argument, if Slack *didn't* ship with these critical features, then he'd have a point. I'd be more inclined to agree with him on the Pavlovian nature of in-app alerts. Constant

---

[*] Pick up a copy of *Slack For Dummies* and you'll see for yourself. #shamelessplug

11 Provide Formal Employee Application Training   243

pings would overwhelm employees, leaving them no choice but to go off the grid to focus.

> ## It's Not You. It's Them.
>
> Here's some free, unsolicited career advice.
>
> Let's say that you enable do-not-disturb mode in an application to focus on your work. Doing so angers your peers and manager. Don't blame tech or yourself. Your company is suffering from a cultural and leadership problem.
>
> It's probably time for you to start looking for a new gig.

Although he's hardly the first person to make the argument, Newport nails the limitations of text-based communication. I've advocated a three-message rule for years. At some point, it behooves everyone to talk to each other—and not just click Reply All.

Misconception #2: Slack Equals Email 2.0

There's another, larger problem with Newport's thesis: Slack is essentially Email 2.0. In his eyes, the former is just a souped-up version of the latter. As a result, he argues that we should use Slack very little—or not at all. In other words, let's throw the baby out with the bathwater.

I've encountered this argument many times before. Again, Newport isn't exactly Neil Armstrong by conflating the two tools.

Yes, colleagues can use both Outlook and Slack to shoot text messages and files back and forth, but that's where the similarities end. (It's kind of like saying that both LeBron James and I play basketball.) Unlike an email client, however, sending asynchronous text messages represents just a small fraction of Slack's robust functionality.

Thousands of organizations have made Slack their *digital headquarters*—a term that Brian Elliott of the Future Forum likes to use.* Forget merely customizing Slack notifications to suit your needs. Those are table stakes. By unleashing the true power of internal collaboration hubs such as Slack, employees can do each of the following:

- Consolidate their application alerts.
- Minimize multitasking.
- Spend less time toggling among different programs.
- Quickly find essential documents and messages.
- Focus while on the clock—the main point in Newport's prior work *Deep Work*.

I could keep going. *Slack For Dummies* isn't a short book, but I'll stay on point here.

> *"Do not attribute to malice that which is adequately explained by stupidity."*
>
> —HANLON'S RAZOR

Newport is a smart cat, and we all make errors of commission and omission. Perhaps his publisher's acquisitions editor was enamored with the success of his previous titles. As a result, the editors and fact checkers involved in his most recent opus failed to ask a simple but essential question about one of his major claims: Is it even true?

---

* Listen to him on my podcast at https://tinyurl.com/rpm-bell.

Underscoring the Need for Formal Employee Training

Despite its dubious premise, *A World Without Email* still became a *New York Times* bestseller. Sales aside, this example illustrates a much larger lesson.

To recap, a venerated and tenured college professor—and, ironically, the bestselling author of a book called *Deep Work*—wants to write a follow-up. He lands on a topical and popular text about the nexus of modern communication and work. He spends *months* researching it and another chunk of dedicated time actually writing it. (Since he's a tenured faculty member, I'd be astonished if he had to teach a single class during this time, never mind a full course load.) In the end, his book fundamentally misrepresents essential functionality of popular communications and collaboration tools.

Now, I'm going to assume two things. First, you're *not* a tenured college professor. Second and more generally, your current job doesn't allow you to dedicate a minimum of six months to researching and writing a book. It's far more likely that you're a busy employee concurrently juggling a bunch of tasks. You're dealing with plenty of work-in-progress.

Against this backdrop, will you have the time to teach yourself the ins and outs of a new application? If not, you may well operate under the same misconceptions as Newport does.

Now, what if your management invested in a proper training class? For its duration, your job entailed learning how to effectively use an essential new workplace application or system. Period. When the class ended, your boss and colleagues would expect you to regularly use that new technology as part of your job.

Bottom line: Expecting busy employees to independently learn the nuances of a new application on their own time is almost always a fool's errand. As we've seen throughout this chapter, it can also be an expensive one.

Proximity, Training, and Employee Loyalty

The need to provide employees with formal application training has never been more acute. After all, thanks to remote and hybrid workplaces, we're working less synchronously with our colleagues. Figure 11.1 displays the relationship between colleague proximity and the extent to which employees rely upon workforce tech.

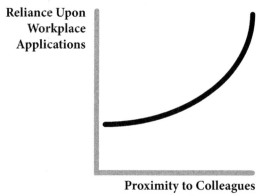

Figure 11.1: The Relationship Between Employee Proximity and Workplace Applications

The idea that employees can just watch YouTube videos as a substitute for proper training and development is absurd. Training—and the signal that management sends to its employees—matters. Again, don't take my word for it.

In 2018 LinkedIn Learning released an extensive report on employee training and development.[11] Among its most interesting findings:

- 94 percent of employees say they would stay at a company longer if it invested in their career development.

11 Provide Formal Employee Application Training 247

- 87 percent of millennials reported that development is an important job characteristic.
- 69 percent of nonmillennials concurred.
- 56 percent of respondents said they would take a course that a manager suggested.

No, Steven won't turn down another job that pays double his current salary just because his manager sponsored his PMP certification three years ago. At the same time, he might pass on a call with a recruiter if he really feels valued—and investing in employee training can send that essential message.

In short, skimping on employee training introduces additional risk to product launches and project management. This is especially true when:

- People increasingly work in remote and hybrid environments.
- Employee engagement is low.
- The labor market is tight and employees can easily switch jobs without relocating.

Basically, that's life right now and for the foreseeable future.

Chapter Summary

- Even smart, successful people underestimate the value of employee training and the power of today's applications.
- The farther we are from our colleagues, partners, managers, and clients, the more we need to rely upon software programs and technology in general. That's why application training is so important.
- Expecting employees to learn on their own time and dime is sanguine at best and dangerous at worst.

Chapter 12

INSTITUTIONALIZE CLEAR EMPLOYEE WRITING

"Words, once they are printed, have a life of their own."

—CAROL BURNETT

In terms of sheer volume, there's at least one category of business books that rivals project management. As I type these words, Amazon lists more than 50,000 texts on *business communication*.[*] My 2015 book *Message Not Received* is a modest contribution to the field. (#shamelessplug) Modify your search to *business writing*, and that number jumps to 60,000.

Those numbers are telling. When publishers and authors pump out tens of thousands of books on a business topic, you can infer a few things: That subject is critical, and the state of it isn't exactly optimal. It's the antithesis of a niche topic that only a few niche authors have nailed.

---

[*] Go nuts at https://tinyurl.com/rpm-bizcom.

In this specific instance, I'll add one more: Project management and business communication are cousins. Business communication is a core PMBOK pillar. It's just as important as the others, if not more so. Our choice of words and medium can dramatically affect whether others comply with our requests.

The move to remote and hybrid work highlights the importance of employees clearly expressing themselves in writing. Nowhere is this need more pronounced than in the context of project management. Fortunately, organizations can take a number of steps to improve their employees' facility with the written word.

Before we go there, though, let's look at some objectively awful writing.

How *Not* to Write: Exhibit A

You've got what you think is a big idea. Here's how you introduce it to the world:

> Building on the arguments of our previous foray into this topic, this book envisions the emergence of the Fifth Wave in American higher education—a league of colleges and universities, spearheaded initially by a subset of large-scale public research universities, unified in their resolve to accelerate positive social outcomes through the seamless integration of world-class knowledge production with cutting-edge technological innovation and institutional cultures dedicated to the advancement of accessibility to the broadest possible demographic representative of the socioeconomic and intellectual diversity of our nation. The Fifth Wave primarily augments and complements the set of American research universities, which, for reasons that will readily become apparent, we term the Fourth Wave, but will also comprise networks of

12 Institutionalize Clear Employee Writing 251

> heterogeneous colleges and universities whose frameworks are underpinned by discovery and knowledge production, and institutional actors from business and industry, government agencies and laboratories, and organizations in civil society.

I'll go out on a limb and assume that previous 'graph either confused or bored you—and probably both. It should. The first discursive sentence clocks in at 85 words. The second is only a smidge shorter at 61. Try to read either sentence in one breath. I can't do it. Sure, Marcel Proust would be proud, but that's no way to write.

So, what exactly did you just read? (Again, context.)

Is that single rambling paragraph the beginning of a nocturnal email from an overzealous colleague who's trying to impress his peers? Try again. What about the output of an artificial intelligence program attempting to churn out what it considers to be sophisticated prose? It certainly reads like that, but that's not the correct answer either.

Give up?

Those unfortunate words represent the beginning of *The Fifth Wave: The Evolution of American Higher Education,* the 2020 book from current president of Arizona State University Dr. Michael Crow and his colleague, William Dabars.

Let me repeat three key words from that previous sentence: *the 2020 book.* This means that editors from Johns Hopkins University Press, an esteemed publisher, recently approved this soporific prose. (See, it doesn't take much effort to drop a 50-cent word.)

No wonder Amazon lists so many books on business writing and communication. Although the company sells the works of verbose and pompous writers, its own internal communication couldn't be more different.

The Six-Pager: How Amazon Promotes Clear Writing

Amazon minimizes project failures by conducting project and product premortems. Although the premortems are largely effective, they represent just one way that the company ensures that future projects and products stay focused.

Cofounder and executive chairman Jeff Bezos famously banned PowerPoint presentations at his company long ago, a policy that current CEO Andy Jassy has intelligently left intact.

If slides are off the table, how does an Amazonian pitch an idea to launch a new product or enter a new market? Not surprisingly, executives follow a different process—one that other companies have started to ape. Specifically, employees write and distribute six-page documents that each member of the company's S-Team—short for *senior team*—read together in silence. When that reading period ends, an informed and spirited discussion immediately begins.

All Amazon bigwigs understand the process they'll have to follow. Because they know all this going in, every word on their six-pagers counts. Returning to the earlier example, assume that Crow and Dabars had distributed their bewildering morass of text at an S-Team meeting. The reaction would be swift and severe. The words *organ rejection* come to mind.

Now, I've never pitched an idea in front of Jeff Bezos, and I've never been in the room while anyone else has. I'm no Colin Bryar or Bill Carr.

In 2021, these two ex-Amazon execs released their book *Working Backwards: Insights, Stories, and Secrets from Inside Amazon.* In it, they explain how company execs routinely spend weeks refining their ideas in preparation for their S-Team meetings. They know that they're not going to get a second bite at the apple.

12 Institutionalize Clear Employee Writing

Carr, now a speaker and advisor like me, appeared on my podcast in March 2021.[*] He discussed how Amazon leadership has long understood the gravity of clear internal communication, especially when working on new endeavors. The company's size and success haven't altered one immutable fact: Launching a new project, service, or product is still inherently risky. Insisting upon clarity minimizes the chances of confusion and failure. (Indeed, lucidly expressing one's ideas doesn't guarantee approval to proceed, much less success down the road. The company's 3D-enabled Fire Phone is a case in point.)

Clarity even extends to standardized line spacing, margins, and font size. In their book, Bryar and Carr detail how Amazon's six-pagers have evolved over time:

> The first few narratives were laughably poor when evaluated by today's standards. Some teams ignored the length limit, which was meant to keep the narratives brief enough so they could be read in the meeting itself. Enthusiastic teams, who felt their idea could not be adequately expressed in such a limited space, came in with 30 or 40 pages of prose. When authors learned that we were serious about a page limit, some squeezed as much text onto a page as possible, using tiny fonts, reducing the width of the margins, and single-spacing the text. We wanted to go back to the benefits of writing, but not to the look of a sixteenth-century document.
>
> Gradually, we settled on a standard format. Maximum length: six pages, no desperate tricks in formatting please. Appendices

---

[*] Yeah, I'm name-dropping a little bit here. Listen at https://tinyurl.com/1rpm-carr.

with further information or supporting detail could be attached, but would not be required reading in the meeting itself.

As is usually the case, Amazon's decision to standardize the format of its six-pager is just plain smart. Plenty of research suggests that our stylistic choices unconsciously affect how others will receive our messages. Unfortunately, no one told Dan Gilbert. He had to learn that lesson the hard way more than a decade ago.

Fonts Matter, Part I

In summer 2010, LeBron James bolted the Cleveland Cavaliers for the Miami Heat as a free agent. ESPN ran a special on it called "The Decision."

Let's just say that the jilted owner of the Cavaliers, Dan Gilbert, was displeased.

Immediately afterward, he wrote a public breakup. Bad move #1. He wrote the letter in the ill-advised Comic Sans font. Bad move #2.

As expected, the internet mocked him mercilessly for it. [1]

Amazon's insistence upon clear writing, especially when undertaking new endeavors, permeates all levels of the company. Several pegs down the org chart, software developers must write press releases before writing a single line of code.[2]

Amazon understands that clarity positively correlates with both success and execution. It's difficult to hit a moving target. The approach minimizes project guesswork and lets everyone begin with the end in mind, to borrow a tip from Stephen Covey's bestselling book *The 7 Habits of Highly Effective People*.

Fonts Matter, Part II

In my days as a college professor, I insisted that all my students use the same template for their papers. This requirement removed a potential source of bias and helped me suss out who couldn't follow simple instructions.

A few students initially demurred. Why couldn't they just use whatever fonts they wanted? Their other professors didn't insist upon uniformity. It was at this point that I would show them a slide with Gilbert's letter and cringe-worthy font choice. Lightbulbs went off.

On Proximity and Clarity of Writing

Amazon might be the most prominent company to imbue clear employee communication into its culture and formal business processes, but it's not the only one. Let's return to Automattic and its CEO, Matt Mullenweg.

During that same February 2022 *Wall Street Journal* interview, Mullenweg spoke about the single biggest challenge that asynchronous work presents:

> Clarity of writing. If you don't have that, you can have people thinking they're on the same page when they actually have [a] different understanding. We've been experimenting with classes and workshops and, of course, books that we recommend for people to improve their writing skills. We also have an editorial team that does our publications, but also does a lot of internal editing. It's incredibly important in an asynchronous organization to invest in your writing.[3]

Mullenweg has long been wise beyond his years. He illustrates a number of simple yet critical points here:

1. Employees—regardless of location—who don't understand how to do something are unlikely to do it correctly.
2. Poor or unclear writing inhibits understanding.
3. At a minimum, trying to launch any new product or update requires clear and common language.
4. The move to distributed, asynchronous, and hybrid work results in less synchronous, in-person communication—not that his company ever relied upon it very much.
5. Less in-person communication accentuates the need for all employees to write clearly.

As a general rule, when all employees work in the same physical office, two things happen. First, employees talk more and write less. A one-hour meeting can obviate 40 emails or Slack messages. Second, they can more easily clarify misunderstandings that stem from poor written communication. Peter could always approach his boss in the hallway and say, "Lumbergh, I don't know what the hell you're talking about."

At the office, hashing things out in person typically doesn't require a ton of prior coordination, much less proper writing. Unfortunately, that's simply not the case with remote and hybrid workplaces; they add friction to matters small and large.

Grabbing a few minutes with a colleague in a hybrid environment is more difficult. Michael *may* luckily catch Gob in the lunch line or in the hallway to discuss obtaining a key building permit, but there's no guarantee. And the farther we work from our colleagues, partners, and clients, the more important clear writing becomes, as Figure 12.1 demonstrates.

Overcoming the Proximity Problem With Clear Writing

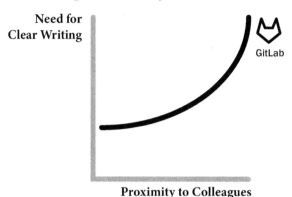

Figure 12.1: Overcoming the Proximity Problem With Clear Writing

The following GitLab sidebar illustrates this truism.

> ### GitLab: Employee Self-Service on Steroids
> —Darren Murph, head of remote at GitLab
>
> Read up on GitLab, and you'll marvel at what it's accomplished since its 2014 inception. The word *extraordinary* comes to mind. In the past eight years, it has built a self-service environment that allows more than 1,500 employees around the globe to search for—and easily find—answers to thousands of policy- and process-related questions *every* day.
>
> Workers don't routinely pester their colleagues with simple queries. New hires quickly learn that you're expected to fish for yourself. Employee communication is less frequent, more meaningful, and more targeted. GitLab employees don't sit in pointless meetings. Its HR folks don't spend their days responding to questions.

> Not surprisingly, compared to industry benchmarks, GitLab's workers are generally happier, less overwhelmed, and less likely to quit their jobs.

Think of clear writing as another *hygiene factor*. In this case, written communication doesn't guarantee a positive outcome. Without it, however, a project or product team will find it virtually impossible to deliver the goods in a timely manner. That goes double when the workplace is hybrid or remote. Clear employee writing is no longer a luxury; it becomes a necessity.

The explosion in remote and hybrid work has increased the sheer number of asynchronous, written messages that employees send and receive in any given day. In March 2021, Microsoft reported that the average Teams user sent "45 percent more chats per week and 42 percent more chats per person after hours, with chats per week still on the rise."[4]

Lucid writing minimizes the number of *total* messages employees receive—and certainly the number of confusing ones. (Ever met anyone who wanted to receive more work-related communication? Me neither.) What's more, clearer communication can reduce employee anxiety and, quite possibly, turnover. But there's another, more recent reason that employees should care more about what they put out there for their peers and partners to read: basic self-preservation.

The Rise of Permanence: Why All Electronic Messages Are No Longer Created Equal

Prior to the pandemic, email served as the *lingua franca* for intraorganizational communication. When was the last time you saw a business card *without* an email address? As proof, "only" 20 million

12 Institutionalize Clear Employee Writing

people used Microsoft Teams every day in November 2019.[5] Email still reigned supreme.

Because employees received so many emails, they generally and understandably viewed them as disposable. (Hence the popularity of philosophies such as Inbox Zero.) Emails ultimately "live" in the inboxes of individual employees, not in any type of enterprise knowledge repository.[*] With rare exception, when workers quit, IT personnel or automated processes promptly disable those email addresses and inboxes. All essential employee decisions, discussions, and content subsequently vanish.

At this point, you may be asking yourself, What's the big whoop?

Dismiss the distinction between these two mediums for written communication as trivial if you want, but that's a mistake. The half-life of a message posted in a hub is much longer than that of a garden-variety email, as the following sidebar illustrates.

Lessons From *The Office*

David joined the small paper company Wernham Hogg in 2014 as its new marketing director. The CEO Jennifer understandably wanted to get him quickly up to speed. As such, she began peppering him with scads of emails and files.

It didn't take long for David to feel overwhelmed. During his first three months, he struggled to catch his breath. Jennifer's messages and attachments kept coming, often in spurts of emails and attachments prefaced with "Found another one."

---

[*] This is one of the many ways in which Teams, Slack, and other internal collaboration hubs crush email.

It wasn't an ideal sitch, but David persevered. During his first performance review, he told Jennifer that her initial email deluge had overwhelmed him.

To her credit, Jennifer took his feedback to heart. In 2018, she moved Wernham Hogg to Microsoft Teams. Internal emails became a relic of the past.

It was a hit. All employees happily used Teams to hold discussions, share files, collaborate, and post announcements.

Three years later, David resigned, one of the many casualties of the Great Resignation.

Later that year, Neil joined Wernham Hogg as David's replacement. Jennifer added Neil to the relevant Teams channels, most importantly #marketing. She told Neil that he could find everything he needed there.

Neil was able to digest the material at his own pace. As he absorbed information about this new role, the company, and his colleagues, he found the comments of Gareth, a marketing analyst, confusing and occasionally unprofessional. Gareth's peers would routinely ask him to clarify previous messages. Naturally, Neil formed a negative initial impression of Gareth.

The previous example revolved around Microsoft Teams, but it would have worked just as well with Slack, Zoom, Workplace from ~~Facebook~~ Meta, Google Workspace, Discord, or any other internal collaboration hub. The change in tools is an important one for a number of reasons:

- ☺ We're increasingly writing our work-related messages with more communal applications. By using email less, our communications are no longer as disposable as they used to be.

12 Institutionalize Clear Employee Writing 261

- ☺ Our future coworkers and managers are more likely to see those messages. As such, they judge us by the clarity and quality of our content. If we write clearly, our words are assets. If not, our words serve as liabilities.
- ☺ Writing clearly can save others time and, even better, minimize the number of times we have to restate our thoughts for others. During projects, these small time savings really add up.

And that's the big whoop.

How to Improve Employee Writing

One doesn't flip a switch or buy a software license and immediately become an effective writer; it's a craft that takes years to *consciously* develop. (It's unlikely to happen by accident.) Still, organizations aren't powerless against the rising tide of jargon and confusing text. They can take concrete steps to improve the level of written communication.

Employers should invest in formal application training. Expecting employees to become proficient in essential communication, collaboration, and PM tools on their own dime and time is foolish. If Surly Susan won't teach herself the ins and outs of Asana on the weekend, what are the odds she'll independently hone her writing skills just for the hell of it?

Not great. To this end, more companies are following Automattic's lead by conducting formal, mandatory writing workshops. In the following sidebar, one of the world's leading authorities on business writing chimes in on how to hold a good one.

Why Writing Workshops Matter

—Josh Bernoff, author of *Writing Without Bullshit* and blogger at withoutbullshit.com

Writing is the lifeblood of the hybrid organization. It's how people communicate, collaborate, and get things done without days chockablock with wall-to-wall meetings.

If the writing is ineffective, that lifeblood is poisoned. Around 6 percent of all the wages in the US are wasted trying to puzzle out poorly written documents.[6]

To help fix this, I've conducted dozens of virtual writing workshops for some of the world's most respected media, technology, industrial, retail, and consulting organizations. I've learned what works. Workshops that work help participants rally around a shared set of writing values that contribute to the organization's effectiveness, culture, and speed.

To start, they must adopt "The Iron Imperative" and treat the reader's time as more valuable than their own. If the workshop is to be more than another tedious chore, its design must help people learn how to do that, and quickly. Some tips:

- **Make it interactive.** You can't learn to drive by reading about it. Writing is the same. Workshops must include exercises in which participants solve real writing problems.
- **Customize the content.** Your organization's problems are unique, so your workshop must be, too. Best practice: Have participants work on real documents from your company.

- **Keep it small.** A virtual workshop should include at most 20 participants. This allows the instructor to get a bead on people's attitudes, involve everyone, and answer questions. To reach more people, repeat the workshop for additional groups.
- **Keep it short.** Holding two 90-minute sessions is ideal. Longer than that, and people balk.
- **Focus on effectiveness.** Key topics include brevity, better titles, and front-loading content to put the most important information at the top.
- **Teach storytelling.** People comprehend, remember, and share stories. Every memo should be a story: We face this challenge, we gathered this evidence, we are going to solve the problem this way, and we all will live happily ever after.
- **Address style issues.** What clogs the lifeblood? Evasive passive voice, incomprehensible jargon, and vague qualifiers. Teach participants to identify and purge these toxic prose elements.
- **Have fun.** My participants get to see some putrid writing samples from other people—and thereby diagnose and recognize what kind of things go wrong and how to fix them. Humor makes learning stick.

A workshop won't solve all your writing problems, but it will get you started in the right direction. Crucially, it gives people a shared vocabulary and a set of tools. If your culture is any good, those things will flourish, your writing lifeblood will become vital, and your organization will run more effectively.

The organization that invests in a proper writing workshop signals to its employees the importance of the topic: Their job during that time involves learning how to write better. Period. In other words, it holds more water than the head of HR uttering a vacuous bromide like, "Be clear with others."

As Bernoff explains, workshop attendees walk away with a greater awareness of what constitutes clear business writing and new skills to hone their own communications. Does that mean that these folks will never send a confusing message to a colleague again? Of course not.

We've all done it, and its effects may be trivial. (I usually blame brain cramps or a lack of coffee.) But we can all be clearer in our written communications. Doing so minimizes the bottlenecks, and that adds to others' work-in-progress—and our own.

Beyond holding workshops for existing employees, companies can take additional steps to raise the level of employee communication. For one, it makes sense to hire employees who write super good. (Yes, my poor grammar in the previous sentence was intentional. Tip your waitress.) Doing so, however, doesn't immediately turn *existing* employees into better writers. Over time, they may learn by osmosis.

Getting All Meta: A Few Final Words on the Written Word

Employees who tell everyone that we all need to "circle back for some blue-sky thinking" should have to contribute to a jargon jar. I'm not kidding.

Jargon, Emojis, and Formality

In February 2022, Slack released the results of a large survey on employee communication.[7] In total, 2,000 remote and hybrid

12 Institutionalize Clear Employee Writing

workers displayed a strong preference for less formal workplace communication. Here are a few other nuggets:

- 73 percent of respondents believe that informal work messages have helped them ease the transition from in-person to remote and hybrid work.
- 63 percent described the use of jargon in messages as off-putting.
- Emojis and animated gifs allow workers to express their tones more accurately—and avoid miscommunications that so often cause problems among colleagues.

You'll get no argument from me that business jargon still sucks. (*Net-net* and *synergy* are just two of my trigger words.) At the same time, don't conflate *less formal* with *completely informal.* A string of borderline-incomprehensible emojis might play for your Twitter followers, but making it your first written interaction with your manager or CEO isn't wise. Read the virtual room.

Brainwriting

Finally, there are benefits from supplanting in-person or virtual meetings with dedicated, asynchronous writing sessions. Speaking with Kara Swisher of the *New York Times,* organizational psychologist and Wharton School professor Adam Grant says:

> We have extensive evidence that if you bring a group of people together to brainstorm, they generate fewer ideas—and less original ideas—than those same individuals working alone. Group brainstorming stifles diversity of thought through production blocking (we can't all talk at once), ego threat (I don't want to look stupid), and conformity pressure (I want to jump on the bandwagon), and those problems are amplified for

people who lack power and status. If you're the most junior person in the room, the only woman of color in a team of white men, or the introvert in a group of extraverts, it's that much harder to overcome those pressures.

An effective solution is called brainwriting. You give people the problem before the meeting or at the start of the meeting, and then let them jot down their own ideas. You get more variety and more quality, and then you can let the wisdom of crowds evaluate and refine. I can't tell you how many meetings I've run in the past two years where I've asked people to type in the chat, and we end up with a much richer set of possibilities than we would've seen otherwise.[8]

The benefits of brainwriting apply well beyond managing projects and launching new products—the primary topics of this book. At the same time, though, I've never seen a successful project run completely sans meetings. And if you think that all future meetings will involve only real-world participants, think again.

In October 2020, Cisco and Dimensional Research released a study on the future of work. The two companies predict that 98 percent of all future meetings will be hybrid. That is, they will include at least one remote participant.[9] Running hybrid, synchronous discussions both intelligently and briefly is a book in itself.*

Chapter Summary

- ⊘ Clear business writing has always been critical. The rise in hybrid and remote work has only accentuated its importance.

---

* Check out *Suddenly Hybrid: Managing the Modern Meeting* by Karin M. Reed and Joseph A. Allen.

12 Institutionalize Clear Employee Writing

- Amazon and Automattic are two prominent companies whose management has taken steps to institutionalize clear employee writing. More firms are coming around to the benefits of holding formal workshops.
- Workshops can pay off in spades, especially since electronic messages are becoming less disposable.

Chapter 13

EMBRACE ANALYTICS

"If you can't measure it, you can't manage it."
—W. EDWARDS DEMING

Selecting a proper PM application—and using it throughout the project—is invaluable. Doing so allows PMs and product owners to get their arms around these challenges.

It's now time to turn the amp up to eleven.

This chapter explains the importance of analytics in the context of project management. We'll see how it can provide insights not only into what's happening, but why. Everyone involved on a project or product launch can benefit from embracing analytics.

MBWA

In 1982, Tom Peters and Robert Waterman published *In Search of Excellence: Lessons from America's Best-Run Companies*. The two authors examined the characteristics of 43 successful American companies from different industries. In the end, they claimed to have discovered the secret sauce for long-term business success.

Despite the authors' considerable methodological shortcomings,[*] *In Search of Excellence* was an immediate hit, selling three million copies in its first four years. In the 1980s and 1990s, it was a staple in top-tier MBA programs. Peters and Waterman turned their book into a string of lucrative consulting engagements from eager CEOs.

Among the book's most popular and enduring lessons was the need for managers to get out of their offices and interact with others—aka *management by wandering around,* or MBWA. Hewlett-Packard managers had lived by that credo since the 1970s.

MBWA was Latin for "I know it when I see it."[†] By randomly strolling around the office in an unstructured manner, managers could check in with individual employees, look at essential physical equipment, identify problems, and develop a sense of the workplace. It quickly became a go-to practice in management circles. The practice was intuitive and simple, and it made sense to people in charge. Executives who lived inside their own bubbles couldn't possibly know what was *really* going on at their companies.

Intuition aside, however, the actual effects of MBWA were decidedly mixed. For instance, a 2013 randomized field study by Anita Tucker and Sara Singer of Harvard Business School found that MBWA negatively impacted performance.[1] One need not be a professor at a prestigious university, however, to poke holes in the basic idea behind MBWA.

---

[*] In his superb 2009 book *The Halo Effect,* my namesake Philip Rosenzweig describes the many problems of this book and *Good to Great* by Jim Collins. It's one of the few business texts that I've read twice.

[†] Justice Potter Stewart popularized this expression by describing his threshold test for obscenity in the 1964 United States Supreme Court case *Jacobellis v. Ohio.*

Consider a stereotypical in-person workplace circa 2013 and the following simple, hypothetical scenario.

> ## Where's Ken?
>
> Ray is a 62-year-old president of a midsized electronics distributor. Every day at 5:15 p.m., he strolls around corporate HQ after his calendar has cleared. He likes to engage employees and take their temperature.
>
> Roseann has carefully played office politics for years and knows where plenty of bodies are buried. She makes it a habit of leaving the office at 6:30 p.m. after taking two-hour lunches and a few 30-minute smoke breaks to boot. Her colleague Ken regularly works through lunch so he can leave at 5 p.m. to see his wife and newborn twins.
>
> Ray always wonders why he never sees Ken during his regular strolls.[*] The former assumes that kids today just lack a strong work ethic. In point of fact, however, Ken is a much more valuable contributor than Roseann will ever be. (Hello again, proximity bias.)

In this example, Ray is neither misguided nor evil. Like all of us to one extent or another, he's just an *empiricist*. At the risk of getting all existential, in philosophy empiricism is the deeply rooted idea that all knowledge stems exclusively or primarily from firsthand, sensory experience. It's tough for *anyone* to shake the belief that "I know it when I see it." If it seems a tad abstract, read the great Michael Lewis book *Moneyball* or watch the movie of the same name.

---

[*] All the more reason to take the strolls at random intervals throughout the day, as MBWA acolytes recommend.

MBWA has *always* been at best a questionable management practice. Now that remote and hybrid workplaces have arrived in earnest, it's downright silly to try to rely upon MBWA to manage a project or launch a new product, much less run an entire enterprise.

Consider Michael. Just because he's out of the office today doesn't mean that he's slacking off; on the contrary, he may be in the zone. Remember that employees will be commuting solely to perform individual and concentrated tasks. This is what our friend from Chapter 11, Cal Newport, calls *Deep Work,* and it represents the very types of tasks that employees should accomplish while away from the office and their peers. For this very reason, companies are leasing less office space than they did prior to the pandemic.[2]

Despite the unequivocal trends from the past two years, however, most old-school managers are still loath to reject their long-held empiricism. Because they're ultimately responsible for their underlings' performance, they tend to believe that work is somewhere you go, not something you do. The idea of letting go makes them especially uncomfortable. Consider the results from a July 2021 report from the Society for Human Resource Management:

> More than two thirds of supervisors of remote workers surveyed by SHRM, or 67 percent, admit to considering remote workers more easily replaceable than onsite workers at their organization, 62 percent believe full-time remote work is detrimental to employees' career objectives, and 72 percent say they would prefer all of their subordinates to be working in the office.[3]

Without empiricism, how are company presidents, PMs, and product owners supposed to know what's going on? Are they just supposed to rely upon blind faith or intuition from a distance?

Fortunately, there's another, better, and decidedly nonempirical way.

Beyond Empiricism: The Case for Analytics

Management fads come and go, and they sometimes come back again. (Can we centralize our workplace tech?) MBWA has gone from *de rigueur* to *passé,* and the field of analytics has taken the business world by storm.[*]

As for why, the reasons vary. *Moneyball* played an enormous role in convincing business leaders that they, too, can reap outsize rewards by analyzing vast amounts of data. Data-driven companies such as Amazon, Netflix, Meta, and Google forced their competitors to raise their game. Data storage costs have plummeted,[†] and a slew of powerful, affordable tools lets nontechies analyze vast amounts of data.

Today, it's no overstatement to claim that the field of analytics permeates just about every discipline. A few examples will illustrate my point:

- **Human resources:** My friend Mike West penned *People Analytics For Dummies* in 2019.
- **Higher education:** Colleges and universities started offering courses on analytics in the mid-2010s. (I should know. I taught one of them for two years.) A friend of mine teaches college courses in *accounting* analytics.
- **Every major and niche sport:** MIT has hosted a sports analytics conference for 15 years.[4] Even golfers[5] and fishing fanatics have embraced data-driven methods.

---

* See for yourself at https://tinyurl.com/mbwa-analytics.

† The drop has been precipitous. See https://tinyurl.com/ps-kryder.

And yes, analytics entered the world of project management long ago as well.

Let's back up, though.

At a high level, all analytics fall into one of the following four buckets:

- **Descriptive:** Describes events that have happened in the past or that are happening now.
- **Diagnostic:** Explains why something happened in the past or is happening now.
- **Predictive:** Forecasts the events that may take place in the future.
- **Prescriptive:** Suggests recommended actions that entities can take to affect future outcomes.

These buckets apply regardless of your specific focus or objective. For example, whether you're trying to predict employee turnover at your company or the weight of the next fish you catch, you're still trying to predict some future event.

Analytics for Project and Product Management

How can analytics help project managers and product owners? At a high level, they help these folks do the following:

- To measure, observe, and analyze project performance.
- To make more rational, data-based project decisions.
- To allocate scarce human and financial resources in an optimal manner.
- To manifest hidden project risks.

Writing for cio.com, Moira Alexander, PMP, details the benefits of applying analytics to individual projects:

Having access to data from past and current projects enables project managers to better allocate resources for current projects and better plan for future ones. By gathering and analyzing data in one place, project managers can identify which resources are being underutilized or overutilized, enabling them to shift resources where necessary and schedule accordingly.[6]

If these objectives and benefits seem a bit vague, consider the following real-world example of how one organization embraced analytics on a failing project.

Analytics in Action

—Adapted from *Project Management Analytics* by Harjit Singh

Kheri Construction (KC) had a problem.

Over the years, the large commercial construction company had built a reputation for successfully completing large private and public works projects in Texas. Examples included skyscrapers, multilane highways, railroad tracks, and shopping malls.

In the spring of 2011, the Texas state government awarded KC a large contract to oversee a highway reconstruction project in Houston. One year after starting, however, things were going poorly. The project was grossly behind schedule and over budget. KC needed to figure out why—and soon.

An extensive, data-driven analysis revealed that the main culprit was high employee turnover—an untenable annualized rate of 52.7 percent. With one out of every two employees leaving every year, KC was spending considerable funds to train new hires. Unfortunately, many newbies soon bolted.

KC hired temps to fill the vacancies, but the company had to train them as well, and the cycle continued.

Compounding the problem, newly trained employees couldn't immediately contribute to the highway reconstruction project. Employees weren't staying long enough for KC to recoup its investment in employee training.

KC engaged an outside consultant to investigate the situation, analyze data related to this project and historical ones, and recommend a remediation plan.

The suggestions included:

- Improving employee pay and benefits.
- Upgrading job classifications—that is, turning part-time, temp positions into full-time, permanent ones.
- Providing hardware and software upgrades for existing employees.

Yes, these changes would immediately increase KC's employment costs. The company was betting, though, that the rewards (decreased employee turnover) would more than justify the additional expenditures. Importantly, KC relied extensively upon data, thus increasing the chances that its big bet would pay dividends.

In short, it did.

Within a month after implementing its action plan, employee attrition began waning. One year later, the annual staff turnover rate had plummeted to a mere 8.6 percent—an improvement of more than 80 percent. Rather than resting on its laurels, KC continued monitoring employee turnover and staff-related issues throughout the duration of the project.

When I interviewed Singh in March 2022, he wholeheartedly concurred with the idea that hybrid workplaces complicate project management. What's more, analytics can help provide much needed transparency into what's going on. In his words:

> Project managers in hybrid or remote settings can no longer rely upon the face-to-face interactions of colocated teams. This complicates their ability to control the essential elements of their projects: scope, schedule, and budget. In order for them to effectively do their jobs, they need to rely upon extensive data to measure project performance.[7]

As the KC example demonstrated, analytics offer far more than basic reporting on project schedules and costs. (As a side note, the KC case study is a decade old. If the external consultant took the same gig today, all the powerful PM tools out there would have made his job much easier.)

Note that analytics don't magically happen in a vacuum or by themselves. They don't turn fundamentally flawed ideas into brilliant ones or solve all the problems related to dysfunctional projects, interpersonal relationships, teams, or companies. This holds true on any project, regardless of its location. Analytics can, however, provide PMs, product owners, and others with invaluable insights, increase visibility, manifest problems, and suggest solutions.

Revisiting Hertz: How Analytics Could Have Helped

Let's return to our Hertz friends. As a refresher, the company forked over $32 million to Accenture to build a new website and mobile app. Three years later with nothing but frustration to show for its money, the company filed a lawsuit and its ex-partner responded in kind. Would the use of analytics have helped both parties avoid such a disastrous outcome?

No one can say with absolute certainty, but I'm betting that the answer is *yes.* Call me a Monday morning quarterback, but here are some suggestions of the very analytics-oriented questions the two parties should have been asking. I've grouped the questions into the four buckets from the previous section.

Descriptive

What percentage of total tasks are currently behind schedule? How does that break down by group, department, and responsible party (read: Accenture vs. Hertz)? Which types of tasks are most commonly behind schedule? Again, how does that break down? Which people, teams, and departments are routinely completing their work? Do the people who are currently struggling to complete their work have anything in common? Same area, manager, or organization?

Diagnostic

Why are so many tasks delayed? When are specific tasks missing their dates? Are many delayed from the start, or is there some type of bottleneck that prevents people from completing their tasks after they start them? Why is a specific person, team, or department so far behind? Why are some individuals, teams, and departments able to routinely complete their work?

Predictive

At its current rate, what are the odds that the team can complete its tasks, project phases, and the entire project? As it stands, when will the team burn through its allocated budget? If Accenture replaces junior employees with more experienced ones, what are the odds that the project will start improving? Judging by reported hours worked, which employees have too much on their plate and

13 Embrace Analytics

are apt to leave? What's the current risk that Hertz management will pull the plug on the project and potentially turn to the courts?

Prescriptive

What are the odds that the team can get the project back on track? What are the odds that adding new team members to the project will help get it back on track? Or will that gambit likely delay the project even more?* Will replacing individual Accenture or Hertz team members address the project's issues? Which ones should stay and go? What are the characteristics of their potential replacements?

Note that the specific answers to these questions aren't as important as the mindset behind asking them in the first place. In this way, the use of analytics builds upon the idea of conducting a project premortem. The biggest difference is that the training wheels are off. The project has moved from theory to practice.

Returning to Chapter 8 for a moment, viewing the state of the project isn't terribly difficult with a mainstream PM application. Figure 13.1 displays a generic dashboard that Basecamp, Asana, and troves of other tools can easily produce today without any technical skill.

AI and the Predictive Future of PM Analytics

Before concluding this chapter, allow me to geek out for a minute.

Wrike—now part of Citrix—is doing some particularly interesting things around predictive analytics and project management. The company's Work Intelligence software analyzes data from millions of projects. Specific attributes include:

- ☺ Project complexity.

---

* Hat tip here to Frederick Brooks's classic book *The Mythical Man-Month*.

- The number of completed and overdue tasks.
- Task activity.
- The task owner's previous projects.

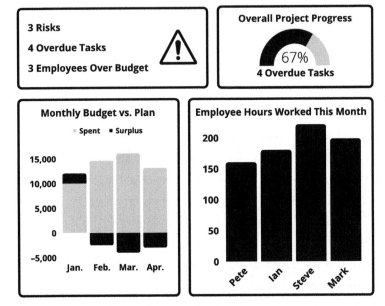

Figure 13.1: Generic Project Management Dashboard

In effect, Wrike is using its trove of anonymized customer data and its proprietary artificial intelligence to predict risks and recommend remediation actions. This invaluable information can help PMs, product owners, and other parties make better real-time decisions—and adjust individual levers as needed.[8]

Smart PM software might seem a little like a *Black Mirror* episode, but the potential consequences are profound. Consider a PM on a hybrid project. She reviews her project dashboard and doesn't view any obvious problems. What if her PM software did the following?

13 Embrace Analytics

- Advised her of a subtle, hidden risk related to a short-term task, contingency, dependency, long-term goal, or individual employee?
- Recommended steps to alleviate an issue that hasn't manifested itself yet?
- *Automatically* accounted for events such as mergers, acquisitions, and employee exits when assessing project risks?

It's not hard to envision PM software in the near future making remarkably insightful recommendations that no human being could. What if it:

- Determined the ideal days of the week that each employee on the team ought to work remotely and in the office?
- Identified the right tasks on which employees ought to be working while at home and in the office?
- Offered hiring recommendations based upon applicant backgrounds, company culture, and the specific work required on the project?

And Wrike is not the only software vendor attempting to figure this out. Asana is also leaning in to machine learning with similar aspirations.[9]

These types of AI-powered features are coming to many of today's popular PM applications. Five years from now, failing to use a dashboard to manage a proper project or launch a new product will become even less defensible.

Chapter Summary

- The advantages of MBWA may seem obvious, but the practice is pointless or even counterproductive in remote and hybrid workplaces.
- A construction company used analytics to turn around a failing project.
- Even the most sophisticated use of analytics guarantees nothing. Analytics can, however, help people make more informed project- and product-related decisions.

Chapter 14

RECONSIDER EMPLOYEE EVALUATIONS AND REWARDS

"Choose uncomfortable expansion over comfortable diminishment."
—OLIVER BURKEMAN

All the candidate vetting, employee application training, writing workshops, premortems, pilots, analytics, and technology in the world don't change one immutable fact: Managing a project or launching a new one is difficult. Pitfalls are everywhere, and remote and hybrid workplaces further complicate matters.

Any experienced PM or business professional knows that there's no universal formula or recipe for delivering a successful product or project. Techniques, technologies, and processes that work for one organization in one context may fail miserably under similar circumstances, much less dramatically different ones.

There may not be a single way to ensure the success of a new product or project, but there's a surefire way to ensure its inevitable failure: Mismanage the people working on it or treat them poorly.

For years, executives have uttered vacuous bromides such as, "People are our most valuable asset." Yawn. A Google search of the phrase reveals more than 517,000 results.[1] Given the sea changes that have taken place in the employment landscape over the past two years, it's time for business leaders to finally preach by example.

This final chapter offers some HR and general management tips. It prescribes additional steps that organizations, teams, and PMs can take to maximize the chances that their remote and hybrid projects succeed and their product launches go smoothly.

The Ugly History of Performance Management

Go ahead and review the existing research on performance management. Three things will immediately stick out. First, the corpus is expansive. As of this writing, Google Scholar lists more than 2.2 million academic studies, articles, and books on the subject.[2] Second, most of this research reflects a far simpler era—one in which the majority of employees worked in the same place at the same time.

Third, employers and managers have generally and consistently failed at performance management. Oodles of studies have found employee-performance reviews "tedious and of low value."[3] Even forced ranking—the preferred system of legendary ex-GE CEO Jack Welch—has fallen out of vogue in recent years.[4]

Samuel Culbert is a management professor at UCLA and the author of *Get Rid of the Performance Review!* As you might expect from the exclamation point in his book's title, Culbert doesn't exactly lack opinions on the subject. Speaking to NPR about performance reviews in 2014, he railed, "They're fraudulent, bogus, and dishonest. And second, they're indicative of and they support bad management."[5] (Other than that, though, they're awesome.)

Oh, and workers have long hated them, too. Prior to the pandemic, between "60 percent and 90 percent of employees, including managers, dislike[d] the performance evaluation."[6]

To be sure, some employees despise performance reviews for two obvious reasons: They have behaved inappropriately or even illegally, and they don't want to face the consequences of their actions. Perhaps their managers had previously put them on performance improvement plans. Then there are those who are about to lose their jobs for entirely legitimate causes, such as:

1. Failing to complete their tasks in a timely manner.
2. Lying to colleagues and managers.
3. Feigning illnesses.
4. Disclosing confidential information to competitors or colleagues.
5. Berating or undermining colleagues.
6. Stealing from the company.[*]
7. Incorrectly using the organization's chosen tools.
8. Refusing to use those tools outright, as the following sidebar illustrates.

A Startup Parts Ways With a New Hire

In 2015, I attended a networking event at a steampunk-inspired coworking space 20 miles from my home in Las Vegas. I struck up a conversation with Frank, an acquaintance of

---

[*] I flew to Florida in the early aughts to run payroll for a local utility that had recently fired its payroll manager. Guess why?

mine who ran a local tech startup. It didn't take long for the two of us to start talking about tech and business.

Frank told me that he had to recently let go of a new hire because she refused to use the company's tools. For example, rather than communicating with her colleagues via Slack, she repeatedly sent everyone emails. This bifurcated conversations and created multiple versions of critical internal documents.

Frank was a smart dude, but his conversations with the employee hadn't changed her behavior. If he'd tolerated this employee's intransigence and insubordination, he'd effectively be sanctioning it. The impact on employee morale and efficiency is self-evident.

Firing a recalcitrant employee is one thing, but how does a manager handle more nuanced employee relations situations in a physical office? Consider two of them:

1. Susan often misses morning meetings. She alternates between blaming traffic and some vague medical issue.
2. While hanging out at the coffee machine, Anthony tells several off-color jokes to Taylor. She promptly reports Anthony to HR. A game of he-said, she-said ensues.

Ask five different people how to handle these scenarios, and you'll probably hear five different opinions. These two situations reflect a larger question: How does any organization ensure that it's fairly assessing the performance its employees?

If answering that question proved challenging in the past, then what about the present and the future? After all, remote and hybrid workplaces are here to stay.

Performance Management in Remote and Hybrid Workplaces

Those eight previous reasons for showing someone the door are still equally valid, and I doubt that many reasonable professionals would disagree with that statement. But consider two slightly different situations involving inappropriate employee behavior:

1. Susan is routinely unavailable during the company's core work hours. Her commuting excuse goes from suspicious to laughable.
2. Anthony posts that same inappropriate joke as a meme or video in Slack or Microsoft Teams. Taylor notifies HR, and its investigation becomes much simpler. The fact that no one personally witnessed Anthony's behavior is immaterial. He did it, and the company can prove as much, although he may speciously claim that hackers seized control of his computer.

These two scenarios are less murky. Managing employee performance in remote and hybrid workplaces will finally cease to be an albatross, right?

Hardly.

In many if not most other cases, it will be trickier for managers, PMs, and product owners to know what is—or isn't—really occurring. The reason is simple: We often don't interact with our colleagues in the same place at the same time.

Sure, we take Zoom calls and share our screens—sometimes paying a steep price for doing so.[7] Employers are increasingly deploying employee surveillance software.[8] Compared to in-person workplaces, though, many of us just can't shake the feeling that we lack real visibility into what our colleagues, managers, and direct reports are doing.

To be fair, internal collaboration hubs like Slack promote transparency when used properly—certainly in a far deeper way than email ever could. What's more, today's PM applications can offer far greater clarity into projects, tasks, and teams than management by wandering around ever could.

At the very least, the logistics of remote and hybrid work muddy the waters of employee performance management. Consider these three simple yet thorny questions:

- ◎ Which employees are really pulling their weight?
- ◎ How can our bosses and peers fairly assess employee performance when they routinely work in different locations—and at different times?
- ◎ How can managers account for the fact that many employees have never met any of their colleagues? After all, our cognitive biases can run rampant.

I certainly don't know all the answers. As I type these words, however, I'm certain that hundreds of researchers are examining these very questions.

Revisiting the Limitations of Project Management Tools

For years any decent PM tool, when used correctly, has been able to identify which people are hitting or missing their goals—and much more. As powerful as monday.com, Smartsheet, Asana, Trello, and Basecamp are, however, by themselves they frequently fail to reveal vital pieces of information to PMs, managers, and other stakeholders. Ditto for the sophisticated analytics that these tools—and supplemental ones—are likely to provide.

For example, John starts his new position in June. He immediately completes his project tasks with vigor. He never misses a single deadline—and he's not exactly shy about advertising that

14 Reconsider Employee Evaluations and Rewards

fact. He's like a bull in a china shop. Whether remotely or in the office, he frequently grates on his colleagues' nerves. A few people have tried to approach him about his ways, but he's not terribly responsive to their feedback.

What to do?

The Need to Conduct Regular Employee Surveys

Before answering, consider that most organizations have historically conducted their annual performance reviews in late March or early April. The timeline coincides with department budgets and the forthcoming fiscal year. In the previous example, John's manager may not give him formal feedback until he's ten months into his tenure. During that time and despite his productivity, he will have burned quite a few bridges—some of them for good.

For decades, employee surveys have proven to be valuable ways of identifying employee and cultural issues. No, they're not perfect, but they remain "one of the best ways to measure engagement."[9] (As a reminder, the word *engaged* hasn't described the stereotypical employee for decades.)

Running surveys exclusively on an annual basis, however, runs the risk of letting tiny issues escalate—and giving rise to new ones altogether. (To quote Kevin Hart, "Small problems become big problems.") Given the ease with which employees can find new jobs today, consider the risks to the project of *inaction*. Remember: Uncertainty is a PMBOK performance domain.

Fortunately, it's never been easier to conduct fast, simple, and routine employee surveys. Consider TinyPulse. The employee engagement tool integrates with popular internal collaboration hubs such as Slack and Microsoft Teams. Rather than just reporting simple statistics like employee satisfaction by department or gender, however, it provides feedback that can help managers coach their employees and address specific areas of improvement.

Putting It All Together

If you think that survey data can significantly benefit project management and new-product launches, trust your instincts. Specifically, timely employee surveys provide valuable complementary information that even robust PM applications aren't designed to track. Think of surveys and PM apps as complements.

Taken together, these tools—and, critically, the data they produce—can provide essential insights and answer questions about the employees who:

- Fail to complete their tasks—and, quite possibly, *why*.
- Knock out their tasks but leave a great deal of collateral damage in the process.
- Butt heads with their peers.
- Require additional training or coaching.
- Need to find another gig. You'll get no argument from me on the necessity of identifying the employees on a project who aren't measuring up and removing them if need be.

Parting Words of Advice

I'll close this book by dusting off my old HR hat and offering some unsolicited advice, some of which transcends the discipline of project management.

I'm willing to bet that, at some point in your career, you felt like your employer, boss, clients, or peers have taken you for granted.

I sure have.

14 Reconsider Employee Evaluations and Rewards

Yeah, We're Gonna Need You to Come in on Saturday

In the mid-aughts, a large hospital in the northeastern United States began the arduous process of replacing its legacy enterprise system with a more contemporary one.

I'll cut to the chase: The project was a mess.[*] The hospital was well on track to complete the failure trifecta: miss its revised deadline, spend at least 50 percent more money than originally anticipated, and deliver the new system without the agreed-upon functionality.

The consultants were working brutal hours, and some couldn't fly home to visit their families on weekends. I was one of the consultants. The PM, Greg, reprimanded people for working only 11-hour days.

One Friday around noon with my luggage already packed in my car to drive home at the end of the day, Greg stopped by my office and informed me that I'd have to come in on Saturday to perform additional system testing. So much for my weekend plans, but I bit the belt and arrived promptly at 8 a.m. the next day. I didn't pull a Peter Gibbons and blow everyone off.

I certainly wasn't thrilled when I walked through the door. I should have been on the practice tee with my friends, getting ready to embarrass myself on the golf course on a beautiful May morning. Instead, I was about to sit in an office with a tie on trying to determine why employee paychecks were inaccurate. Yeah, it was about as fun as it sounds.

---

[*] If you want a much longer explanation, check out my book *Why New Systems Fail.*

> Greg wouldn't be working that Saturday morning, but he could have easily improved my morale. What if he had arranged for a free donut for me at the hotel's front desk as I checked out? That small gesture would have gone a long way toward improving my mood as I headed into the office.
>
> In the immortal words of Homer Simpson, "Mmm ... donuts. Is there anything they can't do?"

The tight labor market has caught many employers by surprise. Key employee departures have hamstrung some organizations and threatened the viability of their critical projects. In the past year, stories have abounded of employers desperately trying to retain their own employees—in some cases countering external job offers with promotions and considerable raises.[10]

Consider Spot Bonuses

The pandemic reset employee priorities around work. Millions of people traded money and prestige for increased flexibility and a better quality of life—and few show signs of reverting to their prepandemic professional situations. Autonomy, mastery, and purpose matter more than ever, to paraphrase from Dan Pink's classic book *Drive: The Surprising Truth about What Motivates Us.*

Still, money matters to workers, and it would be foolish to contend otherwise. A group of neuroscientists discovered in a 2001 study that the anticipation of monetary rewards generates a significant amount of activation in the *nucleus accumbens,* the part of the brain's emotional and motivation circuitry.[11] In the same study, participants reported that the prospect of monetary gain made them feel happier.

14 Reconsider Employee Evaluations and Rewards

The way that companies compensate their employees is starting to change. Some firms are paying employees identical salaries regardless of their locations. Others are issuing more frequent pay increases to combat rising inflation and to placate their employees.[12] The National Law Review notes "the emerging trend in state pay transparency laws."[13]

Spot bonuses have been on the rise for years. Payscale reported in 2018 that these bonuses represent the second most common form of variable pay along with employee referrals.[14] (Annual individual bonuses ranked first.) Google Trends already reflects this increase.[15] Exhibit A: High-end New York law firms are "offering two-part special bonuses as high as $64,000 to retain talent and, in some cases, raising current first years' salaries as high as $205,000."[16] Think of these rewards as prophylactics against employee attrition in a tight labor market.

Powerful forces are challenging the traditional orthodoxy around employee compensation. All of these are encouraging developments. Rigidly adhering to dated pay practices is downright risky today.

Revisit Employee Benefits

Jordan Peace is a cofounder and CEO of employee-benefits startup Fringe. In June 2021, he appeared on my podcast to discuss how employers are increasingly personalizing benefits for their workforces.[*]

Fringe allows employers to easily set up benefit stipends for their employees so the latter can select from a growing array of nontraditional benefits. Forget health and dental insurance. Employees can use their points on delivery services, exercise apps, cleaning services,

---

[*] Give it a listen at https://tinyurl.com/ps-pod-fringe.

and more.[17] Specific examples include Uber, Netflix, Amazon, Hulu, DoorDash, Airbnb, Spotify, and Instacart.

Ending on a Sanguine Note

Will a spot bonus or an innovative benefits program prevent overwhelmed employees from quitting their jobs if they hate their colleagues and company culture? Of course not. These types of programs, however, can serve as part of a larger signal to employees that their employer cares. Coupled with writing workshops, formal application training, and hybrid work, it's not hard to envision more successful projects and product launches, but there's more at stake now.

At a higher level, these trends auger well for the future of work and society. Call me an idealist, but millions of people have discovered that they don't need to let their jobs and careers define them. The Great Reset is making us not only happier, more balanced employees, but better partners, parents, sons, daughters, and citizens.

As I mentioned at the start of this book, at heart I'm an optimist.

Chapter Summary

- ☺ In-person performance management has always proven challenging. It's even harder in hybrid and remote workplaces.
- ☺ Taken together, proper PM and survey tools can help diagnose project issues and identify ways to correct them.
- ☺ Organizations are beginning to creatively reward their employees with nontraditional employee benefits and bonuses. These can improve employee morale, reduce attrition, and potentially mitigate project-related issues.

CODA: A TALE OF TWO COMPANIES

"If you want something new, you have to stop doing something old."

—PETER DRUCKER

We've reached the end of our journey. Before letting you go, however, I'd like to conduct a simple thought experiment.

You're an investor looking at two different companies that just opened their doors.

ABC and XYZ are poised to compete in the same industry: the classic economic example of widgets. The two firms start by employing the same number of people. They both routinely undertake similar projects and launch comparable products. Assume identical organizational structures, initial investor funding, and workplace types. That is, employees at both spend part of their time in a proper physical office and the rest working remotely.

That's where the similarities end.

ABC management regularly conducts project premortems and pilots. It carefully vets new partners, vendors, and employees. It holds in-person kickoff meetings and ensures that everyone involved uses the same tools. ABC invests in employee writing workshops and training—and not just with applications either. On projects, it routinely makes decisions based upon analytics. Not coincidentally, ABC employees are relatively happy. They rarely leave and generally do their jobs well.

For their part, XYZ management doesn't believe in kickoffs, premortems, pilots, and in-person kickoffs. On both internal and external projects, people use a mélange of tools. Top brass view analytics and employee training as wastes of time and money. With respect to training, employees never receive it, apart from taking a mandatory sexual-harassment test. From the beginning, XYZ employees realize that development isn't a management priority. Workers don't feel especially valued. They often bolt at the opportunity to make a little bit more. The ones who do stick around are basically C-players, and they certainly wouldn't qualify as *engaged*.

Equipped with no other information, which company is more likely to be successful?

ACKNOWLEDGMENTS

For making this book happen: Luke Fletcher, Karen Davis, Jessica Angerstein, Vinnie Kinsella, Gary Bennett, and Johnna VanHoose Dinse.

A tip of the hat to the people who keep me grounded and listen to my rants: Dalton Cervo, Rob Hornyak, Hina Arora, Daniel Teachey, Eric Johnson, Steve Putman, Emily Freeman, Chris Olsen, Steve Katz, Bruce Webster, Michael Viola, Joe Mirza, Dave Sandberg, Chris McGee, Scott Berkun, Josh Bernoff, Karin Reed, Alan Berkson, Martin Traub-Warner, Andrew Botwin, Moneet Singh, John Andrewski, Jennifer Zito, Rob Metting, Prescott Perez-Fox, Monica Meehan, Jason Horowitz, Marc Paolella, Peter and Hope Simon, Mark Cenicola, Adom Asadourian, Helen Thompson, Kevin Daly, Sarah Garcia, Jason Conigliari, JR Camillon, Larry English, Mark Pardy, Dustin Schodt, Daniel Green, Matt Wagner, Michelle Gitlitz, Brian and Heather Morgan, Laurie Feuerstein, Lowell Vande Kamp, and especially my *consigliere*, Alan Simon.

Nietzsche once said, "Without music, life would be a mistake." He wasn't wrong.

For decades of incredible music, thank you to the members of Rush (Geddy, Alex, and Neil) and Marillion (h, Steve, Ian, Mark, and Pete). Your songs continue to inspire millions of discerning fans. I'm proud to call myself one of them.

Vince Gilligan, Peter Gould, Bryan Cranston, Aaron Paul, Dean Norris, Anna Gunn, Bob Odenkirk, Betsy Brandt, Jonathan Banks, Giancarlo Esposito, RJ Mitte, Michael Mando, Rhea Seehorn, Michael

McKean, Patrick Fabian, Tony Dalton, and the rest of the *Breaking Bad* and *Better Call Saul* teams have inspired me to do great work.

For making me laugh: Gary Gulman, Nick Griffin, and Taylor Tomlinson.

Finally, to my family: Thank you.

Phil Simon
June 14, 2022
Gilbert, Arizona

BIBLIOGRAPHY

Barrero, Jose Maria, Nicholas Bloom, and Steven J. Davis, 2021. "Why Working from Home Will Stick." National Bureau of Economic Research Working Paper 28731.

Benschop, Nick, Nuijten Arno, Cokky Hilhorst, and Mark Keil. "Undesirable Framing Effects in Information Systems Projects: Analysis of Adjective Usage in IS Project Business Cases." *Information and Management* 59, no. 3 (April 2022).

Berkun, Scott. *Making Things Happen: Mastering Project Management.* Sebastopol, CA: O'Reilly Media, 2008.

Berkun, Scott. *The Year Without Pants: WordPress.Com and the Future of Work.* Nashville, TN: John Wiley & Sons, 2013.

Bernoff, Josh. *Writing Without Bullshit: Boost Your Career by Saying What You Mean.* New York: HarperBusiness, 2016.

Bilton, Nick. *Hatching Twitter: A True Story of Money, Power, Friendship, and Betrayal.* London: Sceptre. 2014.

Brooks, Frederick. *The Mythical Man-Month: Essays on Software Engineering, Anniversary Edition* (2nd Ed.). Addison Wesley, 1995.

Bryar, Colin, and Bill Carr. *Working Backwards: Insights, Stories, and Secrets From Inside Amazon.* London: Macmillan, 2021.

Burlingham, Bo. *Small Giants: Companies That Choose to Be Great Instead of Big.* New York: Portfolio, 2007.

Cappelli, Peter. *The Future of the Office: Work from Home, Remote Work, and the Hard Choices We All Face.* Philadelphia: Wharton Digital Press, 2021.

Carlson, J. R., and R. W. Zmud. "Channel Expansion Theory and the Experiential Nature of Media Richness Perceptions." *Academy of Management Journal* 42, no. 2, (1999): 153–170.

Casnocha, Ben, and Reid Hoffman. *The Start-Up of You: Adapt to the Future, Invest in Yourself, and Transform Your Career.* London: Random House Business Books, 2013.

Cialdini, Robert B. *Influence: The Psychology of Persuasion.* New York: HarperBusiness, 2006.

Covey, Stephen R. *The 7 Habits of Highly Effective People: Powerful Lessons in Personal Change* (15th ed.) New York: Free Press, 2004.

Crow, Michael M., and William B. Dabars. *The Fifth Wave: The Evolution of American Higher Education.* Baltimore: Johns Hopkins University Press, 2020.

Csikszentmihalyi, Mihaly. *Flow: The Psychology of Optimal Experience.* New York: Harper Perennial, 2008.

Daft, Richard L., and Robert H. Lengel. "Organizational Information Requirements, Media Richness and Structural Design." *Management Science* 32, no. 5 (1986): 554–571. https://doi.org/10.1287/mnsc.32.5.554.

English, Larry. *Office Optional: How to Build a Connected Culture with Virtual Teams.* Centric Consulting, 2020.

Fuller, Mark, Joseph Valacich, and Joey George. *Information Systems Project Management: A Process and Team Approach.* Upper Saddle River, NJ: Pearson, 2007.

Glass, Robert L. *Facts and Fallacies of Software Engineering.* Boston: Addison-Wesley Educational, 2002.

Goldratt, Eliyahu. *The Goal: A Process of Ongoing Improvement.* Highbridge Company, 2006.

Gratton, Lynda. *Redesigning Work: How to Transform Your Organization and Make Hybrid Work for Everyone.* London: MIT Press, 2022.

Griffith, Terri L. *The Plugged-In Manager: Get in Tune with Your People, Technology, and Organization to Thrive.* Chichester, England: Jossey Bass Wiley, 2011.

Hsieh, Tony. *Delivering Happiness: A Path to Profits, Passion and Purpose.* London: Grand Central Publishing, 2013.

Kahneman, Daniel. *Thinking, Fast and Slow.* Harlow, England: Penguin Books, 2012.

14 Bibliography

Keating, Gina. *Netflixed: The Epic Battle for America's Eyeballs.* New York: Portfolio, 2013.

Kerzner, Harold R. *Project Management: A Systems Approach to Planning, Scheduling and Controlling: Workbook* (5th ed.) Nashville, TN: John Wiley & Sons, 1995.

Kim, Gene. *The Phoenix Project: A Novel About It, Devops, and Helping Your Business Win* (5th ed.) Portland, OR: IT Revolution Press, 2018.

Lewis, Michael. *Moneyball: The Art of Winning an Unfair Game.* Thorndike Press, 2003.

McLuhan, Marshall. *Understanding Media: The Extensions of Man.* London: MIT Press, 1994.

Mims, Christopher. *Arriving Today: From Factory to Front Door—Why Everything Has Changed about How and What We Buy.* New York: HarperBusiness, 2021.

Newport, Cal. *Deep Work: Rules for Focused Success in a Distracted World.* London: Piatkus Books, 2016.

Newport, Cal. *A World without Email: Reimagining Work in an Age of Communication Overload.* New York: Portfolio, 2021.

Norman, Donald A. *The Design of Everyday Things.* New York: Bantam Doubleday Dell Publishing Group, 1990.

Northcote Parkinson, C. *Parkinson's Law.* Houghton Mifflin, 1957.

Payscale, "Refocusing Compensation's Role in the Great Reevaluation 2022 Compensation Best Practices Report." Retrieved March 19, 2022. https://tinyurl.com/yazdbb8f.

Peters, Tom, and Robert Waterman. *In Search of Excellence: Lessons from America's Best-Run Companies.* HarperCollins, 1995.

Pink, Daniel H. *Drive: The Surprising Truth about What Motivates Us.* New York: Riverhead Books, 2011.

Project Management Institute. *A Guide to the Project Management Body of Knowledge (PMBOK Guide)—Seventh Edition and The Standard for Project Management.* Project Management Institute, 2021.

Putnam, Robert. *Bowling Alone: The Collapse and Revival of American Community.* London: Simon & Schuster, 2001.

Reed, Karin M., and Joseph A. Allen. *Suddenly Hybrid: Managing the Modern Meeting.* Nashville, TN: John Wiley & Sons, 2022.

Ries, Eric. *The Lean Startup: How Today's Entrepreneurs Use Continuous Innovation to Create Radically Successful Businesses.* New York: Crown Publishing Group, 2011.

Rico, David F., Hasan H. Sayani, and Saya Sone. *The Business Value of Agile Software Methods.* Boca Raton, FL: J Ross Publishing, 2009.

Roberts, Simon. *The Power of Not Thinking: How Our Bodies Learn and Why We Should Trust Them.* Chichester, England: BLINK Publishing, 2020.

Rosenzweig, Philip. *The Halo Effect: ... And the Eight Other Business Delusions That Deceive Managers.* Scribner, 2009.

Seidman, Dov. *How: Why How We Do Anything Means Everything.* Nashville, TN: John Wiley & Sons, 2011.

Simon, Phil. *Reimagining Collaboration: Slack, Microsoft Teams, Zoom, and the Post-COVID World of Work.* Motion Publishing, 2021.

Sims, Chris, and Hillary Louise Johnson. *The Elements of Scrum.* Dymaxicon, 2011.

Singh, Harjit. *Project Management Analytics: A Data-Driven Approach to Making Rational and Effective Project Decisions.* Upper Saddle River: Pearson FT Press, 2015.

Tetlock, Philip, and Dan Gardner. *Superforecasting: The Art and Science of Prediction.* London: Random House Books, 2016.

West, Michael. *People Analytics For Dummies.* John Wiley & Sons, 2019.

Wiedeman, Reeves. *Billion Dollar Loser: The Epic Rise and Spectacular Fall of Adam Neumann and WeWork.* Back Bay Books, 2021.

ABOUT THE AUTHOR

Phil Simon is a dynamic keynote speaker and world-renowned collaboration and technology authority. He is the award-winning author of eleven previous business books, most recently *Reimagining Collaboration: Slack, Microsoft Teams, Zoom, and the Post-COVID World of Work*. He helps organizations communicate, collaborate, and use technology better. *Harvard Business Review, MIT Sloan Management Review, Wired,* NBC, CNBC, *Bloomberg BusinessWeek,* and the *New York Times* have featured his contributions. He also hosts the podcast *Conversations About Collaboration*.

INDEX

A

A World Without Email: Reimagining Work in an Age of Communication Overload (Newport), 241–245

Accenture, Hertz and, 220–222
   alternative scenario, 223–225

Adobe Creative Suite, 181

Adobe XD (Experience Designer), 199

Agile methodologies, 106–109

Agilefall, 109

AI (artificial intelligence), analytics and, 279–281

Airtable, 180

Amazon
   clear communication and, 252–255
   labor unions, 26

analytics
   AI (artificial intelligence) and, 279–281
   case study, 275–276
   descriptive, 274, 278
   diagnostic, 274, 278
   Hertz and, 277–279
   predictive, 274, 278–279
   prescriptive, 274, 279
   product management, 274–277
   project management, 274–277
   reach, 273–274

Anatomy of Work Index 2021, 184–186

Apple, SCM (supply chain management) and, 70–71

applications. *See also* tech
   Adobe Creative Suite, 181
   Airtable, 180
   Asana, 180–181, 189
   Basecamp, 180
   Coda, 180
   employee proximity and, 246–247
   Figma, 181
   GitHub, 181
   Google Sheets, 181
   Microsoft Excel, 181
   Microsoft Project, 180
   NHL (National Hockey League) custom apps, 188
   Notion, 180
   number of apps affect, 185
   Numbers, 181
   project size/complexity and, 190
   Smartsheet, 180
   training
      components of good program, 238
      EDMC example, 235–237
      IT and, 235–237
      need, 234–241, 245
      time requirements, 239–240
   Trello, 180
   Workday, 181
   Wrike, 180
   Zendesk, 181

Arrested Development, ii

Asadourian, Adom, 131

Asana, 180–181, 189
   Gantt chart, 105–106

asynchronous work, 133–134
Automattic, 41
   asynchronous work, 133–134
   contract work, 148–149
   in-person meetings, 176

B
Bardzell, Tom, 130
Bart Simpson, 232
Basecamp, 41, 180, 189
Bayes' theorem, 210
Bernoff, Josh, 262–263
Bhajan, Yogi, 67
Bloom, Nicholas, 42–44
Bowling Alone: The Collapse and Revival of American Community (Putnam), 45
brainwriting, 265–266
Breaking Bad, 14, 218
Brittany Runs a Marathon, 222
Bryar, Colin, 252–254
Build-Measure-Learn loop, 110
bullwhip effect, SCM (supply chain management), 69
Burkeman, Oliver, 283
Burnett, Carol, 249
business communications, 250
   Amazon and, 252–255
   brainwriting, 265–266
   email *versus* collaboration tools, 258–261
   emojis, 264–265
   font choices, 254, 255
   formal, 264–265
   improving employee writing, 261–264
   jargon, 264–265
   lucid writing, 258
   proximity and, 255–258
   writing workshops, 261–264
business process, 94

business writing, publication numbers, 249

C
careers, tour-of duty approach, 61–63
Carlin, George, 208
Carr, Bill, 252–254
channel expansion theory, 127–128
chief product officer, 12
Chomsky, Noam, on, corporatization of American universities, 29
Citrix, 180
Cleveland Cavaliers coach firing, 232–233
Coda, 180
coding interviews, 148
cognitive bias, honeymoon effect and, 125
collaboration
   hub-spoke model, 16
   media richness theory, 126–127
   overload, 137–138
   physical space for, 175–176
   PM (Project Management) and, 95
Collaboration in the Gig Economy conference, 185
colleagues, in same space, 6–7
communication, 128
   delays, 129–132
   media richness theory, 126–127
compensation
   compensating wage differential, 57–58
   conversation after giving notice, 61
   employee benefits, 293–294
   inflation and, 58–59
confirmation bias, 124

contract work before full-time
position, 148–149
Cook, Tim, 70–71
core work hours, vetting partners in
work, 153–155
COVID-19 pandemic
distributed companies, 41
productivity in work from home,
32–33
returning to work, 41–42
trends affected, 5
vaccine mandates, 36
work legacy, 36
Cross, Rob, 137–138
Crow, Michael, 251
Culbert, Samuel, 284–285
customer relations reps, 10–11

D

Dabars, William, 251
David, Larry, 109
deep work, 272
Deming, W. Edwards, 269
DeNiro, Robert, 14
descriptive analytics, 274, 278
diagnostic analytics, 274, 278
digital literacy, screening potential
partners, 152–153
digital products, SCM (supply chain
management) and, 77–79
Dion, Celine, 9
distributed companies, COVID-19
pandemic, 41
Dolfing, Henrico, 221–222
"Don't be evil" (Google), 17–18
Drucker, Peter, 295
Dunlap, Al, 26

E

easy answers, 231–233
ecommerce, pandemic effects on, 5

EDMC (Education Management
Corporation), 235–237
education, pandemic effects on, 5
efficiency *versus* resilience, 72
Elliott, Brian, 244
email *versus* collaboration tools,
258–261
emojis in business writing, 264–265
empiricism, 271
employee benefits, 293–294
employee engagement, 27–29
employee stigmas, 60–61
employee surveillance software, 287
employee surveys, 289–290
employer benefits, 23–25
employment prospects
contract work before full-time,
148–149
geography and, 59–60
engagement on the job, 27–29
enterprise tech, 180–187
decentralization from IT, 181–
182
employee response, 183–186

F

face-to-face interactions, social
capital building and, 173–177
"Fast, cheap, and good," 103
Fewell, Jesse, 98
*The Fifth Wave: The Evolution of
American Higher Education*, 251
Figma, 181
firings, 139–140
fitness programs, pandemic effects
on, 5
FMLA (Family and Medical Leave
Act), 23–24
formal writing, 264–265
Friedman, Milton, 119
Fringe, 293–294

G

Gandhi, Mahatma, 65
Gantt charts, 105–106
Gardner, Howard, 231
Gilligan's Island pilot, 218
GitHub, 181
GitLab, 41, 257–258
Glass, Robert, 205
Goldratt, Eliyahu
    The Goal: A Process of Ongoing Improvement, 102
    Theory of Constraints, 102
Google, 229
    "Don't be evil," 17–18
    "Ruthless" Ruth Porat, 101
Google Sheets, 181
Great Reset, 30
Great Resignation, 30

H

halo effect at work, 122–123
Hamm, John, 23
Hanlon's Razor, 244
HCM (human capital management), 65, 80
    academia example, 81–88
    balanced approach, 81
    efficiency, 88
head of product, 11
healthcare, pandemic effects on, 5
Hertz, 220–222
    alternate scenario, 223–225
    analytics and, 277–279
    expectations and, 226–228
Hogarth, Steve, 179
Homer Simpson, 68, 292
Homestead Strike, Carnegie Steel, 25
honeymoon effect, 124–125
Hsieh, Tony, 111

hub-spoke model of collaboration, 16
hybrid work
    asymmetries of, 49–50
    difficulties, 63–64
    performance management, 287–288
    proximity bias, 49–52
    social capital and, 45–51

I

In Search of Excellence: Lessons from America's Best-Run Companies (Peters & Waterman), 269–270
in-app notifications, 242–243
income, compensating wage differential, 57–58
individual contributors, 13
inflation, wages and, 58–59
information systems, SCM (supply chain management) and, 67
interruptions, 241–242
interviews, coding interviews, 148
IT
    application training and, 235–237
    IT-business divide, 104

J

Jackson, Samuel L., 217
jargon in business writing, 264–265
JIC (just-in-case), 71
    golf analogy, 74
JIT (just-in-time), 71
    golf analogy, 74
job changes
    job-hopper stigma, 60
    long-timers, 61
job satisfaction. *See* employee engagement
Judge, Mike, *Office Space,* 120

Index 309

K
Kahneman, Daniel, 208
Kanban, 73
Kerzner, Harold, 100

L
labor legislation, 24
labor markets, 55–58
labor unions, 25–27
Lake Wobegon effect, 209
Langer, Ellen, 47
layoffs, 138
lean manufacturing, 69–72
efficiency *versus* resilience, 72
JIC (just-in-case), 71
JIT (just-in-time), 71
Toyota, 73
WIP (work-in-progress), 72
Lean methods, 110–112
Leonard, Amy, 174–175
logistics
partners in work, vetting, 155–156
SCM (supply chain management) and, 66
long-timers at jobs, 61

M
Mad Men, 14, 23, 53, 202, 218
Malkovich, John, 171
Marillion, 96, 179
Mathrani, Sandeep, 39
MBWA (management by wandering around), 269–273
McLuhan, Marshall, 157
media richness theory, 126–127
meeting days, 154–155
Microsoft Excel, 181
Microsoft product morgue, 229
Microsoft Project, 180
Microsoft Teams, 134–135, 193–194

Mims, Christopher, 66
Miranda Priestly *(The Devil Wears Prada),* 56
Moneyball, 271, 273
Mullenweg, Matt, 255–256
multiple organizations, 134–135
Murph, Darren, 41, 257–258
Musk, Elon, 39–40

N
negative interactions
medium choice, 172
relationship lack and, 169–170
Netflix, pilots and, 218–220
Newport, Cal, 241–245
NHL (National Hockey League)
custom apps, 188
no-meeting days, 139
Norman, Don, 186
Notion, 180
Numbers, 181
Nurse Jackie example, 80–81

O
Office Space, 120, 128
offshoring, time zone issues and, 153–154
Okta, 183–184
online dating, 225–226

P
paid leave, 23–25
paradox of technology, 186–187
Parkinson, C. Northcote, 103
Parkinson's Law, 103
partners in work
Simon's Law of Tool Overlap, 194–197
tech and, 194–202
vetting, 145–147
core work hours, 153–155

digital literacy screening, 152–153
location, 155–156
preferred tools, 150–152
Peace, Jordan, 293–294
Pearl Lemon, 151
Peart, Neil, 1
performance management, 284–286
employee surveys, 289–290
hybrid workplaces, 287–288
remote workers, 287–288
spot bonuses, 292–293
Peters, Tom, 269–270
Phase-Gate process, 105–106
physical office
benefits, 53
colleagues in same space, 6–7
elimination, 51–52
future of, 53–55
returning after pandemic, 41–42
work/location pendulum, 56
pilot. *See also* project pilot
definition, 217
Playfair Data, 174–175
PM (Project Management)
Agile methodologies, 106–109
analytics, 274–277
business communications and, 250
collaboration and, 95
dashboard, analytics and, 280
definition, 94, 96
difficulty, poll results, 116
lean methods, 110–112
number of published works, 2–3
Phase-Gate process, 105–106
project charter, 114
RACI matrix, 114–115
remote workers and, 51
SOW (statement of work), 112–113

students, 14
success rates, 115–117
Systems Development Life Cycle, 105–106
tools (*See* tech)
Waterfall method, 105–106
PMBOK (Project Management Body of Knowledge)
business communications and, 250
hypothetical issues, 99
knowledge areas (v6), 97–98
premortems and, 210
project performance domains (v7), 98–100
Delivery, 99
Life Cycle, 99
Measurement, 99
Planning, 99
Project Work, 99
Stakeholder, 99
Team, 99
Uncertainty, 99
PMI (Project Management Institute)
business process term use, 94–96
IT-business divide, 104
PM (Project Management), definition, 94
project performance domains, 98–99
Talent Triangle, 115–116
PMOs (project management office), 103
PMP (Project Management Professionals)
certification, 2–3
of the past, 3–4
postmortems, 207
predictive analytics, 274, 278–279
Wrike and, 279–280

premortems, 206–207
  as litmus test, 214–215
  persuading others, 213
  PMBOK and, 210
  project size and, 214
  reasons for, 208–212
prescriptive analytics, 274, 279
prestige television, 219
product management, analytics,
  274–277
product manager, 12
product peeps, 11–12
productivity
  during early COVID, 32–33
  interruptions and, 241–242
project categories, 96
project charter, 114
project failure, premortems, 206–
  207
project management. *See* PM
  (Project Management)
*Project Management: A Systems
  Approach to Planning,
  Scheduling, and Controlling*
  (Kerzner), 100
Project Management Analytics
  (Singh), 275–277
project performance domains, PMI,
  98–99
project pilots
  factors, 228
  Hertz and, 220–222
    alternate scenario, 223–225
  Netflix and, 218–220
  RACI matrix, 229
  as test run, 223
project remediation, 205–206
proximity, 271
  applications and, 246–247
  clarity of writing clarity, 255–258
  project/product complexity and,

173–177
proximity bias, 49–52
Pulp Fiction, 217
Putnam, Robert, 45

Q
Quibi, 229

R
RACI matrix, 114–115
  project pilot, 229
recruiting, 147–148
  coding interviews, 148
Reimagining Collaboration (Simon),
  7
relationships
  medium choice, 172
  negative/positive interactions,
    169–170
remote natives, social capital and,
  159–160
remote work, 41–44. *See also* WFH
  (work-from-home)
  increase in companies offering,
    45
  inequities with in-person
    workers, 50–51
  job prospects and, 59–60
  performance management,
    287–288
  PMs problems with, 51
Rudd, Paul, 93
Rush, 1

S
SAFe (Scaled Agile Framework
  efforts), 109
salary. *See* compensation
Salesforce, Trailblazer Ranch,
  175–176
Schorr, Jason Alvarez, 41–42

SCM (supply chain management), 65. *See also* HCM (human capital management)
  Apple and, 70–71
  bullwhip effect, 69
  car orders, 76
  digital products and services, 77–79
  efficiency *versus* resilience, 72
  future of, 74–75
  information systems and, 67
  lean manufacturing and, 69–72
  logistics, 66
  physical books, 76–77
  The Simpsons example, 68–69
  stocking options, 70–71
  substitute goods, 75, 77
second shift, 139
Seinfeld, Jerry, 101, i
self-employment, Great Resignation and, 30
service providers, 12
  hirers of, 13
shelfware, 184
SHRM (Society for Human Resource Management), 24
  report on remote work/workers, 272
Singh, Harjit, 275–277
The Simpsons, 232
  example of SCM (supply chain management), 68–69
six-pagers, Amazon, 252–254
Slack, 163–164, 193–194
  digital headquarters, 244
  as distraction, 241–242
  Email 2.0 attitude, 243–244
  notifications, 242–243
slamming others
  medium, 172
  relationships and, 169–170

Smartsheet, 180, 189
social capital, 45–51
  building
    face-to-face interactions, 173–177
    proximity and project/ product complexity, 173
  influence on interactions, 169–170
  remote natives and, 159–160
  stranger, interactions with, 47–48
  unconscious cognition and, 123
  WFH and, 122–123
    case study, 160–169
    deterioration, 158–159
    future of, 159
SOW (statement of work), 112–113, 201
Spaulding, Dan, 57
Spears, Britney, 9
sport coach firings, 231–234
spot bonuses, 292–293
sprints, 107–108
Story Matters Here, 14–15
strangers, interactions with, 47–48
Streisand, Barbra, 79
substitute goods, SCM (supply chain management) and, 75, 77
Succession, 160
Sun Tzu, 217
Swinmurn, Nick, 111
Systems Development Life Cycle, 105–106

T
Talent Triangle (PMI), 115–116
Tarantino, Quentin, 217–218
tech. *See also* applications
  dissenters, 191–192

employee response, 184–186
resistance, 183
enterprise tech, 180–187
increased use in workplace, 184–186
paradox of technology, 186–187
PM tools, 187–192
limitations, 288–289
TinyPulse, 289–290
potential partners and, 194–202
shelfware, 184
Simon's Law of Tool Overlap, 194–197
varied users, 192–193
test runs. *See* project pilots
Theory of Constraints, 102
time zone issues, offshoring and, 153–154
TinyPulse, 289–290
tools
limitations, 288–289
partners in work, vetting, 150–152
Pearl Lemon, 151
TinyPulse, 289–290
tour-of duty approach to careers, 61–63
Toyota, lean manufacturing and, 73
Trailblazer Ranch (Salesforce), 175–176
training for applications
components of good program, 238
EDMC example, 235–237
IT and, 235–237
need, 234–241, 245
time requirements, 239–240
Travolta, John, 217
Trebek, Alex, 23
Trello, 163–164, 180
triple-peak day (Microsoft), 139

Tuckman, Bruce, 228
Twitter, VP of Product, 12

U
UberX, 1–2
unconscious cognition, 123
universities
as corporations, 29
HCM (human capital management) and, 81–88
UOL (Universo Online), 54
Upwork, 31
user stories, 107

V
VP of Product (Twitter), 12

W
wages. *See* compensation
Wagile, 109
Waterfall method, 105–107
Waterman, Robert, 269–270
Waystar Royco case study, 160–169
Webster, Bruce F., 211–212
WFH (work-from-home). *See also* remote work
employee preferences, 42–43
productivity during early COVID, 32–33
reasons for, 35–36
second-order effects, 119
channel expansion theory, 127–128
communication, delays and, 129–132
confirmation bias, 124
halo effect, 122–123
honeymoon effect, 124–125
media richness theory, 126–127

work preferences, 121–122
   trust, social capital and, 163–165
   willingness to return to office, 34
   work/life balance, 36
WFH Research, 42–43
Winchell, Walter, 145
WIP (work-in-progress), lean
   manufacturing and, 72, 133
   Toyota and, 73
work hours. *See also* core work
   hours
work legacy of COVID-19, 36
Workday, 181
*Working Backwards: Insights, Stories,
   and Secrets from Inside Amazon*
   (Bryar & Carr), 252
work/life balance, WFH (work-
   from-home) and, 36
work/location pendulum, 56
workplace
   pandemic effects on, 5
   physical office, elimination,
      51–52
   unknowns about colleagues, 7–8
   WFH during COVID, 32–34
   willingness to return, 34
workspace
   colleagues in same space, 6–7
   geography and, 59
Wrike, 180
   predictive analytics and, 279–280
writing skills
   brainwriting, 265–266
   clarity, proximity and, 255–258
   examples, 250–251
   hygiene factor, 258
   improving, 261–264
   lucid writing, 258
Writing Without Bullshit (Bernoff),
   262–263
writing workshops, 261–264

Z
Zappos, 111
Zendesk, 181
Zillow, compensating wage
   differential and, 57–58
Zoom, 136–137

ENDNOTES

Introduction

1. CFA Exam Results and Pass Rates, https://tinyurl.com/z-cfa-RPM.

2. Amazon.com, accessed March 10, 2022, https://tinyurl.com/amzn-30k.

3. Eric Wicklund, "AMA Survey Charts Explosive Growth of Telehealth Services in 2020," healthintelligence.com, accessed March 24, 2022, https://tinyurl.com/yh4t42bf.

4. International Trade Administration, "Impact of COVID Pandemic on ECommerce," trade.gov, accessed March 24, 2022, https://tinyurl.com/yawn4je8.

5. Hamza Shaban, "The Pandemic's Home-Workout Revolution May Be Here to Stay," January 7, 2021, https://tinyurl.com/y7pgrc8f.

6. Doug Lederman, "New Data Offer Sense of How COVID Expanded Online Learning," insidehighered.com, September 16, 2021, https://tinyurl.com/y9kxddtq.

7. Tom Bateman, "Belgium Approves Four-Day Week and Gives Employees the Right to Ignore Their Bosses After Work," February 2, 2022, https://tinyurl.com/RPM-ignore.

8. US Bureau of Labor Statistics, Occupational Employment and Wage Statistics, May 2020, https://tinyurl.com/yb4jltld.

9. Noam Scheiber, "Plugging Into the Gig Economy, From Home With a Headset," November 17, 2017, https://tinyurl.com/y7xorqb8.

10. Penny Reynolds, "Exploring Call Center Turnover Numbers," June 30, 2015, https://tinyurl.com/y9x4yucu.

11. "Project Management Job Growth and Talent Gap 2017–2027," pmi.org, accessed March 27, 2022, https://tinyurl.com/y7dxqm46.

12. Daisuke Wakabayashi and Katie Benner, "How Google Protected Andy Rubin, the 'Father of Android,'" October 25, 2018, https://tinyurl.com/yce7of9a.

13. Kate Conger, "Google Removes 'Don't Be Evil' Clause From Its Code of Conduct," May 18, 2018, https://tinyurl.com/y2qg45x4.

Chapter 1

1. Society for Human Resource Management, "New SHRM Research Shows Employers Offering Paid Leave Has Increased," September 15, 2020, https://tinyurl.com/y77xbcvz.

2. Jamie Ballard, "Seven in Ten Americans Say Both Mothers and Fathers Should Get Paid Parental Leave, April 15, 2021, https://tinyurl.com/ybxfozqo.

3. Barbara A. Butrica et al. "The Disappearing Defined Benefit Pension and Its Potential Impact on the Retirement Incomes of Baby Boomers," *Social Security Bulletin* 69, no. 3 (2009), https://tinyurl.com/yy2zv2pq.

4. CNN Money, "Ultimate Guide to Retirement," accessed February 23, 2022, https://tinyurl.com/y2uxyxyf.

5. US Bureau of Labor Statistics, "News Release," January 20, 2022, https://tinyurl.com/jeprcmx.

6. Noam Scheiber, "Canada Goose Workers Vote to Unionize in Winnipeg," December 1, 2021, https://tinyurl.com/y6g7c5rh.

7. Anna Kramer, "Amazon Workers in Staten Island Are Voting on a Union Today," Protocol, March 25, 2022, https://tinyurl.com/ybden7aw.

8. David Streitfeld, "How Amazon Crushes Unions," March 16, 2021, https://tinyurl.com/yey5ph2k.

9. John Ydstie, "On Jobs, U.S. Ranks Worse Than Similar Nations," September 4, 2010, https://tinyurl.com/yb6u26bk.

10. Jim Harter, "Employee Engagement on the Rise in the U.S.," August 26, 2018, https://tinyurl.com/y2ed8td2.

11. Georgi Gyton, "Just One in 10 Brits Feel Engaged at Work, Says Gallup," October 18, 2017, https://tinyurl.com/y7jtshyh.

12. Emma Goldberg, "You Quit. I Quit. We All Quit. And It's Not a Coincidence," *New York Times,* January 21, 2022, https://tinyurl.com/y74cd7sv.

13. Eli Rosenberg, "A Record 4.4 Million Americans Quit Their Jobs in September as Labor Market Tumult Continued," November 12, 2021, https://tinyurl.com/yelebu79.

14. Elise Gould, Economic Policy Institute, October 12, 2021, https://tinyurl.com/yaeh84v2.

15. Rani Molla, "Why More Americans Than Ever Are Starting Their Own Businesses," January 26, 2022, https://tinyurl.com/y75cxjyq.

16. Dr. Adam Ozimek, "Freelance Forward Economist Report," 2021, https://tinyurl.com/yckm3u7x.

17. Edward Ongweso Jr, "How Fast Food Workers Are Finally Getting $15 an Hour," May 10, 2021, https://tinyurl.com/yfyum26w.

18. Sean Bryant, "How Many Startups Fail and Why?," November 9, 2020, https://tinyurl.com/ycquzmqq.

19. Valerie Bolden-Barrett, "Nearly 3 Out of 4 Workers Would Leave Their Current Job for One Offering Remote Work," Sept. 20, 2017, https://tinyurl.com/ya2qcy2y.

20. Kim Parker et al. "COVID-19 Pandemic Continues to Reshape Work in America," February 16, 2022, https://tinyurl.com/yafm5oaw.

21. Kathy Frankovic, "Americans Tend to Support Biden's Vaccine Mandates for Health-Care Workers and Large Companies," January 7, 2022, https://tinyurl.com/yagtbxqq.

22. Reuters, "Latvia Bans Unvaccinated Lawmakers from Voting, Docks Pay," November 12, 2001, https://tinyurl.com/yz9gona6.

Chapter 2

1. Elon Musk, "Tesla is restarting production today against Alameda County rules. I will be on the line with everyone else...," Twitter, May 11, 2020, https://tinyurl.com/rpm-musk2.

2. Allana Akhtar, "WeWork's CEO Said People Who Are Most Comfortable Working from Home Are the 'Least Engaged' with Their Job," May 12, 2021, https://tinyurl.com/yj9wc2cm.

3. Aarian Marshall, "Elon Musk Defies Lockdown Orders and Reopens Tesla's Factory," May 11, 2020, https://tinyurl.com/y77zztfo.

4. Darren Murph, personal conversation with author, February 27, 2022.

14 Endnotes

5. Callum Borchers, "Sorry, Bosses: Workers Are Just Not That Into You," February 24, 2022, https://tinyurl.com/y7dh9wlj.

6. Derek Thompson, "The Five-Day Workweek Is Dying," February 23, 2022, https://tinyurl.com/y8njmh4p.

7. Christopher Mims, "How the Pandemic Broke Silicon Valley's Stranglehold on Tech Jobs," March 12, 2022, https://tinyurl.com/yb5rpnsv.

8. George Anders, "Employers Catch On: Remote Job Posts Rise 357% as Tech, Media Lead the Way," May 26, 2021, https://tinyurl.com/yhepleep.

9. Chenda Ngak, "Then and Now: A History of Social Networking Sites," CBS News, July 6, 2011, https://tinyurl.com/ybqnoh3e.

10. Pew Research Center, "In a Politically Polarized Era, Sharp Divides in Both Partisan Coalitions," December 17, 2019, https://tinyurl.com/y5gjrm6f.

11. M. Mahdi Roghanizad and Vanessa K. Bohns, "Ask in Person: You're Less Persuasive Than You Think over Email," *Journal of Experimental Social Psychology* 69 (2017): 223–226, https://doi.org/10.1016/j.jesp.2016.10.002.

12. Charter Newsletter, "Physical Proximity and the Future of Work," February 21, 2021.

13. Future Forum, "Pulse Survey," January 25, 2022, https://futureforum.com/pulse-survey.

14. Singh Ankita, "Project Management Features Report: Is 2019 the Year to Replace Your Current Solution?," April 17, 2019, https://tinyurl.com/y7zmx86p.

15. Jennifer Liu, "PwC Announces Nearly 40,000 U.S. Employees Can Work Remote from Anywhere in the Country," October 1, 2021, https://tinyurl.com/ygss77gc.

16. Caitlin Mullen, "Office Changes in 2021: Smaller Headquarters, More Satellite Locations Could Replace Large Offices," January 13, 2021, https://tinyurl.com/ych55wzl.

17. Melissa Kravitz Hoeffner, "Co-Working Spaces Are Back. And There Are Many, Many Options.," July 15, 2021, https://tinyurl.com/ye6fop62.

18. Nitin Nohria, "The Post-Pandemic Office Should Be a Clubhouse," January 6, 2022, https://tinyurl.com/y7pqxz9y.

19. Chip Cutter, "The Death of the Office Desk Is Upon Us," January 13, 2021, https://tinyurl.com/ydfntcus.

20. Kellen Browning, "Big Tech Makes a Big Bet: Offices Are Still the Future," February 22, 2022, https://tinyurl.com/ycta9her.

21. Sara Sneath, "Offshore Oil and Gas Worker Fatalities Are Underreported by Federal Safety Agency," Southerly, August 18, 2021, https://tinyurl.com/y8jqcjpy.

22. Dan Spaulding, "Why Zillow Group Is De-Emphasizing Location as a Component of Compensation, Making It Easier for Employees to Move," September 15, 2021, https://tinyurl.com/y7o2uvdb.

23. Rani Molla, "Nice Raise. Too Bad About Inflation.," February 16, 2022, https://tinyurl.com/yddggfzr.

24. Drew Desilver, "For Most U.S. Workers, Real Wages Have Barely Budged in Decades," August 7, 2018, https://tinyurl.com/y2ok8x9z.

25. Bureau of Labor Statistics, "Number of Jobs, Labor Market Experience, Marital Status, and Health: Results from a National Longitudinal Survey," August 31, 2021, https://tinyurl.com/y5xzrjxb.

318   Project Management in the Hybrid Workplace

26. Charlie Wells, Claire Ballentine, and Paulina Cachero, "Pay Me More or I Quit: Workers Play Risky Game with Their Bosses," February 4, 2022, https://tinyurl.com/ybq375dl.

27. Reid Hoffman, Ben Casnocha, and Chris Yeh, "Tours of Duty: The New Employer-Employee Compact," June 2013, https://tinyurl.com/nh8bm8t.

Chapter 3

1. Matthew Boyle, "Forget Finance. Supply Chain Management Is the Pandemic Era's Must-Have MBA Degree," September 3, 2021, https://tinyurl.com/yd4fs5xl.

2. Dan Mihalascu, "Tesla Now Has More Than 1.25 Million Pre-Orders for the Cybertruck," August 3, 2021, https://tinyurl.com/ev-rpm-cyb.

3. Constance Grady, "The Great Book Shortage of 2021, Explained," October 6, 2021, https://tinyurl.com/rpm-books.

4. Martin Pengelly, "Josh Hawley Finds New Publisher After Simon & Schuster Cancels Book," January 18, 2021, https://tinyurl.com/yxnqujw2.

5. Thad McIlroy, "AI Comes to Audiobooks," October 29, 2021, https://tinyurl.com/pw-ai-audio.

Chapter 4

1. Google search by author, accessed March 24, 2022, https://tinyurl.com/google-pm.

2. Jessica Lee, "No. 1 Position in Google Gets 33% of Search Traffic [Study]," Search Engine Watch, June 20, 2013, https://tinyurl.com/y79kf47g.

3. Project Management Institute, "What Is Project Management?," accessed February 21, 2022, https://tinyurl.com/pmi-pm-def.

4. Jesse Fewell, "144: PMBOK Guide 7th Edition: A Principles-Based Approach," January 3, 2022, produced by Velociteach, podcast, MP3 audio, 0:36, https://tinyurl.com/yavoa2fz.

5. Max Chafkin and Mark Bergen, "Google Makes So Much Money, It Never Had to Worry About Financial Discipline—Until Now," December 8, 2016, https://tinyurl.com/zcvn9bv.

6. J. A. Miller, "What Is a Project Management Office (PMO) and Do You Need One?," October 19, 2017, https://tinyurl.com/ya9hurd4.

7. M. Duddy and M. P. Perry, APM, Business Focused PMO Setup, PMI survey 2010.

8. Olivia Erlanger and Luis Ortega Govela, "The Origins of Silicon Valley's Garage Myth," November 27, 2018, https://tinyurl.com/ybqb5gwh.

9. Brian Sommer, personal conversation, February 28, 2022.

Chapter 5

1. Future Forum, "Pulse Survey," January 25, 2022, https://futureforum.com/pulse-survey.

2. Matthew D. Lieberman, David Rock, and Christine L. Cox, "Breaking Bias," *Neuro Leadership Journal* 5 (May 2014), https://www.scn.ucla.edu/pdf/Lieberman(2014)NLI.pdf.

3. R. L. Daft and R. H. Lengel, "Organizational Information Requirements, Media Richness, and Structural Design," *Management Science* 32, no. 5 (1986): 554–571, doi:10.1287/mnsc.32.5.554.

4. "Usage Statistics and Market Share of WordPress," W3techs.com, March 2022, https://tinyurl.com/y9sa74aa.

14 Endnotes   319

5. Te-Ping Chen, "This CEO Lets His Employees Work Whenever They Want—From Wherever They Want," February 4, 2022, https://tinyurl.com/y9cz3hz9.

6. Rob Cross, "Beyond Collaboration Overload," December 13, 2021, in *Author Talks,* produced by McKinsey & Company, podcast, MP3 audio, 11:21, https://tinyurl.com/ycznf2b5.

7. Anneken Tappe, "Record 20.5 Million American Jobs Lost in April. Unemployment Rate Soars to 14.7%.," May 8, 2020, https://tinyurl.com/ydzbsqhf.

8. Jessica Dickler, "Despite Rising Wages, 61% of Americans Are Still Living Paycheck to Paycheck, Report Finds," CNBC, February 17, 2022, https://tinyurl.com/ybax2ov8.

9. Jack Kelly, "Nike Is Closing Its Corporate Offices, Giving Workers a Week Off to 'Prioritize Mental Health," August 30, 2021, https://tinyurl.com/y96nucnf.

10. Kristy Threlkeld, "Two-Thirds of Workers Say the Pandemic Has Worsened Employee Burnout," March 11, 2021, https://tinyurl.com/ycqdeghk.

11. "State of Remote Work 2021," owllabs.com, accessed March 19, 2022, https://tinyurl.com/y93cdv55.

Chapter 6

1. Rebecca Knight, "When to Take a Chance on an Imperfect Job Candidate," *Harvard Business Review,* March 8, 2021, https://tinyurl.com/y9aubcth.

2. Automattic, "How We Hire," accessed March 10, 2022, https://automattic.com/how-we-hire/.

3. "Offshoring Gains Popularity," CIO Insight, September 28, 2010, https://tinyurl.com/y7qdq3hq.

4. Jennifer Dikler, "Reshoring: An Overview, Recent Trends, and Predictions for the Future," *SSRN Electronic Journal* (August 19, 2021), KIEP Research Paper, World Economy Brief 21–35, https://tinyurl.com/y85wfm4x.

5. Susie Neilson and Nami Sumida, "The San Francisco Exodus Isn't Over, According to New Migration Data. Here's Where People Are Moving.," *San Francisco Chronicle,* December 15, 2021, https://tinyurl.com/yc4rcdvj.

6. Paul Gray, "How to Use a Core Hours Policy to Improve Employee Experience," TechRepublic, July 29, 2021, https://tinyurl.com/y8ozs5nc.

7. Laura Vanderkam, "The Scheduling Secret That Will Make Your Team More Productive," Fast Company, August 18, 2015, https://tinyurl.com/y924v2lh.

8. Aiyana Ishmael, "Too Many Zoom Meetings? 'Core Hours' Keep Some Remote Workers Productive and Sane," *Wall Street Journal* (Eastern Ed.), July 20, 2021, https://tinyurl.com/y92ap9wv.

9. Aiyana Ishmael, 2021. "Too Many Zoom Meetings? 'Core Hours' Keep Some Remote Workers Productive and Sane," *Wall Street Journal* (Eastern Ed.), July 20, 2021, https://tinyurl.com/y92ap9wv.

Chapter 7

1. Nancy Baym, Jonathan Larson, and Ronnie Martin, "What a Year of WFH Has Done to Our Relationships at Work," *Harvard Business Review,* March 22, 2021, https://tinyurl.com/y8zz43hz.

320 Project Management in the Hybrid Workplace

2. Jennifer J. Deal and Alec Levenson, "Figuring Out Social Capital Is Critical for the Future of Hybrid Work," *MIT Sloan Management Review*, July 1, 2021, https://tinyurl.com/y9z4m6xr.

3. Paul Keegan, "Remote-Work Experts Are in Demand as Return to Office Begins Anew," March 8, 2022, https://tinyurl.com/ycz6veen.

4. Katherine Bindley, "Forget the Office—Salesforce Is Making a Wellness Retreat for Workers," *Wall Street Journal* (Eastern Ed.), February 10, 2022, https://tinyurl.com/y8r3fq52.

5. "Introducing Trailblazer Ranch: Igniting the Next Chapter of Salesforce's Culture," Salesforce News, February 10, 2022, https://tinyurl.com/ydafzb6d.

Chapter 8

1. Singh Ankita, "Project Management Features Report: Is 2019 the Year to Replace Your Current Solution?," April 17, 2019, https://tinyurl.com/y7zmx86p.

2. "Asana Announces Record Third Quarter Fiscal 2022 Revenues; Surpasses $100 Million Quarterly Revenues," asana.com, December 2, 2021, https://tinyurl.com/y9qoydyc.

3. Lizzy Lawrence, 2022, "Slack or Bust: How Workplace Tools Are Becoming Job Deal-Breakers," Protocol, February 9, 2022, https://tinyurl.com/y7lvonrh.

4. Lizzy Lawrence, 2022. "Slack or Bust: How Workplace Tools Are Becoming Job Deal-Breakers," Protocol, February 9, 2022, https://tinyurl.com/y7lvonrh.

5. Ron Miller, "Okta's 8th 'Businesses at Work' Cloud Usage Report Shows Increasing Heterogeneity," TechCrunch, January 25, 2022, https://tinyurl.com/y7ts5ft5.

6. Asana, "Anatomy of Work 2021—Rise of Work Management," accessed March 15, 2022, https://tinyurl.com/ygvomjyy.

7. Ashley Abramson, "Burnout and Stress Are Everywhere," apa.org, January 21, 2022, https://tinyurl.com/y7yacd29.

8. "Customer Story: NHL," monday.com, accessed March 20, 2022, https://monday.com/customers/nhl.

9. Jordan Mirchev, "Project Reporting Made Easy with Trello's New Dashboard View," trello.com, February 16, 2021, https://tinyurl.com/yadqp7gd.

10. Matthew Finnegan, "Slack or Teams? Many Businesses Opt for Both," Computerworld, June 20, 2019, https://tinyurl.com/y27klere.

11. Todd Bishop, "Microsoft Teams Surpasses 270M Monthly Active Users, as Growth Slows from Early Days of Pandemic," January 25, 2022, https://tinyurl.com/ycbfckyf.

12. Ulia Herbst, "91 of the 100 Largest U.S. Companies Are on Microsoft Teams," March 10, 2020, https://tinyurl.com/v72o6ss.

13. "Windows 95 Remains Most Popular Operating System," CNET, January 2, 2002, https://tinyurl.com/y9qnt35f.

Chapter 9

1. Gary Klein, "Performing a Project Pre-Mortem," September 2007, https://tinyurl.com/ojfgtpp.

2. Bruce F. Webster, *The Art of 'Ware: Sun Tzu's Classic Work Reinterpreted*, M&T Books, 1995.

14 Endnotes 321

Chapter 10

1. Rebecca Greenfield, "The Economics of Netflix's $100 Million New Show," February 1, 2013, https://tinyurl.com/m35q8fx.

2. Emily Steel, "How to Build an Empire, the Netflix Way," November 29, 2014, https://tinyurl.com/ybbdv2lt.

3. Lesley Goldberg, "'Marco Polo' Canceled at Netflix After Two Seasons," December 12, 2016, https://tinyurl.com/y6uuu5b6.

4. Kieren McCarthy, "Accenture Sued Over Website Redesign So Bad It Hertz: Car Hire Biz Demands $32m+ for 'Defective' Cyber-Revamp," April 23, 2019, https://tinyurl.com/y7r995aj.

5. Henrico Dolfing, "Case Study 8: How Hertz Paid Accenture $32 Million for a Website That Never Went Live," October 18, 2019, https://tinyurl.com/yaymvqn5.

6. Apple Developer Documentation, "Running Your App in the Simulator or on a Device," accessed March 28, 2022, https://tinyurl.com/ya7fgtbm.

7. Alex Shashkevich, "Meeting Online Has Become the Most Popular Way U.S. Couples Connect, Stanford Sociologist Finds," August 21, 2019, https://tinyurl.com/yxgtmgxz.

8. Andrew Francis-Tan and Hugo M. Mialon. "'A Diamond Is Forever' and Other Fairy Tales: The Relationship Between Wedding Expenses and Marriage Duration," *SSRN Electronic Journal,* September 15, 2014, https://tinyurl.com/yb352tza.

9. Ron Ashkenas and Nadim Matta, "How to Scale a Successful Pilot Project," January 8, 2021, https://tinyurl.com/y7szz8ta.

10. B. W. Tuckman, "Developmental Sequence in Small Groups," *Psychological Bulletin* 63, no. 6 (1965): 384–399, https://tinyurl.com/ycohetfv.

11. Amazon.com, "AMS Responsibility Matrix (RACI)," accessed March 17, 2022, https://tinyurl.com/ybxb3ko9.

12. Marcus Wohlsen, "The Amazon Fire Phone Was Always Going to Fail," January 6, 2015, https://tinyurl.com/yaex8a9r.

13. "Facebook-Funded Cryptocurrency Diem Winds Down," BBC News, February 1, 2022, https://tinyurl.com/yahvocoo.

14. Julia Alexander, "Quibi Has Raised Close to $2 Billion, and It Hasn't Even Launched Yet," March 4, 2020, https://tinyurl.com/wv9d8na.

15. Jordan Hoffman, "Quibi Fire Sale: Roku Head Says It Was a Good Deal," June 18, 2021, https://tinyurl.com/yc33ggee.

Chapter 11

1. *The Simpsons,* season 2, episode 19, "Lisa's Substitute," directed by Rich Moore, written by Matt Groening, James L. Brooks, and Sam Simon, featuring Dustin Hoffman, aired April 25, 1991, in broadcast syndication, FOX.

2. Dave McMenamin and Ian Begley, "David Blatt Fired as Cavaliers Coach; Tyronn Due to Take Over Team," January 22, 2016, https://tinyurl.com/y7pdnodd.

3. Oriana Bandiera et al. "CEO Behavior and Firm Performance," *The Journal of Political Economy* 128, no. 4 (2020): 1325–1369, https://tinyurl.com/y8xas6wq.

4. "Work with New Electronic 'Brains' Opens Field for Army Math Experts," *Hammond Times* (Hammond, IN), Nov. 10, 1957, https://tinyurl.com/y7xy82lf.

322   Project Management in the Hybrid Workplace

5. Training Industry, "Size of the Training Industry," April 20, 2017, https://tinyurl. com/ycceozyz.

6. Aaron De Smet, Monica Mcgurk, and Elizabeth Schwartz, "Getting More from Your Training Programs," October 1, 2010, https://tinyurl.com/y8wn5g2w.

7. Gartner, "Setting L&D Leaders Up for Success," April 19, 2019, https://tinyurl.com/ y9ckpvz3.

8. Mckinseyquarterly.com, "Building Organizational Capabilities: McKinsey Global Survey Results," March 2010.

9. Linkedin.com, "2018 Workplace Learning Report," 2018, https://tinyurl.com/yaozv7tx.

10. Cal Newport, "Slack Is the Right Tool for the Wrong Way to Work," *New Yorker,* December 20, 2020, https://tinyurl.com/mwaaabt5.

11. LinkedIn Learning, "2018 Workplace Learning Report," November 20, 2018, https:// tinyurl.com/y4cmesuj.

Chapter 12

1. John D. Sutter, "Cavs Owner's Letter Mocked for Comic Sans Font," July 9, 2010, https://tinyurl.com/y89gn3vs.

2. Jillian D'Onfro, "Why Amazon Forces Its Developers to Write Press Releases," March 12, 2015, https://tinyurl.com/y8d62988.

3. Te-Ping Chen, "This CEO Lets His Employees Work Whenever They Want—From Wherever They Want," February 4, 2022, https://tinyurl.com/y9cz3hz9.

4. Microsoft, "The Next Great Disruption Is Hybrid Work—Are We Ready?" March 22, 2021, https://tinyurl.com/yg296gkf.

5. Jared Spataro, "5 Attributes of Successful Teams," November 19, 2019, https://tinyurl. com/y7p2epkp.

6. Josh Bernoff, "Bad Writing Costs Businesses Billions," April 13, 2017, https://tinyurl. com/y8sq5uz3.

7. Slack, "From Jargon to Emoji, the Evolution of Workplace Communication Styles," February 16, 2022, https://tinyurl.com/y9cyqyqb.

8. Kara Swisher, "Opinion," *New York Times,* March 17, 2022, https://tinyurl.com/ya9aexcn.

9. Dimensional Research and Cisco, "The Rise of the Hybrid Workplace: A Global Survey of Executives, Employee Experience Experts, and Knowledge Workers," www.cisco. com, October 2020, https://tinyurl.com/ycrjv8lo.

Chapter 13

1. Anita L. Tucker and Sara J. Singer, "The Effectiveness of Management-by-Walking-Around: A Randomized Field Study," ebs.edu., September 14, 2013, https://tinyurl. com/yd5szd7q.

2. Kristin Broughton and Nina Trentmann, "Companies Cutting Office Space Predict Long-Term Savings," *Wall Street Journal* (Eastern Ed.), July 5, 2021, https://tinyurl. com/yel6l3gh.

3. SHRM, "SHRM Research Reveals Negative Perceptions of Remote Work," July 26, 2021, https://tinyurl.com/yayledlu.

4. Massachusetts Institute of Technology, "MIT Sloan Hosts Sports Managers at Conference on Role of Analytics," MIT News, February 7, 2007, https://tinyurl.com/y7arbrfd.

14 Endnotes

5. Taylor Soper, "Meet the PGA Tour's Geekiest Golfer: Bryson DeChambeau on His Passion for Tech, Physics, Data," GeekWire, February 17, 2017, https://tinyurl.com/yd4hrldf.

6. Moira Alexander, "The Data-Driven Project Manager: Using Analytics to Improve Outcomes," March 23, 2021, https://tinyurl.com/y77b87cq.

7. Harjit Singh, personal conversation with author, March 25, 2022.

8. Brandon Weaver, "Wrike's Work Intelligence Gets Even Smarter," wrike.com, December 16, 2021, https://tinyurl.com/y8kg34ah.

9. Ingrid Lunden, "Asana Introduces Timeline, Lays Groundwork for AI-Based Monitoring as the 'Team Brain' for Productivity," TechCrunch, March 30, 2018, https://tinyurl.com/y92nvlbd.

Chapter 14

1. Google search, "People Are Our Most Valuable Asset," accessed March 19, 2022, https://tinyurl.com/y9ruamue.

2. Google Scholar, "Studies Employee Performance Management," accessed March 21, 2022, https://tinyurl.com/scholar-ps-epm.

3. Elaine D. Pulakos, Rose Mueller-Hanson, and Sharon Arad., "The Evolution of Performance Management: Searching for Value," *Annual Review of Organizational Psychology and Organizational Behavior* 6, no. 1 (2019): 249–271, https://tinyurl.com/y9zntlgq.

4. Sarah O'Connor, 2021. "Why Ranking Employees by Performance Backfires," April 6, 2021, https://tinyurl.com/ye6j24r4.

5. Yuki Noguchi, "Behold the Entrenched—and Reviled—Annual Review," NPR, October 28, 2014, https://tinyurl.com/y9e7xpl2.

6. Yuki Noguchi, "Behold the Entrenched—and Reviled—Annual Review," NPR, October 28, 2014, https://tinyurl.com/y9e7xpl2.

7. David K. Li and Sasha Urban, "University of Miami Professor Resigns After Reportedly Sharing Porn Bookmark on Zoom," NBC News, April 29, 2020, https://tinyurl.com/y55fm8l4.

8. Matthew Finnegan, "Rise in Employee Monitoring Prompts Calls for New Rules to Protect Workers," Computerworld, November 30, 2021, https://tinyurl.com/yyhb7g7v.

9. Scott Judd, Eric O'Rourke, and Adam Grant, "Employee Surveys Are Still One of the Best Ways to Measure Engagement," *Harvard Business Review,* March 14, 2018, https://tinyurl.com/y93hnggq.

10. Ray A. Smith, "These Workers Wanted to Quit Their Jobs. They Got Promoted Instead.," *Wall Street Journal* (Eastern Ed.), January 7, 2022, https://tinyurl.com/yaadgz92.

11. R. McKell Carter et al. "Activation in the VTA and Nucleus Accumbens Increases in Anticipation of Both Gains and Losses," *Frontiers in Behavioral Neuroscience* 3, no. 21 (2009), https://tinyurl.com/yastg66f.

12. Rani Molla, "Nice Raise. Too Bad About Inflation.," Vox, February 16, 2022, https://tinyurl.com/yddggfzr.

13. "The Emerging Trend in State Pay Transparency Laws," *The National Law Review* XII, no. 105 (2021), https://tinyurl.com/y8jhc3zy.

14. Payscale, "Will They Stay or Will They Go? Employee Retention and Acquisition in an Uncertain Economy," 2018, https://tinyurl.com/y947wsfn.
15. Google Trends, accessed March 19, 2022, https://tinyurl.com/y7dfphan.
16. Caroline Spiezio, "Elite N.Y. Firms Are in a Battle for Talent. Could They All Be Losing?," Reuters, June 15, 2021, https://tinyurl.com/y7rturac.
17. Jonathan Shieber, "Fringe Pitches a Monthly Stipend for App Purchases and Subscriptions as the Newest Employee Benefit," TechCrunch, July 10, 2020, https://tinyurl.com/ycjpotgh.

Printed in Great Britain
by Amazon